The Social Costs of Underemployment

Inadequate Employment as Disguised Unemployment

Going beyond the usual focus on unemployment, this research explores the health effects of other kinds of underemployment, including such forms of inadequate employment as involuntary part-time and poverty-wage work. Using the National Longitudinal Survey of Youth, this study compares falling into unemployment versus inadequate employment relative to remaining adequately employed. Outcomes include low self-esteem, alcohol abuse, depression, and low-birthweight babies. The panel data permit study of the plausible reverse causation hypothesis of selection. Because the sample is national and was followed over two decades, the study explores cross-level effects (individual change and community economic climate) and developmental transitions. Special attention is given to school leavers and welfare mothers, and, in cross-generational analysis, the effect of mothers' employment on babies' birthweight. There emerges a new way of conceptualizing employment status as a continuum, ranging from good jobs to bad jobs to unemployment, with implications for public policy on issues related to work and health.

David Dooley is Professor of Psychology and Social Behavior, Department of Psychology and Social Behavior, University of California, Irvine.

JoAnn Prause is Lecturer and Research Specialist, Department of Psychology and Social Behavior, University of California, Irvine.

The Social Costs of Underemployment

Inadequate Employment as Disguised Unemployment

DAVID DOOLEY
University of California, Irvine

JOANN PRAUSE
University of California, Irvine

PUBLISHED BY THE PRESS SYNDICATE OF THE UNIVERSITY OF CAMBRIDGE
The Pitt Building, Trumpington Street, Cambridge, United Kingdom

CAMBRIDGE UNIVERSITY PRESS
The Edinburgh Building, Cambridge CB2 2RU, UK
40 West 20th Street, New York, NY 10011-4211, USA
477 Williamstown Road, Port Melbourne, VIC 3207, Australia
Ruiz de Alarcón 13, 28014 Madrid, Spain
Dock House, The Waterfront, Cape Town 8001, South Africa

http://www.cambridge.org

First published 2004

Printed in the United States of America

Typeface Palatino 10/12 pt.   *System* LATEX 2$_\varepsilon$ [TB]

A catalog record for this book is available from the British Library.

Library of Congress Cataloging in Publication data

Dooley, David.
The social costs of underemployment : inadequate employment as disguised
unemployment / David Dooley, JoAnn Prause.
   p.   cm.
Includes bibliographical references and index.
ISBN 0-521-81014-0
1. Underemployment.   2. Underemployment – Health aspects.   3. Underemployment –
Psychological aspects.   I. Prause, JoAnn, 1953–   II. Title.
HD5709.D66   2003
362.85'2–dc21   2003043948

ISBN 0 521 81014 0 hardback

Contents

Preface

This book reports a decade of research on underemployment. Our present approach grew out of an earlier program of research that focused narrowly on job loss and its psychological and physical health costs. A century of unemployment studies had corroborated the conventional wisdom that job loss could harm well-being, particularly the mental health of dislocated workers and their immediate family members. But the suspicion remained that some forms of employment might also carry social costs that were being ignored.

Our initial efforts to study the consequences of various forms of underemployment were frankly exploratory. But positive findings from the study of one outcome stimulated further research on other outcomes. Findings of the adverse effects of underemployment on self-esteem among school leavers invited follow-up analyses of alcohol abuse, depression, and birthweight. Parallel findings for these different indicators appeared across different survey years, representing different life stages of the respondents and different economic environments in which they worked or sought jobs. The data seemed to insist that not only unemployment but also inadequate employment had a strong and pervasive connection to all of the outcome measures that were available for our study.

Those of us who conduct research on employment status have had to recognize the importance of the prevailing economic climate. It defines the opportunity structure that determines the risks of individual job change, both good and bad. It also provides the environment for comparison and self-assessment in which individuals judge their relative well-being and future prospects. So it comes as no surprise that the economic climate, by setting a context in which to choose study topics and interpret research findings, influences researchers.

Although the data reflect varying conditions beginning in the early 1980s, we conducted the present analyses largely during the 1990s, in the midst of the longest economic expansion in American economic history.

Unemployment levels fell year after year, while the stock market was multiplying millionaires as fast as new companies could be created. This was an era in which unemployment seemed to be disappearing as a social problem. At the same time, however, a closer look at the labor market revealed massive job churning, along with flat or falling real wages for middle- and lower-income workers. This historical moment demanded that we give attention to the economically inadequate jobs that were being eclipsed in the public eye by the falling unemployment rates.

This book begins with an introduction to the problem of underemployment as it has emerged in the changing labor market (Chapter 1) and locates our approach in the long tradition of research on unemployment (Chapter 2). The program of studies described in this book could not have been mounted without the extraordinary data provided by the National Longitudinal Survey of Youth (NLSY), gathered and maintained by the Center for Human Resource Research (CHHR) at The Ohio State University and sponsored by the Bureau of Labor Statistics, U.S. Department of Labor. We describe this panel survey and our approach to analyzing it in Chapter 3.

The middle chapters describe a series of hypothesis tests on the relationship between various forms of underemployment and various psychological, behavioral, and health outcomes. Chapter 4 considers the rival hypothesis of reverse causation – that preexisting dysfunction causes people to become underemployed. The remaining chapters test the social causation hypothesis – that adverse employment change predicts decreased well-being (or that favorable employment change predicts increased well-being). Chapters 5 through 7 deal with different mental health outcomes during different life stages: effects on self-esteem, alcohol abuse, and depression. Chapter 8 extends the logic of our approach by considering welfare transitions as special cases of employment transitions. Chapter 9 extends our approach across generations by measuring the connections between a mother's employment experience and her child's well-being, indexed by birthweight. The final two chapters summarize the overall nature of our findings (Chapter 10) and consider their implications for the next steps in research and policy (Chapter 11).

This research program required the help of many people. We are grateful for the generous financial support provided by grants from the W. T. Grant Foundation, the California Wellness Foundation, and, in recent years, the Robert Wood Johnson Foundation's Substance Abuse Policy Research Program. We appreciate the long friendship and intellectual stimulation of Ralph Catalano, who collaborated on the early unemployment studies that provide a methodological foundation for this research. We acknowledge the assistance provided by Steve McClaskie at the CHRR, who has been extremely helpful over the past decade in answering our many questions about the NLSY data. Over the years we have benefited from the encouragement and stimulation provided by many colleagues and students in the School of Social Ecology at the University of California at Irvine, and we thank them all for their support. We thank one of our students, in particular, for helping us to polish this manuscript as well as for collaborating with us on some of the research analyses: Kathleen A. Ham-Rowbottom. We especially thank our spouses, Braddie Dooley and George Prause, for their understanding and encouragement.

1

Disguised Unemployment and Changing Forms of Work

Since there can be little doubt that some types of jobs under some modern conditions are psychologically destructive, a controversy has arisen over the question of whether current indicators of social pathology are better explained by prevailing employment conditions or by rates of unemployment.

Jahoda, 1982, p. 43

... a transition is occurring in industrial society from a uniform system of lifelong full-time work organized in a single industrial location, with the radical alternative of unemployment, to a risk-fraught system of flexible, pluralized, decentralized underemployment, which however, will possibly no longer raise the problem of unemployment in the sense of being completely without a paid job.

Beck, 1992, p. 143

INTRODUCTION

The Paradox

A funny thing happened on the way to economic utopia. At the turn of the millennium, Americans were enjoying an economic expansion of record length that had begun in 1993. But a shadow hovered over the celebration of rising stock prices and falling unemployment rates. It was not the obvious fear that the next economic bust was lurking around the corner. Of course, there was a contraction in 2001, even before the September 11 terror attacks. But along with the threat of recession, there was a rising suspicion that even the best of economic times are somehow flawed. The conventional wisdom assumes that an economy that minimizes unemployment must be good. But during the late twentieth century, signs appeared that the postindustrial, downsized, restructured, and globalized economy had not banished the old unemployment but had only replaced it with an inadequate type of employment – a kind of disguised unemployment.

Over a century of research has explored both the effects on individual health and the societal effects of unemployment, providing a departure point of theory and method from which we can begin to study other adverse employment statuses. But researchers who investigate unemployment and health have seldom extended their work in this direction. Similarly, economists have devoted considerable attention to measuring aggregate unemployment and explaining its role in the overall economy, while leaving the study of its human costs to others. Governments routinely publish official unemployment rates, and politicians and news commentators just as routinely discuss their meaning for the chances of incumbents' reelection. But these analysts pay little attention to inadequate types of employment, and even less to their health consequences for individuals. This book fills a gap in the literature by measuring the social costs of such inadequate employment.

Low Unemployment

The economy of the United States, as usually measured, provided little reason for concern during the last decade of the twentieth century. On the contrary, its remarkable expansion during the late 1990s set records for length. The unemployment rate in the last recession peaked in 1992 at 7.5% and declined every year thereafter, reaching 4.2% in 1999, and it continued falling into early 2000 (United States Department of Labor, 2000). To find such a low unemployment rate, one has to go back a generation to the 1960s. As the Dow and the NASDAQ repeatedly hit new highs, new millionaires emerged as fast as new initial public offerings (IPOs) could be released. While the Fed chairman worried that a "wealth effect" could create a bubble economy, some mental health professionals identified a new disorder – "sudden wealth syndrome."

Surprisingly, the low unemployment rates of the late 1990s were not accompanied by rising inflation. Economic theory suggests that when the supply of labor becomes tight, employers, competing for more workers, will bid up wages and pass along their cost increases to consumers in the form of higher prices. This trade-off between unemployment and inflation has been summarized in the Phillips curve (Phillips, 1958), and it helps to explain the seeming paradox of stock price increases following reports of flat or rising unemployment. Such news is often taken as insurance against rising interest rates and inflation and thus as encouragement for more investment in the stock market. When the unemployment rate threatens to fall to new lows, some people worry that too few people are out of work.

Our history of economic cycles warns against generalizing from either very good or very bad times. The apocalyptic titles of some books on this topic illustrate the danger of overly pessimistic predictions – for example,

The Economic Horror (Forrester, 1999) and *The End of Work* (Rifkin, 1995). These books argue that in the postindustrial, computerized economy, the need for workers will decline or even vanish altogether. In the economic context of the 1990s, these catastrophic predictions seem rather premature. On the other hand, there is ample evidence that not all is well for many workers, even in the boom years, and hyperbolic book titles can also be found to illustrate overly optimistic economic expectations – for example, *The End of Unemployment* (Miller, 1988). Among competing book titles, the one that may come closest to capturing the emerging situation is *The New Insecurity: The End of the Standard Job and Family* (Wallulis, 1998).

Income Inequality and Poverty

One troubling sign is rising income inequality. One measure of income inequality is the ratio of real (inflation-adjusted) wages of those at high levels (say, the seventy-fifth percentile) to those at low levels (the twenty-fifth percentile). For American males, who contribute the majority of earnings to the income of households with prime working-age heads (18–64), this ratio rose from about 1.9 in 1967 to 2.4 in 1997 (Reed, 1999). This could have occurred if everyone had earned more over time (the rising tide lifting all boats), with the "haves" rising more than the "have-nots." But this was not the case. Only men above the median in 1967 enjoyed rising real wages. Men in the twenty-fifth percentile earned less in real terms in 1997 than their twenty-fifth percentile peers did in 1967. (Note that such data do not describe income changes for the same persons over time, but rather are based on different samples for each year. Thus particular individuals whose earnings were at the twenty-fifth percentile in 1967 might well have risen to a higher percentile by 1997. These findings compare the incomes of different people with the same relative standing in different years).

Efforts to describe and explain rising wage inequality have produced large and expanding literatures in several fields. For example, one study compared two cohorts of young white men, one entering the workforce in the mid-1960s and the other, after the onset of the current economic restructuring, in the early 1980s (Bernhardt et al., 1998). Wages for these young workers were monitored over a period of sixteen years in each cohort to compare intragenerational mobility during these two eras. One finding was that although the two groups started off at similar wage levels, the growth of wages with increasing age was slower during the later than during the earlier period. Another finding was that the natural polarization in wages between high and low earners over time was greater in the later than in the earlier cohort. This pattern of rising wage inequality was only partially explained by such factors as education, job tenure, worker's industry, and hours worked. The authors conclude that a "new generation is entering a transformed labor market, and especially for those without a college degree, the prospects for a living wage and stable employment are not at all certain" (Bernhardt et al., 1998, p. 21).

To appreciate the seriousness of this economic trend, consider the magnitude of drops in earnings, which were more dramatic in some states than in the nation as a whole. In California, for example, the weekly earnings of men in the twenty-fifth percentile (in 1997 dollars) were $526 in the business cycle peak year of 1969. They then fell to $345 in the cycle peak year of 1989 and to a low of $291 in the cycle trough year of 1993, before making an anemic recovery to $308 by 1997 (Reed, 1999). This loss of $218 per week in real earnings represents a 40% drop between 1969 and 1997. In sum, the increase in income inequality does not result from everyone getting richer at different speeds. It derives, rather, from our poorest workers experiencing stagnant wages or, in some places, actual losses in real terms. This pattern has serious implications for poverty.

In 1997, well into the longest economic expansion in U.S. history, 35.6 million Americans (13.3%) lived at or below the poverty line (U.S. Department of Labor, 1999a). This level is defined not for individual earnings but rather in terms of the family unit and is adjusted for the number of family members (e.g., $16,400 for a family of four in 1997). Of those in poverty, 7.5 million (21%) had been in the workforce for at least twenty-seven weeks during the past year. The working poor tend to experience one or more of the main employment problems: intermittent unemployment, involuntary part-time work, and low wages. Even at its most successful, the American economy still has difficulty providing adequate employment for all workers.

The result is a large gap between the number of living-wage jobs and the number of people needing them. A living wage, as distinct from a poverty-level wage, is one that allows families to meet their basic needs without public assistance, to deal with emergencies, and to plan ahead. One study estimated that for a family with one adult and two children, a living wage in 1996 would be at least $30,000 in one of the northwestern states, varying according to housing and childcare costs (Northwest Policy Center and Northwest Federation of Community Organizations, 1999). The median wage in the Northwest was then slightly greater than the living wage of an individual (assuming full-time work for a full year), but it was only two-thirds of the living wage for an adult with two children. It was estimated that for every job opening that paid a living wage for an adult and two children, there were on average ten to seventeen job seekers in the Northwestern states. Despite variation in details according to local living costs and industries, a similar shortfall probably exists in other regions.

Different explanations for the gap between the number of workers and the number of adequate jobs have emerged. For example, one perspective is that we have evolved into a "winner-take-all society," where the best in each field takes the lion's share of the rewards, leaving everyone else with a pittance (Frank & Cook, 1995). With the emergence of mass media, consumers can elect not to attend their local opera house or minor league ballpark to see the available singers or athletes. Instead, they can choose to see and reward only the very best talent by buying CDs or purchasing cable connections. Thus the "best" performers get most of the audience and remuneration, leaving little for the rest.

Whatever validity this view has for certain jobs, such as those in sports and entertainment, it may be less applicable to the more mundane types of blue- and white-collar work. But another explanation addresses these categories by reference to the economic globalization that occurred after the end of the cold war, when capital became freely mobile to go anywhere in the world (Wolman & Colamosca, 1997). In this view, the unexpected (from the Phillips curve) absence of wage increases despite full employment derives from the capacity of multinational companies to shift jobs overseas at the first sign of unwanted wage demands. In other words, job insecurity can help hold down wages.

Job Churning and Insecurity

Whatever the full explanation for rising income inequality, high job turnover seems to be a hallmark of the modern American economy. We expect substantial job displacement during recessions, but it has continued on, albeit somewhat abated, during the most recent expansion as well. Thus the low unemployment rates of recent years have emerged by a process of job churning. In a kind of musical chairs, high numbers of workers were displaced and then reemployed. A workforce snapshot each time the music stopped would show low levels of unemployment, but such snapshots would miss the stressful flurry of job leavings and seekings that many workers experienced.

The U.S. Department of Labor has conducted special surveys of job displacement since 1984, including a report covering the expansion period 1995–97 (U.S. Department of Labor, 1998). Displaced workers are defined as those over nineteen years old who lost or left jobs for economic reasons (e.g., plant closed or moved, position or shift abolished, insufficient work). A total of 8 million workers were displaced during the survey period 1995–97 (out of about 125 million total employed workers in 1995). Of these, 3.6 million had long tenure, defined as three or more years in the same job. By January 1998, 76% of the long-tenured displaced workers were reemployed, with the remainder either unemployed (i.e., actively trying to find work – 10%) or out of the labor force (discouraged workers, retired, or other).

Of the 2.7 million long-tenured workers who found new jobs, about 2.4 million had lost full-time wage or salary jobs. Of these previously full-time workers, about one in five were working either part-time (11%) or in self-employed or unpaid family work (7%). Of those reporting new full-time positions, only 47% reported wages equal to or better than their lost jobs. The remainder either reported a decline in wages (38%) or did not report prior wages (15%). In sum, large numbers of American workers experience job displacement even in good times, and although most can find new work, a substantial number of these new jobs are economically inferior to their old jobs.

Not surprisingly, surveys of American workers reveal a persistent anxiety about their job security (Herzenberg, Alci, & Wial, 1998; Mishel, Bernstein, & Schmitt, 1999). Compared to results from 1989 at a similar point in the business cycle, the proportion of workers in 1996 who thought it unlikely that they would lose their jobs was sharply down. And it was not just that workers feared losing their jobs; their confidence that it would be easy to find an equally good job was also down. In past expansions, workers typically took the opportunity to leave undesirable jobs voluntarily, but in the most recent expansion, the voluntary share of unemployed workers stayed low (Mishel et al., 1999, p. 239). Workers apparently suspect that job changes in the present labor market can have adverse effects not only on their incomes but also on benefits such as health insurance and pension plans. This picture of a fully employed but anxious workforce suggests a distinction between full employment and "good employment."

From the perspective of traditional unemployment research, the impact of downsizing should fall mainly on those who are dislocated from their jobs. But from a perspective that includes inadequate employment, the survivors of downsizing may also suffer harm. That is, the "stayers" who retain their jobs may face health consequences not unlike those of the "leavers" (Kivimäki et al., in press). Adverse effects, including self-reported health and emotional difficulties, have been reported for survivors of downsizing (Kivimäki et al., 2001; Woodward et al., 1999). Explanations for such effects on stayers include increased job demands, decreased employment security, and a reduction in job control (Kivimäki et al., 2000). Having just seen some of their coworkers downsized, stayers have good reason to worry about their own jobs. Simultaneously, they are expected to make up the production slack left by the leavers, leading to job strain (Karasek & Theorell, 1990).

In addition to the ongoing reorganization of work determined by the private sector, the U.S. government added a new factor to the labor market in 1996. Under the Personal Responsibility and Work Opportunity Reconciliation Act of 1996, Aid to Families with Dependent Children (AFDC) was renamed Temporary Assistance to Needy Families (TANF) and required that states make major changes in welfare programs. Unlike AFDC grants, federal funds for TANF assistance are cut off after two years unless the parents engage in approved work or job training, and these funds have a five-year cumulative lifetime limit regardless of employment status. What will happen when welfare recipients approach the time limit on their TANF benefits? The Nobel Prize–winning economist Robert Solow offers this answer:

> ...More important is the possibility that competition for jobs by ex-welfare re-cipients and their successors will drive down the wages for unqualified workers by enough to induce some employers to hire them to replace slightly more qual-ified incumbents who do the job better but have to be paid more.... In principle, the process does not stop here. The erosion of wages of second-level, slightly skilled, workers makes them more competitive with third-level, slightly more skilled workers.... So the costs of adjusting to the influx of former welfare recipients spreads to the working poor, the working just-less-poor, and so on, in the form of lower wages and heightened job insecurity. (Solow, 1998, pp. 28–29)

In short, the welfare reform may contribute to the existing trend toward stagnant wages, job dislocation, and insecurity among low-earning groups. But there exists still another aspect to this changing labor market – the dissolution of the old social contract between workers and employers.

Changing Employment Relationships

New technologies and management techniques have always changed the process of work. For example, computerization, just-in-time inventory con-trol, and heightened competition from all corners of the globe have each contributed to the most recent work changes (Wall & Jackson, 1995). But some argue that the present changes go beyond evolutionary adjustments of the work process and now threaten to overthrow the very nature of jobs and careers.

From a historical perspective, the "job" is a social construction that arose only in recent centuries with the industrial revolution (Bridges, 1994). The job served to provide the employer a fixed number of the worker's hours at the work site on a fixed schedule, in return for which the worker got fixed wages regardless of the amount of work produced. This familiar employee-employer relationship is now beginning to disappear. Although plenty of work remains to be done, it is no longer being packaged in the familiar envelope of activities called jobs. Instead, organizations are said to be "dejobbing" in favor of more flexible arrangements in order to get work done at less cost. The problem from a psychological perspective is that people have come to base their sense of identity and security on their jobs. Thus the gains in efficiency for the new flexible organization will likely entail some "social breakage" for the affected workers (Bridges, 1994).

This shift in the nature of jobs in turn implies changes in the nature of careers. A career consists of one or a series of jobs in the same occupation, and workers traditionally made their entire career with the same employer.

At one point, careers were even multigenerational, with fathers and sons working at the same job for the same employer. Then careers became a single lifetime in length, and now individuals may have several careers in the same lifetime – different occupations with different employers (Hall & Mirvis, 1995).

The chances of having a career with one employer for most of one lifetime have fallen with the emergence of new outsourcing arrangements. In the three-part "shamrock organization" model, one segment consists of a small number of core workers who serve as the leaders of their organization and provide its institutional memory (Handy, 1989). Only they enjoy the long-term employer-employee relationship that we associate with the traditional job and career. A second section of the organization consists of outside organizations or individuals who perform most of the actual work under contract to, and at the direction of, the core section. Such outside contractors may in turn use a shamrock-style organization guided by a small core leadership group. The third section consists of temporary workers brought in by the core group on a part-time basis to cover peak production periods. Thus most of the organization's production comes from workers with little or no commitment to it.

Not only is the employer-employee relationship changing, but for many the nature of work itself is changing – becoming more cognitive, complex, and fluid (Howard, 1995a). With dejobbing, workers are paid not for their availability to provide fixed hours of labor but rather for the performance of some task. The availability of this work is uncertain, and its location is variable. Like musicians, workers increasingly are paid by the "gig," and getting the gig may be just as difficult as performing it well. This new organizational environment requires workers with high intelligence and special abilities and may increasingly differentiate the workforce into those in the core sections of successful organizations and the multitude of peripheral, contingent workers (Howard, 1995b).

We are witnessing not the end of work but the end of traditional jobs and careers seen as marriagelike bonds between employee and employer. As more of us become contingent workers in one fashion or another, the few who can exploit this new environment will reap high rewards. But workers who are not well equipped to compete are likely to experience continued wage stagnation, insecurity, and the "social breakage" of lost job and career identities. As Beck says, in this new environment, "unemployment in the guise of various forms of underemployment is 'integrated' into the employment system, but in exchange for a *generalization of employment insecurity* [emphasis in original] that was not known in the 'old' uniform full-employment system of industrial society" (1992, pp. 143–144). In the old system, when employees came to work, the employer assumed the risk that there would not be enough work to occupy them or that their efforts would not yield a profitable amount of production. The workers still got full pay for full hours, unless and until the company foundered and had to lay them off. Under the new work arrangements, the employer buys a contracted product of completed labor from the contingent employee, leaving to the worker or subcontracting work group the details of work arrangements and time of labor. This flexibilization of work (the worker can choose the location, timing, and production procedures) may be attractive to some workers, but it comes with a price, the "privatization of the physical and mental health risks of work" (Beck, 1992, p. 143). The extent of this price in health costs provides the focus for our research.

THE TASK

The Question

If inadequate employment is really supplanting unemployment, is that so bad? Surely any job, even a bad one, is better than no job. Put another way, is inadequate employment really harmful and a health threat, or merely unpleasant, something necessarily tolerated for the greater good provided by economic efficiency? The answer, of course, varies depending on one's point of view. From an economic perspective, both unemployment and inadequate employment may be regarded as necessary evils, inevitable side effects of a dynamic labor market continually seeking equilibrium between the supply of and demand for workers. However, although the efficiencies of a free labor market may benefit everyone in theory, the costs of underemployment fall most heavily on only a few.

From an ethical perspective, what are the interests of the harmed individuals, those who must experience job loss or inadequate employment for the greater good? These individuals can and do claim the right to be protected against or indemnified for their loss of dignity, security, and standard of living. How shall we resolve this tension between the economic benefits to the many and the personal costs to the few? This is where the political process comes into play – balancing the electorate's sympathy for the pain of the underemployed with its interest in keeping taxes for social safety-net programs low and productivity high. This balance is itself dynamic, tending more to sympathy when rising unemployment rates give a taste of joblessness and insecurity to more of the electorate. For this reason, U.S. presidential candidates pay great attention to unemployment rates during election years (Monroe, 1984).

While each of these perspectives is important, we will focus on a different one here – the health effects of inadequate employment. What are the social costs, measured in mental health terms, of adverse employment change? Are the effects of being inadequately employed more like those of adequate employment or of unemployment? We must constantly remind ourselves of the plausibility of the null hypothesis, namely that falling from

adequate to inadequate employment produces no significant psychological harm. From this latter perspective, workers in the free enterprise system know, or should know, their risks of adverse employment change and
should be expected to exercise appropriate coping skills in order to adapt
to and overcome such challenges. Thus the present study extends the long
tradition of research on unemployment and health described in the next
chapter.

Key Terms

Studies on the health effects of economic stress have focused on the construct of unemployment but have operationalized it in different ways.
Merely not working does not constitute unemployment. Those who cannot
work (e.g., young children, the disabled) or who do not want paid employment (e.g., retired persons, full-time students, full-time homemakers) are
considered out of the labor force (OLF). The U.S. Bureau of Labor Statistics
(BLS) officially defines an unemployed person as one who is not employed,
wants a job, and has actively tried to find work in the past four weeks (U.S.
Bureau of Labor Statistics, 1994). This measure provides the basis for the
aggregate unemployment rate, the most widely reported single indicator
of how the economy is doing. However, this BLS unemployment measure
excludes those nonworking people who want employment but have given
up hope of finding it. Such people are officially counted as OLF and commonly termed "discouraged workers," even though they may be at highest
risk for the adverse effects of joblessness.

Another approach defines unemployment as receiving unemployment
compensation, but not every job provides unemployment insurance. Moreover, unemployment insurance has time limits (typically about six months
in the United States), with the result that long-term unemployed people
stop receiving such compensation before they find reemployment. Other
approaches have varied with the research design. For example, a study of
the effects of a plant closing could define the unemployed as those who
lost their jobs in the closure. Some specialized surveys base their sampling
on the rolls of job placement agencies. Regardless of the variety of methods used to characterize unemployment, all such studies typically share
a common limitation – the dichotomous distinction between employed
and unemployed.

Despite the prominence of this dichotomous approach, there is another perspective that recognizes more variation in employment status.
Robinson (1936) coined the term "disguised unemployment" early in the
last century to reflect the fact that some jobs have economic characteristics intermediate between adequate employment and unemployment. Disguised unemployment has no standard definition or official governmental recognition. However, it has an important connotation for the present

analysis. Because past research and public attention have concentrated almost exclusively on unemployment, it might now be useful to refocus on inadequate employment by first recognizing its kinship to unemployment.

Over the past three decades, a detailed system for operationalizing a range of employment statuses has developed (see Jensen & Slack, in press). In response to shortcomings in the prevailing approaches to labor statistics, the International Labor Office sponsored a series of conferences to develop better measures. The goal was to improve the counting of visible (e.g., involuntary part-time work) and invisible (e.g., poverty wages) forms of underemployment. To remedy this situation, Philip Hauser (1974) developed a conceptual framework termed the Labor Utilization Framework or LUF. This approach recognizes both the official BLS form of unemployment (derived from the Current Population Survey or CPS) as well as discouraged workers (later called sub-unemployment). It went beyond unemployment to recognize different categories of economically inadequate employment based on hours (involuntary part-time work) and wages (poverty-level pay). Following the approach taken in the LUF, the term "underemployment" will be used here to include *both* unemployment (official CPS-based and discouraged workers) and economically inadequate employment. The LUF evolved in subsequent years and now has both a substantial literature and a more elaborated set of subcategories (Clogg, 1979; Sullivan, 1978). Our operational adaptation of the LUF for purposes of this study will be detailed in Chapter 3.

Of course, there are other facets of work that can be used to differentiate employment status. For example, one approach contrasts nonstandard or contingent employment relationships (on-call, temporary help) from standard employment (Kalleberg, Reskin, & Hudson, 2000). Another approach has concentrated on the health consequences of certain psychological characteristics of work, such as job satisfaction, decision latitude, and demand (Karasek et al., 1998). Still others have contrasted overwork (too many hours per week) with adequate work (Schor, 1991). These other approaches are complements rather than alternatives to the LUF system. For example, a contingent worker might be a poorly paid clerk (inadequate employment) or a highly paid professional. In contrast to the special survey instruments required to assess the psychological dimensions of work, the LUF system has the advantage of drawing on the standard items of the Current Population Survey used to gather official government statistics about the workforce.

Prevalence of Underemployment

Is inadequate employment a serious problem? The answer to this question depends on two other questions. First, does inadequate employment have serious health consequences? Answering this question is the focus of the

remainder of this book. Second, is inadequate employment a widely prevalent working condition? The answer to this question is complicated by the
absence of routine publication of rates for LUF employment categories
other than CPS unemployment. However, nongovernmental researchers
have calculated rates for some of the LUF statuses for selected years.

For example, rates for several LUF categories were calculated for the
years 1969 to 1980 (Clogg & Sullivan, 1983). Unlike the BLS approach, which
considers discouraged workers as out of the labor force, the LUF includes
them (the sub-unemployed) in the denominator, with the effect of reducing the apparent unemployment rate below the officially reported levels.
During the twelve years studied, unemployment averaged 6.2%, ranging
from 3.4% in 1969 to 9% in 1975. Sub-unemployment averaged 1.4%, low
hours 3.2%, and low income 7.1%, with the sum of these three forms of
underemployment averaging almost twice the level of unemployment.

These types of underemployment were unevenly distributed throughout the population. Women tended to have higher rates in each of these
categories than males. The gender discrepancy was smallest for unemployment, with nearly equal levels by 1980. But the ratio of female to male rates
was consistently higher for the other underemployment categories in that
year: 3.3 for sub-unemployment, 1.3 for low hours, and 2.0 for low income.
Younger workers typically experience higher unemployment rates than
all others with the exception of retirement-age workers. For example, in
1980, the 16–19 age group experienced 16.1% unemployment, compared
to 3.5% for those in the 50–64 age group. Similarly, younger workers also
had higher rates of sub-unemployment, involuntary part-time work, and
low-wage work compared to older workers. The racial discrepancy was
also apparent throughout this period. In 1980, the ratio of black to non-
black rates was 2.1 for unemployment, 3.9 for sub-unemployment, 1.7 for
involuntary part-time work, and 1.4 for low income.

Researchers have also calculated the rates in the various LUF categories
for more recent years. Jensen and Slack (in press) used the March CPS data
for the years 1990 to 2000 to estimate rates of unemployment, discouraged workers, low-wage underemployment, and involuntary part-time
underemployment. Their analysis shows that the total of these four underemployment categories tracked the changing economic situation in the
country. Total underemployment rose from about 17% at the beginning of
the decade to over 20% during the recession years, before falling steadily
to around 14%. These data reflect the general principle that all of these underemployment categories tend to move together, rising during recession
years and falling during economic expansion years.

These LUF categories have also been calculated for the time frame that
includes the period during which our study sample was born, grew up,
and reached adulthood. Employment estimates were generated at five-year
intervals from 1968 to 1993 (Jensen et al., 1999). In 1993, the last of these

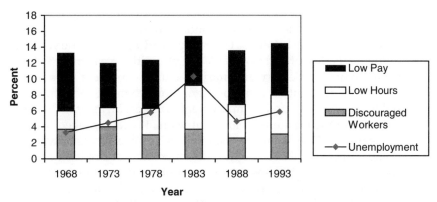

FIGURE 1.1. Levels of different types of underemployment. *Source:* Based on Jensen et al. (1999).

six data points (and the year before our study's final well-being measures were collected), the LUF unemployment level was 7.1%, or about half of the total of the other three categories: sub-unemployment, 1.2%; low hours, 4.9%; and low income, 7.2%. Figure 1.1 graphically summarizes the relationship among the various underemployment categories over the studied years.

This study also considered the employment transitions of individuals surveyed in the CPS, analyzing the characteristics of those who fell from adequate employment to underemployment over the entire period. As one would expect, the risk of such adverse change was higher during periods when the economy was weakening. Interestingly, after controlling for the strength of the economy (location in the business cycle), there was a significant trend: increasing risk of adverse employment change over time. Males, younger workers, people living in nonmetropolitan areas, those with less education, and blacks and Latinos all had greater risk of such adverse change.

These data also reveal something about the covariation between the routinely publicized labor force measure, the unemployment rate, and those other forms of underemployment that seldom get public attention. As indicated earlier, these more- and less-publicized measures tend to move roughly together, moving up or down with recessions and expansions. But they do not necessarily move precisely in parallel. It is possible that some forms of underemployment are proportionately greater in some economic circumstances than in others. If the less-publicized forms of underemployment moved exactly in proportion to unemployment, we would expect the ratio of the sum of the former (i.e., discouraged workers plus low pay plus part-time) to the latter (i.e., unemployment) to be the same in both low-unemployment and high-unemployment years.

Consider the six years spanning three decades described in Figure 1.1. Three of those years reflected good economic times during which the unemployment rates were below 5% (1968, 1973, and 1988). In those years, the unemployment rates ranged from 3.3% to 4.7%, with a mean of 4.1%. In the other three years (1978, 1983, and 1993), the unemployment rates ranged from 5.8% to 10.3%, with a mean of 7.4%. Now, compare the ratio of the less-publicized forms of underemployment to unemployment in these two sets of years. In the high-unemployment years, the ratio ranged from 1.5 to 2.5 (mean 2.0). That is, in the "bad" years, for every person who was unemployed there were two people with other kinds of employment difficulty (discouraged worker, low pay, or involuntary part-time). But because the routinely reported unemployment rate was high during those years, it was no secret that the economy was suffering and that many people were having employment difficulties. By contrast, in the low-unemployment years, the ratio ranged from 2.7 to 4 (mean 3.2). That is, in those years in which Americans read about very low unemployment rates, for every person who was unemployed, there were over three people with the less-publicized forms of employment difficulty. In sum, the true challenges faced by workers may be less visible in the "good" years than in the "bad" years, as the forms of "disguised" unemployment may be proportionately higher in the former than in the latter.

The uneven pattern of underemployment in different population subgroups also persisted during the most recent economic expansion. In 1999, the overall unemployment rate for all workers over age sixteen was just 4.2% (U.S. Bureau of Labor Statistics, 2000a). But for men, the unemployment rates ranged from 3.6% for whites to 5.6% for those of Hispanic origin to 8.2% for African Americans. For women, the comparable rates were 3.8%, 7.6%, and 7.8%. For the 16–19 age group, the unemployment rates were 12.6% and 11.3% for white men and women, but 30.9% and 25.1% for African American men and women. Inadequate employment showed parallel variations. For example, the rates of involuntary part-time employment ranged from 1.2% and 1.8% for white men and women to 2.1% and 2.9% for African American men and women. In sum, even the best economy in a generation has not erased these persistent subgroup underemployment differentials, and inadequate employment remains a serious problem despite falling unemployment.

The Plan of the Book

Inadequate employment appears to be quite prevalent and seems intuitively to be undesirable and unpleasant. But is it a serious threat to health and well-being? This book offers an empirical test of the hypothesis that falling into inadequate employment has health consequences similar to those associated with job loss. The next chapter will locate this relatively new question in the context of the older unemployment research tradition. Scholars prominent in that tradition have long recognized that some forms of employment might have negative health consequences similar to those of job loss (e.g., Feather, 1990; Fryer, 1986; Jahoda, 1982; Warr, 1987), and we build on that perspective to provide a theoretical and methodological foundation for our project.

The database for the research reported in this book comes from the unique National Longitudinal Survey of Youth (NLSY) that began with a representative sample of young Americans and followed them for over two decades. Chapter 3 describes this data set and the analytic approaches to be applied. A major strength of this data set is its panel design, which allows us to assess two rival explanations for any association between adverse employment and distress or dysfunction. One of these explanations is selection – the drifting of poorly functioning individuals into less adequate employment or unemployment. Chapter 4 will summarize our findings on this rival explanation.

The following chapters consider in more detail the other explanation – that is, the social causation of distress by adverse employment change, controlling for prior functioning. Each chapter explores a different type of well-being indicator at different points in the maturation of this panel, including self-esteem in recent school-leavers (Chapter 5), alcohol abuse in early adulthood (Chaprter 6), and depression in the early thirties (Chapter 7).

In Chapter 8, we extend the employment continuum by considering the effects on poor women with small children of transitions into and out of welfare (Aid to Families with Dependent Children or AFDC). In Chapter 9, we extend our research approach by testing the hypothesis that adverse employment transitions in mothers-to-be carry intergenerational consequences for their first-born children as reflected in low birthweight. The final chapters summarize the conclusions that can be drawn from these analyses and their implications for research and policy.

2

The Social Costs of Unemployment

Work is life, you know, and without it, there's nothing but fear and insecurity.
John Lennon quoted from BBC-TV, December 15, 1969, by Herzenberg
et al., 1998, p. 21

INTRODUCTION

History

A century of research on the health effects of employment stress has focused
largely on just one aspect of underemployment – job loss or unemployment.
But this literature also provides a theoretical framework for understanding
the health consequences of other forms of underemployment, such as inadequate employment. And it provides empirical guidelines for designing
new research on these understudied forms of underemployment.

Durkheim's (1966) analysis of suicide, published in 1897, provided one
of the earliest studies of economic stress and health. Durkheim suspected
that one cause of suicide was anomie, the disorientation and alienation consequent on losing the supportive structure of social norms. He theorized
that anomie increased during periods of great change, including economic
turbulence. In contrast to the later focus on adverse employment change,
Durkheim suspected that change per se, economic expansions as well as
contractions, would increase anomie and, in turn, suicide. He offered empirical data showing an association between absolute economic change and
suicide rates. This hypothesis received further attention from researchers
using modern econometric methods, generating evidence both pro (Pierce,
1967) and con (Marshall & Hodge, 1981).

This sociological debate about the relative importance of absolute versus adverse economic change has a parallel in the psychological literature
on the impacts of different kinds of life events. One early position held that

any life event, regardless of its desirability, would require adjustment and therefore produce some distress (Holmes & Rahe, 1967). However, later research has found that desirable events added little to the prediction of distress by undesirable events (e.g., Lei & Skinner, 1980; Ross & Mirowsky, 1979). Although Durkheim helped to pioneer the empirical study of the link between economic stress and health, most of the subsequent research on this topic has concentrated, in both the psychological and the aggregate economic literatures, not on change per se but rather on undesirable change, such as unemployment.

The Concept of Unemployment. The perception of unemployment has varied over time and across societies and scholarly disciplines (Garraty, 1978). The present concept of unemployment could appear only with the modern concept of employment as waged labor. The first appearance of the term "unemployment" in the *Oxford English Dictionary* did not occur until 1888, although the term is used in various official reports in England going back at least to the 1830s (Burnett, 1994).

Although it might be expected that they would be among the first to consider unemployment, economists actually had little to say about this topic until the twentieth century (Eltis, 1996). One reason for this inattention was the classical economic assumption that the labor market would clear any surplus labor by the operation of supply and demand. Unemployed workers were expected to compete for scarce jobs by offering to work more cheaply, thus bidding down the prevailing wage. As labor costs fall below the level at which employers can afford to hire new workers and still make a profit, employers should take on more workers. The market should find a new equilibrium point at which more people have employment at a lower average wage that corresponds better to the marginal rate of return of labor. From this economic perspective, unemployment should be a temporary phenomenon but one necessary to the achievement of maximum productive efficiency. By definition, only those people who voluntarily withhold their labor at the prevailing wage would be out of work. To the extent that unemployment was a problem, this economic analysis viewed it as a moral problem caused by the "work shy."

Note that this analysis implies the existence not only of unemployment but also of other types of underemployment. For example, some people who want to work may give up on finding employment at acceptable wage levels (called the "reservation wage," – the point at which they will reserve their labor from the job market). In modern parlance, these are discouraged workers. Farm workers typically have seasonal work, with bouts of joblessness during the winter between harvesting and planting. The current jargon refers to this as intermittent unemployment. Classical economics expected low-wage employment, which was considered a crucial element in finding the equilibrium point for labor supply and demand. Over the past two centuries, references have been made not only to unemployment but also to inadequate employment in the form of "lowness of earnings" and "irregularity of work" (Burnett, 1994). Nevertheless, concern for the problem of underemployment has most often focused on unemployment.

Unemployment as a Political Problem. That the equilibrium wage that cleared the labor market might fall below a life- or health-sustaining level or that some workers had to suffer lengthy bouts of unemployment while waiting for the labor market to clear appeared initially as more of a political than an economic problem. Periodically, underemployed workers have threatened political stability, forcing governments to acknowledge the unpleasant facts of joblessness and poverty. For example, changes in English farming communities during the early 1800s produced the Last Labourers' Revolt of 1830–31 (Burnett, 1994). Earlier, small farms with low ratios of workers to employers had allowed close personal bonds marked by mutual respect and even affection. As farms grew larger, more impersonal labor relations accompanied increasing ratios of workers to employers. Becoming more commercially oriented, these larger farms enclosed lands on which peasant workers previously had enjoyed common rights. Larger-scale farms could afford to replace workers with the new threshing machines, and the more socially distant owners felt less obliged to keep the remaining workers on during the slack seasons. Unemployed and lowpaid workers began to riot, destroy threshing machines, and cut fences to demand better pay and steadier employment. The government's initial response was suppression: Almost 2,000 rioters were brought to court, with the majority found guilty and given sentences ranging up to execution (nineteen received the death penalty).

Observers recognized that the underemployed people of this era had a wretched lot, but they differed on whether their plight derived from an insufficiency of employment or from an overgenerous and demoralizing poor relief system. This debate about the proper interpretation and management of unemployment has echoed through the eras. Witness the recent expressions of concern about growing wage inequality, the changing social contract between employers and workers, and, in the political arena, the debate over the revision of the U.S. welfare laws in 1996. Policy makers have tried for generations to find a balance that preserves both flexibility for economic change (i.e., allowing unemployment to occur as an aid to market efficiency) and social stability (i.e., protecting people and institutions against the dislocating effects of unemployment).

One set of trade-offs involves the nature of the social safety net that governments provide their workers. European countries have typically been more generous than the United States in both the benefits that governments or strong unions require employers to provide to their employees (job security, paid vacation) and the benefits that the state provides to the unemployed. But higher requirements for worker benefits may discourage employers from adding new employees, and generous state-provided safety nets require higher taxes that may reduce the incentive for economic expansion, resulting in higher unemployment. "Chronic unemployment is higher in Europe than in the United States, but the low pay and frequent periods of lay-offs in the United States are the functional equivalents" (Hage, 1995, p. 486). In sum, the insufficiency of demand for labor may be expressed, depending on fiscal and labor policy, more in the form of unemployment (as in Europe) or more in the form of inadequate employment (as in the United States). However expressed, underemployment seems destined to remain a fact of life.

Unemployment as an Economic Problem. As politicians grappled with the disruptive social effects of underemployment, economists began to look at unemployment as more than a necessary evil. Economists before Keynes largely assumed that decreased demand for labor would produce lower wages but not widespread or enduring unemployment (Eltis, 1996). Failures of the labor market to clear could be attributed to unions or to other institutional rigidities that resisted lowering wages. The Great Depression of the 1930s cast doubt on the assumption that unemployment was temporary and caused by such rigidities and invited a new economic theory to explain it. Keynes's perspective saw unemployment as a problem but one that proper economic management might control. However, Keynesian policies designed to reduce unemployment, after apparent successes in the 1950s, later seemed to bring inflation and stagflation and the need for a better paradigm (Eltis, 1996).

From one perspective, unemployment has the useful effect of holding wage inflation in check, a relationship summarized in the Phillips curve (Phillips, 1958). A reserve of unemployed workers ready to take jobs at the present wage level will inhibit workers in those jobs from bargaining for higher wages. As unemployment decreases, inflation increases. Presumably, some "natural" level of unemployment will hold inflation steady. Economists call this the "non-accelerating-inflation rate of unemployment" (NAIRU) and estimate it to be in the range of 4% to 6%. Although controversial among economists (Gordon, 1988), this NAIRU hypothesis offers one argument against Keynesian full-employment policies that might raise inflation and still not achieve zero unemployment. Thus the policy challenge for economists has become not so much eradicating underemployment but rather minimizing it and proportioning it between joblessness and various forms of inadequate employment.

Unemployment as a Health Problem. The classical economic view saw unemployment as a natural mechanism for regulating the labor market and therefore necessary for the greater good. This is analogous to generals' acknowledging that some soldiers must die on the battlefield as the price required for victory. However, while societies laud their military casualties as heroes and sometimes generously provide for them and their surviving family members, they tend to ignore their economic counterparts until they rise up in protest. Of course, one may argue that being laid off hardly compares to being wounded in battle. Indeed, if unemployment produced mainly inconvenience and discomfort, then a different analogy would be in order. Perhaps unemployment more resembles being drafted into a peacetime army. In this case, the draftee bears the cost of a temporary decrease in freedom and comfort but experiences no serious harm other than a delay in getting on with his or her civilian career. In this case, the issue becomes one of fairness, distributing the military obligation in a way that seems unbiased – for example, by a lottery. In contrast, the experience of unemployment is not randomly distributed. Similar to the composition of the current U.S. volunteer military, the unemployed tend to be young, less educated, and members of minorities.

But, aside from the equity of its distribution, the question remains whether underemployment is essentially harmless, albeit inconvenient and uncomfortable, or has serious health effects. Certainly, during previous eras, a falling demand for labor could have major impacts on health.

The analysis of the great classical economists indicated that lower wages would produce increased mortality at the poorer end of the income scale, and if wages fell far enough, there would be extra deaths among the young, the old and indeed the able-bodied in many labouring families. . . . By the mid-19th century, the wages of the averagely skilled and even the unskilled had risen to a level where a reduction in the real pay of the employed would no longer produce a significant increase in mortality. Only the casually employed remained vulnerable. . . . (Eltis, 1996, pp. 138–139)

Perhaps the adverse effects of underemployment on health, however severe in prior centuries, have been largely eliminated in the modern era. But if not, underemployment would warrant attention not only as an economic and political issue, but also as a public health threat. Indeed, governmental debates about employment policies have sometimes explicitly weighed the health impacts of underemployment. Evidence that rising unemployment leads to increased suicide or mental hospitalization rates quickly becomes an argument for reducing joblessness. For example, the late Senator Hubert Humphrey made just this connection in support of the Humphrey-Hawkins full employment legislative proposal (Preface to Brenner, 1976). Opponents of such policies naturally challenge the epidemiologic studies underlying such arguments, as illustrated by the counterattacks in England on such research (Bartley, 1992). The following sections will consider the literature on the health effects, especially the mental health effects, of unemployment.

Focus of Health Research on Unemployment

Studies of Unemployment versus Underemployment. The concepts of un-employment and other forms of underemployment emerged as recognized social problems well before professional research societies, such as those of public health, psychology, and sociology, had developed large-scale scholarly publication systems. Thus, we might expect similar levels of research attention to unemployment and other forms of underemploy-ment by the end of the last century. Instead, scholarly attention seems to be disproportionately weighted toward unemployment. A search of the medical literature for 1999 (in Medline) found 231 citations for the keyword "unemployment" but only 5 for "underemployment." A similar search of the sociological literature for 1999 (in *Sociological Abstracts*) found 193 citations for "unemployment" but just 12 for "underemployment." Of course, these results might reflect an unusual year that is not representative of a more balanced scholarly interest in underemployment.

The psychological literature lends itself especially well to studies of the history of research topics because of its computerized publication files going back to the late 1800s. The key words "unemployment" and "under-employment" were searched for the period 1897 to 1998 in the PsycINFO database. The first "unemployment" reference appeared in 1917, but the first "underemployment" reference did not appear until 1960. During the search period, a total of 2,782 dated items appeared on the topic of "unem-ployment," but just 92 on "underemployment." Searches using alternative terms such as "involuntary part-time employment," "low-wage employ-ment," and "poverty-wage employment" ("work," "job") produced even fewer citations. Figure 2.1 displays the persistent historical discrepancy between these two literatures.

Unemployment Research and the Economic Climate. The explosion of re-search publications during the last few decades was not unique to the field of unemployment research but rather reflects the general increase in publication outlets and active scholarship in all branches of the social and medical sciences. Besides this general upward trend in publications, the "unemployment" citation time series might reflect cyclic patterns tuned to the prevailing economic climate. Perhaps scholarly work on unemploy-ment rises and falls with actual unemployment rates. We would expect high levels of unemployment to attract the concern of lay people and the curiosity of researchers. Moreover, one might expect the government to in-crease research funding for the problems of unemployment in proportion to levels of actual unemployment. On the other hand, politicians might also want to minimize public attention to unemployment to the extent that it harms their electoral chances.

Figure 2.2 provides data on the possible link between unemployment rates and scholarship. In order to remove the upward trend and better

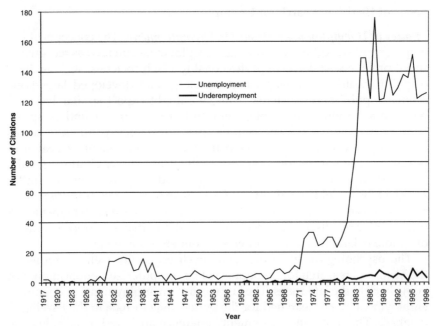

FIGURE 2.1. PsycINFO citations for key words "unemployment" and "underemployment." *Source:* Dooley (in press), Figure 1.

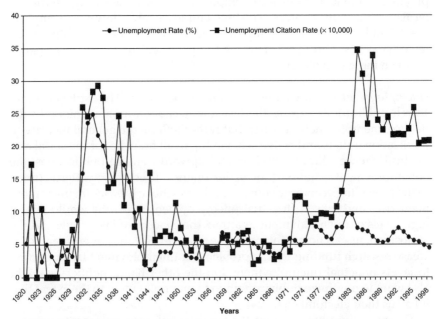

FIGURE 2.2. Unemployment rate and PsycINFO "unemployment" citation rate. *Source:* Dooley (in press), Figure 2.

reveal possible cycles, PsycINFO citations on unemployment are plotted as proportions of total citations. Alongside appear the actual annual average unemployment rates for the United States (before 1929 from Lebergott, 1964; after 1928 from U.S. Department of Labor, 1990; 1999b). The clearest connection between actual unemployment and unemployment research appears during the Great Depression era, when the number of citations jumped for the first time from single to double digits. With unemployment dropping during World War II and remaining low during the 1950s and 1960s (peak unemployment of 6.8% in 1958), the number of annual unemployment citations fell back to single digits for the period 1946–70. Apparently, substantial sustained unemployment levels are necessary to trigger expanded research on this topic. The number of citations moved again into double digits with the recession of the early 1970s (peak unemployment of 8.5% in 1975) and into triple digits with the recession of the early 1980s (peak unemployment of 9.8% in 1982). Time-series analysis of these data showed that this apparent association was statistically significant, controlling for other regularities in the series (Dooley & Catalano, in press).

Does this phenomenon help to explain the differential scholarly attention paid to unemployment versus underemployment? As developed in the first chapter, actual levels of inadequate employment have consistently exceeded actual levels of official unemployment over the last several decades. Were researchers devoting their efforts to the actual prevalence of economic problems, we would expect to see more research on inadequate employment than on unemployment. It seems more likely that researchers' attention follows perceived economic problems as emphasized in official government reports and echoed in the media, that is, the published unemployment rates. When unemployment reaches high levels, it seems imperative to deal with joblessness, and any job seems precious. When unemployment falls, the society breathes a sigh of relief and turns its attention to noneconomic priorities.

For whatever reason, scholars have amassed a large literature on unemployment and a much smaller one on other forms of underemployment. Nevertheless, the findings and methods of the former literature might serve to inform and accelerate the development of the latter.

RESEARCH ON UNEMPLOYMENT

Findings

Why So Many Studies? The numerous studies on unemployment in the psychology literature have taken many forms. Some merely mention unemployment descriptively as an incidental element in studies devoted to other topics. Of those including unemployment as a vital structural factor, some treat unemployment as an outcome of some prior disabling personal characteristic. But the most relevant studies for our purposes treat unemployment as the cause of health effects. Even this narrowing of the unemployment literature to the social causation category leaves us with hundreds of studies over the last century.

Why did it require so many studies to test the seemingly simple hypothesis that unemployment causes ill health? One reason is that the relationship at issue is not a fixed target but rather moves with such surrounding variables as the economic climate, labor market structure and rigidities, cultural attitudes, and social safety nets. Another reason is that the health effects of job loss do not lend themselves to the most decisive research designs, that is, true experimental manipulations with random subject assignments. Finally, we are interested not just in the simple main effects of employment change on well-being but also in the processes by which mediating variables transmit the effects and in the conditioning of these processes by potential moderating variables.

The many studies on this question have appeared during different eras, used different research approaches, and included different sets of explanatory variables. A few examples can illustrate this methodological variety. As early as 1910, researchers went door to door in the city of York, England, to count the unemployed and to assess the nature and causes of their unemployment (Rowntree & Lasker, 1911). During the Depression of the 1930s, a team of qualitative researchers studied the effects of unemployment on both individual and community life in the town of Marienthal in Austria (Jahoda, Lazarsfeld, & Zeisel, 1971). In the early 1970s, modern econometric techniques were used to estimate the covariation in aggregate employment and mental hospitalization time series for the state of New York (Brenner, 1973). A quasi-experimental research design was used to compare individuals who lost their jobs at a closing plant with those who retained their jobs at a plant that stayed open (Cobb & Kasl, 1977). More recent research has followed a panel of Australian school-leavers to explore the developmental effects on young people of their success or failure in getting jobs (Winefield et al., 1993). Not surprisingly, these different studies have sometimes reached different conclusions, or at least different magnitude estimates of the focal relationship.

Literature Reviews. There is no need to add still another review to the dozens that have already attempted to make sense of this complex literature. A small portion of those appearing over the past two decades include the following: Brenner & Mooney, 1983; Catalano, 1991; Dew, Penkower, & Bromet, 1991; Dooley & Catalano, 1980; Dooley, Fielding, & Levi, 1996; Feather, 1997; Horwitz, 1984; Kasl, Rodriguez, & Lasch, 1998; Lennon, 1999; Liem & Rayman, 1982; Murphy & Athanasou, 1999; Platt, 1984; Warr, 1987; and Winton, Heather, & Robertson, 1986.

These reviews typically report adverse health effects associated with unemployment. The magnitude of such effects varies from study to study depending on the research design, the studied population, and the evaluated outcome. For example, mental health indicators such as depression and alcohol abuse have been studied more often and, perhaps not coincidentally, have shown stronger links to unemployment than have physical health indicators. In order to estimate the usual magnitude of the effect of employment change on mental health outcomes, one review used meta-analysis (Murphy & Athanasou, 1999). This review included only the sixteen recent studies that used longitudinal designs and standardized psychological tests of mental disorder. Of these studies, fourteen provided evidence of an adverse effect of job loss on mental health, and five provided data suitable for estimating an average effect size or "d." The resulting value of the weighted d was .36, indicating that those who lost their jobs showed an increase of .36 of a standard deviation in mental symptom scores relative to those keeping their jobs. Although statistically significant (standard error of the weighted d = .06), an effect of this size is usually regarded as "small" in magnitude, although it does have potential practical significance. However, as the authors note, the estimate is based on a very small number of studies representing a tiny fraction of the entire literature.

Rather than adding another overall summary of this literature, we will identify the major design dimensions along which the literature has evolved and their implications for new research on other forms of underemployment. In later chapters, we will revisit relevant portions of the unemployment literature as it relates to each of our outcome variables.

Research Challenges and Design Responses

Of the various dimensions used for categorizing unemployment studies, we are interested primarily in those that provide guidance for new research on other forms of underemployment. There are, of course, social research standards that, if applicable, would govern the design of such new research. For example, the true experimental design is widely accepted as the gold standard for ensuring internal validity – that is, confidence that the observed effect (e.g., increased depression) is due to the presumed causal variable (e.g., job loss). However, true experiments require the authority to assign subjects randomly to differently treated groups. For both ethical and practical reasons, such designs seldom if ever prove feasible for studying the effects of unemployment. Instead, unemployment researchers have had to rely on more practical but less internally valid designs that risk the challenge of rival hypotheses. Two of these challenges and their design responses identify dimensions that can help us to map the unemployment literature. One involves the temporal nature of the analysis, either cross-sectional or longitudinal. The other concerns the level of analysis, either individual or aggregate.

Selection and Longitudinal Research. A long-standing challenge to research on unemployment and health involves the direction of the causal process. An association between being unemployed and being unhealthy could appear at some point in time by any of three different mechanisms. First, some other variable could cause people both to lose their jobs and to become unhealthy. For example, growing up in poverty with little education or material resources might dispose individuals to a higher risk of intermittent unemployment and of illness. Called "confounding," this rival explanation can be controlled by different research procedures. Research on unemployment usually relies on statistical adjustment of potential confounding variables, such as parental income and social status. If the apparent link between unemployment and illness disappears with such adjustment, we consider the relationship spurious rather than causal.

But suppose the association between two variables persists after controlling for potential confounding variables. In this case, the other two mechanisms become plausible. One explanation, called social causation, holds that the stress of job loss leads to increased symptoms of disorder. The rival explanation, called selection, holds that preexisting dysfunction leads to dysfunction in the occupational setting and to subsequent job loss. Choosing between the social causation and selection explanations is a common challenge for studies of unemployment and health. In cross-sectional research, critics can offer the plausible rival hypothesis that the only people who lose their jobs are those with prior health problems.

Fortunately, there exists a response to this challenge other than the usually impractical true experiment – longitudinal designs. By measuring the respondents both before and after the employment status change (e.g., job loss), it is possible to adjust for any selection effects of prior symptoms. Longitudinal data can measure the difference in symptom change between those losing and those keeping their jobs. An increase in symptoms in the unemployed relative to the continuing employed, after adjusting for earlier symptoms and other confounding variables, would favor the social causation hypothesis. For this reason, unemployment researchers generally prefer longitudinal designs.

Note that research designed to control for selection does not imply an either/or choice between social causation and selection. In principle, both mechanisms may operate. High-symptom individuals may be more vulnerable to job loss, and people who lose their jobs may experience increased symptoms of distress. Both processes should interest us, and longitudinal designs permit us to investigate both. In Chapter 4, we will focus on selection by examining whether prior symptoms predict later adverse employment change, in order both to estimate the magnitude of this phenomenon and to check possible interactions of the selection effect by moderator variables. However, our primary interest in the subsequent chapters will concern the existence and magnitude of the social causation effect net of any such selection.

The Ecological Fallacy and Individual-Level Research. Longitudinal research can analyze data at either the individual or the aggregate level. Aggregate-level data characterize spatial and temporal units – for example, time series such as annual unemployment and mental hospitalization rates for a state. Such data may originate from individual-level interviews or records, but the aggregation process shears off the individuals' personal characteristics. Studies of such concomitant time series provide good protection against the rival explanation of selection or reverse causation. No one would argue that increases in rates of mental hospitalization or suicide cause increases in the unemployment rate. However, these aggregate-level studies have raised questions of two different sorts.

One challenge pertains to the econometric procedures used in aggregate time-series analysis, particularly those linking unemployment to mortality, such as those produced by Brenner (1976; 1979). His strikingly positive evidence linking health and the national economy came under strong criticism around a host of technical statistical issues (e.g., Cohen & Felson, 1979; Gravelle, Hutchinson, & Stern, 1981). The complex details of this debate need not concern us here (for more in-depth treatment, see Wagstaff, 1985). Despite such difficulties, a persuasive logic for the general approach of aggregate time-series analysis and an alternative statistical strategy based on Box-Jenkins methods have been offered for use in unemployment studies (Catalano, 1981; Catalano, Dooley, & Jackson, 1983). But regardless of how one comes down on this dispute, a second challenge to such aggregate methodology remains.

The second major concern about aggregate time-series research arises not from its statistical procedures but rather from the fundamental limits on the interpretations that it can support. Correlations between unemployment and mortality rates can inform us about the community (or state or national) health responses to economic change. But any interpretation of such correlations linking an individual's health to that individual's job loss would risk the ecological fallacy (Robinson, 1950). For example, evidence that the suicide rate rises following an increase in the unemployment rate cannot assure us that the additional suicides were people who had lost their jobs. Although the extra suicides may be people who recently suffered job loss, they could as well be family members of those laid off, people not currently in the workforce but feeling discouraged about their prospects for reentering the labor market, or others with even more distant connections to the economy.

The ecological fallacy does not imply that aggregate-level estimates never describe actual individual-level relationships. Aggregate- and individual-level patterns may or may not coincide, depending on such factors as the grouping process by which the individual-level data were aggregated (Firebaugh, 1978). The problem is that individual-level inference, which is often the primary concern of psychological and medical studies, cannot be drawn safely from aggregate data. Conversely, and for similar reasons, aggregate-level inferences cannot be based on individual-level data without risking the individual differences fallacy (Richards, 1990). Scholars working in public health or economic policy and interested in community-level phenomena may well want aggregate-level inferences that can be safely based only on aggregate-level data.

Economic Climate and Cross-Level Research. Given our primary focus here on the individual-level relationship between adverse employment change and well-being, should we disregard aggregate-level data? On the contrary, a full understanding of the individual-level connections between employment and health may require the inclusion of a measure of the community's economic climate. Aggregate economic conditions may influence individual well-being indirectly, through personal employment change. Moreover, the surrounding economic climate may also condition or moderate the relationship between personal employment change and well-being. Fortunately, a cross-level design permits exploration of such indirect and interactive effects. This approach expands the usual individual-level design to include measures of the presumed employment stressor at both levels (e.g., the unemployment rate for the respondent's community and the individual's personal employment status) as well as a term representing their interaction.

Various mechanisms for such an interaction between aggregate and individual employment variables have been suggested. One possibility is that unemployed individuals make attributions in the context of the prevailing economic climate and thus blame themselves less when those around them are also experiencing high unemployment. Consistent with this view, one study found that personal unemployment proved less stressful during high-unemployment periods (Cohn, 1978). The opposite pattern would appear if unemployed people experience more stress when their hopes for reemployment are dimmed by high prevailing unemployment. Consistent with this view, another study found that more health problems were reported during high-unemployment periods, particularly by the less-educated unemployed, who would face more difficulty competing for scarce jobs (Turner, 1995). However, other studies have found no evidence for any interaction between aggregate and personal unemployment (Dooley, Catalano, & Rook, 1988; Dooley, Catalano, & Wilson, 1994).

This absence of a clear pattern of cross-level interactive effects may reflect the lack of research attention to this issue, which may in turn stem from the difficulty of mounting a proper test. Conducting a cross-level study requires adequate variability in the key variables, including the measure of economic climate. But economic climate will have little variability in studies conducted in one community over a short time. Studies that take place in either high- or low-unemployment climates may, to the extent that the local unemployment rate does function as a moderator, find quite different individual-level relationships between employment status and well-being. Unfortunately, if the moderating role of the economic climate goes unrecognized, these discrepant results may appear as failures to replicate the main effect of adverse employment change.

For example, consider another basis for anticipating such an interaction (suggested by Winefield & Fryer, 1996). At any point in time, the people who both are unemployed and have severe health problems can be divided into two groups – those experiencing health problems caused by their job loss and those selected into unemployment by their prior health problems. The ratio of these two groups should, in theory, vary directly with the unemployment rate. During high-unemployment periods, many usually well-functioning people experience layoffs and subsequent health problems, but during low-unemployment periods, only the already dysfunctional will be left out of work. Thus a longitudinal study that adjusts for prior symptoms should find a stronger social causation effect of personal job loss on health during high-unemployment periods but a smaller effect during low-unemployment periods, when selection dominates.

The economic climate might also influence studies of job loss in an opposite way. Recall that the adverse effect of unemployment appears as a contrast to the relative well-being of those who retain their employment. However, the satisfaction of employed people also appears to vary with aggregate conditions (Fenwick & Tausig, 1994; Tausig & Fenwick, 1999). As the unemployment rate rises, workers may experience a weakened bargaining position, making it harder for them to maintain wages or working conditions at the same time that employers feel compelled to trim production costs in the face of falling demand. Workers already unhappy with their bosses, coworkers, or labor conditions may feel increasingly trapped between rising job insecurity and the absence of alternative positions. Thus during a recession, increased symptoms on the part of job losers may show less contrast with the declining well-being of the continuing employed. This argues not only for using cross-level designs where possible but also for dividing the continuing employed into those experiencing continued adequate employment and those falling into less-adequate employment.

In summary, unemployment and health studies have used mainly correlational and quasi-experimental research designs. Of these, one type responds best to the potential challenges of both selection and the ecological fallacy. This design uses individual-level data gathered longitudinally and, where possible, adds aggregate measures of economic climate in order to allow cross-level analyses. The next chapter describes a data set that meets these criteria and summarizes the analytic approach that we take in the remaining chapters. Despite its advantages, this approach cannot guarantee perfect internal validity because of the ever-present possibility of spuriousness. Researchers must routinely include in their models potential confounding variables and also search for other variables that might either explain the impact of adverse employment change or moderate it. Guidance for choosing and categorizing such variables must come from theory.

THEORY

The Costs of Underemployment

General Framework: Stressful Transitions. A comprehensive theory for the unemployment-health relationship would include multiple direct, indirect, reciprocal, and interacting causal pathways (see for example, Dooley & Catalano, 1980). Unemployment studies sometimes treat the focal event of personal job loss as an entirely random event with no prior causes. In fact, individual-level employment transitions take place in an economic context and derive, at least in part, from such phenomena as changes in the local economic climate, the individual's industry, the employer's need for the individual's particular skills, and the individual's work performance. These variables not only help to predict a person's job loss but may also moderate its impact, to the extent that they render it more or less expected, discounted, and planned for. Thus an increase in the unemployment rate in a person's industry may serve as a direct cause of that person's job loss and both an indirect cause and a moderator of any resulting health effects.

Similarly, if the job loser experiences increased symptoms, this is seldom the last or only outcome of unemployment. Adverse job change can have effects on the individual other than personal health problems. It may delay or derail the individual's employment career growth, resulting in lowered lifetime earnings, loss of health insurance, and decreased resources to cope with other health risk factors. Adverse job change may also affect other persons. For example, it may produce intrafamily tensions, with spillover effects on the spouse (e.g., Rook, Dooley, & Catalano, 1991) or children (Steinberg, Catalano, & Dooley, 1981). Changes in personal health symptoms, whether of the job loser or of others in his or her family, can lead to increased demand for health services, such as admissions to mental hospitals as measured in the aggregate. Extremely high levels of unemployment may produce demoralization at the community level by a process of social contagion (Jahoda et al., 1971). Thus, the many causal pathways that can link economic and health changes make it difficult to specify the total effect of unemployment on health, from aggregate unemployment rate changes through personal job loss to personal, family, and community outcomes. One way to limit this complexity is to focus on a subset of the full array of possible links between employment and health.

Most researchers have concentrated on the link between personal job loss and personal health outcomes. Of the various general theories that might explain this link, the stress model has been among the most widely employed. According to this model, as articulated by the physiologist Hans Selye (1956), any life change taxes adaptive resources and threatens to throw the individual out of equilibrium. Selye viewed stress as a response, part of a three-part sequence called the general adaptation syndrome. In the first or "alarm" stage, the person mobilizes to deal with the adaptive challenge. In the second or "resistance" stage, the person's body replenishes itself physiologically to deal with the threats. And if the stressor persists, the person reaches the third or "exhaustion" stage, where the body's resources become depleted, thus limiting further adaptation and leaving the person vulnerable to illness.

Although Selye based his model on animal analogue research, subsequent human research using this paradigm has explored the health sequelae of various kinds of stressful life events. Holmes and Rahe pioneered this approach with their development of the self-report life event checklist called the Social Readjustment Rating Scale (1967). Virtually all of the many subsequent variants on this life-event methodology have ranked job loss as among the most demanding of such events. Although different types of stressful events may result in similar adverse health outcomes, the specific mechanisms by which they operate may vary not only from event to event (as between unemployment and divorce) but also from individual to individual for the same event. The stress model allows for the investigation of both the mediating processes by which different events produce disorder and the moderating processes by which different individuals respond differently to the same event.

Stress models emphasize the association between stressful events and subsequent illness but often do not explain the mechanism for this connection. Selye explained the physical health consequences in terms of physiological exhaustion. But however plausible this mechanism may be for explaining physical illness, it seems insufficient to explain the psychological and behavioral costs of stressful events. The job loss literature consistently finds that there are mental health effects resulting from unemployment (e.g., depression), but it more rarely finds clear physical health outcomes. Is there a psychological mechanism that can explain the link between adverse employment transitions and such outcomes as low self-esteem, alcohol abuse, and depression?

One conceptually attractive approach, that of Jutta Heckausen and her colleagues, explains the stressfulness of such events in terms of control theory (Heckhausen & Schulz, 1995). They begin with the assumption that people want to have primary control over their environments, that is, they want to be able to change the world to fit their needs (based on the primary/secondary control approach of Rothbaum, Weisz, & Snyder, 1982). When people are unable to exert primary control, according to this model, they will compensate by resorting to secondary control. Secondary control involves modifying one's cognitions or changing oneself so as better to fit the world – for example, reorganizing one's goals in an effort to regain primary control by pursuing more reachable outcomes. One or the other of these control types will come into play when people encounter transitional events. Such an event consists of a temporally discrete change that affects a person's ability to reach important goals. Failure to exert primary control in response to such transitions may produce frustration, loss of self-esteem, and loss of confidence in one's ability to control events, leading to feelings of helplessness and depression. The likelihood that a transition will produce such negative consequences depends on the effectiveness of the person's secondary control repertoire. Unfortunately, some adaptive responses may actually prove dysfunctional – for example, alcohol misuse (Jones & Berglas, 1978).

This theory provides an overarching psychological framework for understanding the mental health consequences of the full range of adverse employment changes (including not only job loss but also falling into inadequate employment). This model allows for variation from person to person in the psychological meaning of such employment transitions. For example, job loss may mean loss of status to one person and loss of income and standard of living to another. The model subsumes these different types of loss under the common rubric of net loss of ability to attain important goals, whatever those particular goals are for each person. However, researchers who have focused narrowly on job dislocation as a stressor have looked beyond the general loss of control to identify the particular types of loss brought about by unemployment.

Benefits of Employment. For unemployment to be stressful implies that employment provides desirable benefits or assets that help workers to achieve their various goals and are, therefore, painful to lose. Different theories have emphasized different sets of these benefits or functions (for an overview, see Winefield, 1995). The most obvious loss arising from unemployment involves decreased income and the consequent fall in the worker's standard of living. Some studies have offered support for the view that financial strain mediates the connection between unemployment and ill health (Kessler, Turner, & House, 1988). However, losing certain psychosocial functions of work may also affect well-being. For example, to work's manifest function of providing income, Jahoda (1982), in her Deprivation Theory, added five latent functions: time structure, social contacts, social purpose, status, and activity. Losing one's job might be expected to deprive workers of one or more of these functions, and researchers have offered empirical support for the adverse impact of losing some of these functions (e.g., Isaksson, 1989).

Taking a different approach, Fryer, in his Agency Theory, argues that Jahoda's latent functions may sometimes operate not only as benefits but also as costs (Fryer, 1986). For example, the time structure imposed by the employer may conflict with the employee's human needs. At the extreme, working excessive overtime hours might lead to health or behavioral problems (Schor, 1991). Fryer also argues that Jahoda's supposed psychological benefits, or their deprivation by unemployment, seem to be imposed on passive workers. By contrast, he contends that workers are proactive agents with initiative and independence, for whom unemployment is harmful mainly to the extent that loss of income restricts their agency.

In his Vitamin Theory, Warr (1987) offers another model that treats employment as an environment that can be analyzed on various dimensions. Some of these involve unalloyed benefits, the loss of which should prove stressful to anyone – for example, the provision of money and status. Others could prove either beneficial or harmful depending on their degree, including opportunities such as those for control and interpersonal contact. Just as vitamins can be taken in dosages that may be too small or too large, so some work environments can be too high or low on Warr's dimensions. As he says, "some people's jobs are worse in terms of environmental 'vitamins' than are some settings of unemployment" (Warr, 1987, p. 291). This perspective accords well with the perspective of the research described in this book. Jobs in the economically inadequate categories of underemployment may be lacking in the virtues identified in each of the theories just noted. They may lack some of Jahoda's latent functions, may lack the agency desired by Fryer, and may be too high or low on some of Warr's vitamin dimensions. Thus such forms of employment may resemble unemployment more than adequate employment with respect to mental health outcomes. Falling from adequate employment into such forms of underemployment could, therefore, serve as an adverse transition that threatens workers' sense of control.

Complex Effects

Variation in Effects of Job Change. From two different perspectives, job loss should constitute more of an adaptive challenge for some people than for others. First, if employment provides substantial manifest and latent benefits, as Jahoda argues, or "vitamins," in Warr's terminology, their loss will be felt more or less acutely depending on the workers' access to other sources of these functions. For example, workers with large savings or living in countries with generous unemployment insurance should feel less financial strain than do workers without savings or access to such benefits. Benefits that are lost with employment operate as mediators of subsequent health problems. If the same benefits are available to workers from other sources, they operate as buffers to reduce the adverse effects of job loss. Similarly, workers equipped with effective coping skills may compensate for adverse employment change with secondary control.

Second, some jobs may feel inherently stressful, for the reasons given by Fryer and Warr. Kasl pointed out that losing an undesirable job "may not be the trauma which facile generalizations from the 'stressful life events' literature would seem to dictate" (1979, p. 195). If the role, whether an employment role or a marital role, is sufficiently aversive, losing it may seem more a blessing than an adaptive challenge; and some research supports this hypothesis (Wheaton, 1990).

From this latter perspective, there is no qualitative psychological distinction between employment and unemployment. Unemployment may be demoralizing and dreadful, but proactive people may turn it into a positive experience (Fryer & Payne, 1984). Employment may be satisfying or not; some people dissatisfied with their jobs report as much distress as people out of work (Feather, 1990; Winefield et al., 1993). The stress-model approach to job loss thus rests on the assumption that, in general, most people enjoy more benefits economically and psychologically when employed than when unemployed. The central question that this book asks is whether a significant subset of the employed, those in economically inadequate jobs, more resemble the unemployed than the adequately employed.

Favorable Employment Change. If losing employment produces distress, does finding a job improve health? Although such a symmetric relationship seems intuitive, it does not follow that favorable employment change produces a gain in well-being equivalent to the loss of well-being brought about by adverse employment change (Lieberson, 1985). Some kinds of symptomatic response to job loss may be relatively labile and easily reversed. For example, one study of emotional functioning found that reemployment reversed the symptoms of depression (Kessler et al., 1988). However, some maladaptive responses may result in established habits (e.g., substance abuse) or major changes in the individual's social support system (e.g., divorce). In such situations, reemployment may not return the individual to the pre-crisis level of functioning.

The beneficial effects of reemployment have received much less attention than the social costs of job loss. One review did find seven studies on the impact of moving from unemployment to employment (Murphy & Athanasou, 1999). The expected beneficial effects of such change varied across studies, perhaps reflecting variations in the nature of the outcome variables (*d* effect sizes ranged from o to .76). However, the weighted average (*d* = .54) clearly supported an overall benefit of reemployment. The theoretical mechanisms for a beneficial employment effect have received even less attention than the existence of the effect.

One theoretical question involves the most likely beneficiaries of reemployment. Perhaps those individuals who experience the greatest loss of well-being due to job loss will enjoy the greatest gains upon reemployment. If reemployment did prove restorative in this manner, it would serve a therapeutic function, reducing the symptoms brought on by the job loss. On the other hand, perhaps unemployed individuals who did not suffer health effects or present new symptoms are the ones responding most favorably to reemployment. In this case, reemployment would function not as therapy but as primary prevention of disorder, promoting good health. This is an open research question that can be answered by checking the effect on later symptoms (after reemployment) of the interaction between prior symptoms (while still unemployed) and reemployment.

Another issue derives from the earlier analyses of the costs and benefits of employment. If undesirable employment can prove unhealthful, then the benefit of reemployment should vary with the quality of the new job. One study of unemployed workers found that those moving into less satisfactory jobs reported no mental health benefits, while those moving into satisfactory jobs did report such benefits (Wanberg, 1995). Just as the study of adverse employment change cannot be simplified to research on job loss, so favorable employment change will prove more complicated than reemployment. On an employment-status continuum ranging from very desirable jobs to inadequate jobs to unemployment, there exist many potential favorable and unfavorable transitions. Does a marginally favorable change from unemployment to employment with inadequate pay or hours match the benefits of change from such an inadequate job to an economically adequate one?

Perhaps the best antidote for the ills of unemployment is a good job. But an economic policy aimed at providing that antidote would benefit from research that addresses such issues as those just identified. In later chapters where we explore the costs of adverse job change, we will consider the benefits of favorable job change as well.

3

Data Sources and Methods

Unemployment and mental health researchers have frequently proceeded by contrasting the better mean mental health of employed people with the worse mean mental health of unemployed people in both cross-sectional and longitudinal designs. However, it may now be only a matter of time until the deteriorating mean mental health of employed people obliterates this formerly largely reliable difference.

Fryer, 1999, p. 1

INTRODUCTION

Overview

Longitudinal Design. This chapter will describe the longitudinal research design, the data sources, and the key measures used throughout this book. In contrast to cross-sectional designs, which measure all subjects at a single point in time, longitudinal research includes a variety of different designs, each having differently timed measurement periods as a common component. Longitudinal approaches that assess a different group of individuals at each point in time are called "trend" designs. In contrast, a "panel" design measures the same individuals at multiple points in time (for further details on such designs, see Babbi, 1995; Bijleveld et al., 1998; Kleinbaum, Kupper, & Morgenstern, 1982; Menard, 1991). All of our analyses employ panel designs.

Panel designs are particularly useful because they characterize change over time within individuals (intraindividual change) as well as between individuals (interindividual change). Clarification of the temporal sequence of events is central to the study of complex causal relationships between variables. Experimental research designs deal with this problem by arranging for the presumed cause (a manipulated independent variable) to take place before the presumed effect. But such experimental approaches are not feasible in the study of naturally occurring economic swings and employment shifts. Because we must rely on passively observed variables, the panel design is essential for the determination of event order.

Although the temporal order of events is one criterion for establishing causal relationships (the causal variable must precede the outcome variable), it is not the only consideration. Two other important criteria involve establishing association (or covariation) between the variables under study and controlling confounding variables. This latter criterion requires ruling out possible alternative explanations that might explain the observed association between the study variables (Dooley, 2001). For this reason, statistical analysis plays a central role in nonexperimental studies of causal processes by estimating the association between variables and adjusting for potential confounding variables. We will describe the multivariate methods used here after first introducing the data to which these statistical techniques will be applied.

Data Sources. The National Longitudinal Survey of Youth (NLSY) offers a unique data set for exploring complex relationships among employment, mental health, and alcohol disorder. First, because it is a panel survey, it permits tracking change over time in the same group of individuals in changing economic contexts. Second, findings generated from the NLSY are widely applicable (i.e., have high "external" validity), because the sample is nationally representative of all youths residing in the United States in 1979 (see the next section for a more detailed description of the NLSY sample). Third, the NLSY collected data from a relatively large number of respondents, which in most cases provides adequate statistical power for making confident between-group comparisons.[1] Lastly, the survey collected a very rich set of data that profiles work transitions, family life, physical health, and emotional well-being, as well as other life transitions experienced by the panel.

National Longitudinal Surveys. The National Longitudinal Surveys (NLS) include several different surveys, each representing a different population. The original surveys sampled four groups that were first interviewed during the mid-1960's: 5,020 older men surveyed from 1966 to 1983 and again in 1990; 5,083 mature women interviewed from 1967 until 1992; 5,225 young men surveyed from 1966 until 1981; and 5,159 young

---

[1] Statistical power is the ability to detect existing differences between groups or existing relationships between variables, i.e., effects that are sufficiently large that they are probably not due to sampling error. Sample size is only one determinant of power. Others include the actual size of the effect being studied, the level of significance chosen for the test (i.e., the risk one is willing to run that the effect is due to chance), and, if applicable, the balance between the sample sizes in the subgroups being compared.

women interviewed from 1968 until 1993. Two additional surveys began in 1979 and 1997 and are referred to as the NLSY79 and the NLSY97, respectively. The NLSY97 followed a sample of 8,984 youths who were twelve to sixteen years old when first interviewed in 1997. The NLSY79 began with an initial sample of 12,686 individuals who were fourteen to twenty-two years old when first interviewed in 1979. This latter survey, the NLSY79, serves as the basis for all analyses presented here and will be described in detail.

The Bureau of Labor Statistics of the United States Department of Labor sponsors the NLS. Many other federal agencies have contributed funding for special supplements to the survey questionnaires, including the National Institute of Child Health and Human Development, the Department of Defense, the Department of Education, the Department of Justice, the Department of Health and Human Services, the Social Security Administration, the National Institute on Aging, the National School-to-Work Office, the National Institute on Drug Abuse, the National Institute on Alcohol Abuse and Alcoholism, and the Women's Bureau and the Pension Welfare Benefits Administration of the Department of Labor (Center for Human Resource Research, 2000). The NLS contracts with the Center for Human Resource Research (CHRR) at The Ohio State University, the National Opinion Research Center (NORC), and the Census Bureau for data collection, production, and distribution; user services; and overall survey management (CHRR, 2000).

National Longitudinal Survey of Youth 1979

Sampling Design. The NLSY79 was designed to represent the entire population of youth residing in the United States on January 1, 1979, who were born between January 1, 1957, and December 31, 1964. Three probability samples comprise the NLSY79 (CHRR, 2000): (1) a primary sample designed to be representative of the noninstitutionalized civilian segment of young people living in the United States in 1979; (2) a supplemental group that oversampled civilian Hispanic, African American, and economically disadvantaged non-Hispanic, non–African American youth; and (3) a military sample designed to represent the population born January 1, 1957, through December 31, 1961, and serving in the military as of September 30, 1978. The primary sample, as well as the Hispanic and African American supplemental samples, has been eligible for reinterview at each survey. However, due to budgetary considerations, the military and economically disadvantaged non-Hispanic, non–African American samples were dropped after 1984 and 1990, respectively.

Beginning in 1986 – with funding from the National Institute of Child Health and Human Development (NICHD) and other private foundations – all children born to females of the NLSY79 have been surveyed on a biennial basis in order to collect detailed information regarding their cognitive, socioemotional, and physiological development. These children, referred to as "Children of the NLSY79," now comprise a separate survey offering a unique opportunity to study relationships between parental variables and child outcomes. During 1998, 7,067 interviews were conducted with members of the "Children of the NLSY79" survey. These children and young adults (fifteen years old and older) are considered a representative sample of all children born to females fourteen to twenty-two years old in 1979. We use one measure of these children, the birthweight of firstborns in the 1980s, to provide an illustrative test of possible intergenerational effects of adverse employment change. The details of that analysis appear in Chapter 9.

The NLSY79 data are available on compact disc – with or without the confidential geocode data, which contain detailed geographic data. Accessing the survey data with the geocode option requires that individuals satisfactorily complete the BLS geocode agreement procedure (CHRR, 1999).[2]

Data Collection and Sample Retention. The NLSY79 is a panel survey with interviews conducted annually from 1979 through 1994, after which interviews have been conducted every other year. All respondents were surveyed using traditional pencil-and-paper interviews (PAPI), in a face-to-face interview format, from 1979 through 1986. In 1987, budgetary constraints required that respondents be interviewed via phone, with personal interviews resuming in 1988. In 1993, computer-assisted personal interviews (CAPI), using laptop computers and an electronic version of the survey questionnaire, replaced the more traditional PAPI. The NLSY reported improved data quality as a result of adopting the CAPI interview process (Baker & Bradburn, 1992; CHRR, 2000).

In 1979, 14,575 sample members were initially designated for interview, of whom 12,686 were actually interviewed, yielding a base-year completion rate of 87% for the total sample (90% for the primary sample, 89% for the supplemental sample, and 72% for the military sample). The base-year completion rate for the NLSY compares favorably to another large and frequently used panel survey, the Panel Study of Income Dynamics (PSID), in which only 76% of the families designated for interview in the base year (1968) were actually interviewed (Hill, 1992).

---

[2] Several important pieces of documentation (e.g., the NLS handbook, the NLS user's guide) are included in the purchase price of the compact discs, with other documentation available for purchase (e.g., the NLSY survey questionnaires). The NLS User Services Office can be contacted at: 921 Chatham Lane, Suite 100, Columbus, OH 43221-2418; phone: (614) 442-7366; fax: (614) 442-7329; e-mail: ⟨usersvc@postoffice.Center for Human Resource Reseach.ohio-state.edu⟩, or see the NLS web homepage, ⟨http://stats.bls.gov/nlshome. htm⟩.

TABLE 3.1. *NLSY79: Number of interviews and retention rates by sample type*

	Sample Type			
	Primary	Supplemental	Military	Total
Year	Total/Retention Rate (%)	Total/Retention Rate (%)	Total/Retention Rate (%)	Total/Retention Rate (%)
1979	6,111 –	5,295 –	1,280 –	12,686 –
1980	5,873 (96.1)	5,075 (95.9)	1,193 (93.2)	12,141 (95.7)
1981	5,892 (96.4)	5,108 (96.5)	1,195 (93.4)	12,195 (96.1)
1982	5,876 (96.2)	5,036 (95.1)	1,211 (94.6)	12,123 (95.6)
1983	5,902 (96.6)	5,093 (96.2)	1,226 (95.8)	12,221 (96.3)
1984	5,814 (95.1)	4,040 (95.2)	1,215 (94.9)	12,069 (95.1)
1985	5,751 (94.1)	4,957 (93.6)	186[a] (92.5)	10,894 (93.9)
1986	5,633 (92.2)	4,839 (91.4)	183 (91.1)	10,655 (91.8)
1987	5,538 (90.6)	4,768 (90.1)	179 (89.1)	10,485 (90.3)
1988	5,513 (90.2)	4,777 (90.2)	175 (87.1)	10,465 (90.2)
1989	5,571 (91.2)	4,853 (91.7)	181 (90.0)	10,605 (91.4)
1990	5,498 (90.0)	4,755 (89.8)	183 (91.0)	10,436 (89.9)
1991	5,556 (90.9)	3,281[b] (89.9)	181 (90.0)	9,018 (90.5)
1992	5,553 (90.9)	3,280 (89.8)	183 (91.0)	9,016 (90.5)
1993	5,537 (90.6)	3,293 (90.2)	181 (90.0)	9,011 (90.4)
1994	5,457 (89.3)	3,256 (89.2)	178 (88.6)	8,891 (89.2)

[a] A total of 201 military respondents were retained from the original sample of 1,260; 186 of the 201 participated in the 1985 interview.
[b] Of the economically disadvantaged non–African American/non-Hispanic male and female members of the supplemental sample, 1,643 were not eligible for interview as of the 1991 survey.
Source: Center for Human Resource Research (2000), p. 28.

Table 3.1, taken from the NLS Handbook (CHRR, 2000), gives the number of individuals interviewed and the retention rate for each survey year. The NLSY calculates the retention rate by dividing the number of individuals interviewed by the number eligible for interview. All subjects interviewed in the baseline year (1979) and not permanently dropped from the sample are considered eligible for interview in subsequent years. Because deceased respondents are considered eligible for interview, retention rates provided by the NLSY tend to be conservative. For example, in 1998, the NLSY reported 51 deceased Hispanic respondents, 115 deceased African American respondents, and 129 deceased non–African American/non-Hispanic respondents (CHRR, 1999, p. 31).

The NLSY reports retention rates ranging from 89.2% for the total sample in 1994 to 84.3% as of the 1998 interview (CHRR, 1999, p. 25). This relatively high level of retention is in part due to the intensive efforts made by the NLSY staff to locate and interview all eligible members of the panel during each survey year. The occasional respondents who miss interviews in some years are reinterviewed in subsequent years. As a small incentive, respondents received $10 upon completion of the interview in the 1979–94 survey years. The personal interview takes approximately one hour to complete (CHRR, 1999).

Attrition, or loss of subjects over time, is commonly recognized as a potential drawback to panel studies (Babbi, 1995; Menard, 1991). If subjects who are lost to follow-up (interviewed during one year and not others) are systematically different from those remaining in the study, results produced by the study may have substantial bias. The NLSY compares favorably in this regard to the PSID, where cumulative attrition as of 1989 was 51% (49% of the sample interviewed in the baseline year was interviewed in 1989). Despite the considerable attrition in the PSID, its sample as of 1989 is not considered greatly distorted (Fitzgerald, Gottschalk, & Moffitt, 1998).

In a study of sample representativeness and attrition in the NLSY, similar retention rates were reported across racial groups as of 1998: 82.7% for Hispanic respondents, 84.5% for African American respondents, and 84.3% for non–African American/non-Hispanic respondents (CHRR, 1999, p. 31). Analyses of data from panel studies frequently rely on subsets of respondents who are interviewed during continuous years of the study. The NLSY reports that 66.9% of the respondents in 1998 had completed eighteen consecutive surveys (all possible interviews from 1979 to 1998 – CHRR, 1999). A greater percentage of female respondents than male respondents completed all eighteen surveys – 72.0% and 61.9%, respectively. There was also variation by race in the number of respondents completing all eighteen surveys: 59.6% of Hispanic respondents, 66.4% of African American respondents, and 70.1% of non–African American/non-Hispanic respondents. The NLSY cautions that these statistics may overstate the amount of missing information, because respondents are asked to reconstruct retrospectively some information that might have been missing in prior interviews – for example, work history, education, training, marital status, and family composition. Therefore, much of the information lost because of a missing interview in one year is obtained in subsequent interviews.

Approximately 89% of the respondents in 1998 had completed fourteen or more surveys (not necessarily in consecutive years) since the start of the study in 1979. This figure differed little by sex (88.2% for males and 90.5% for females) or race (88.1% for Hispanic, 90.4% for African American, and 89.2% for non–African American/non-Hispanic respondents) (CHRR, 1999).

One detailed analysis of attrition and its potential effects on earnings and other labor-market variables in the NLSY found no differences in attrition patterns between men and women, but it did identify some wage and employment differences between "prospective" and "retrospective" attriters (MaCurdy, Mroz, & Gritz, 1998). Retrospective attriters leave the sample but subsequently return. Prospective attriters leave the sample permanently and, thus, can only be described using data obtained prior to their exit. These authors found that prospective attriters, compared to those remaining in the sample, were less likely to be nonemployed prior to leaving the sample. After age twenty, attrition patterns appeared to be randomly distributed across wage and earnings distributions. Retrospective attriters tended to work less and earn less upon their return, when compared to the rest of the panel. Thus, for both types of attrition, there appears to be some risk of underestimating the prevalence of underemployment. After age twenty, differentials in labor force participation rates tended to be higher for females than for males when comparing retrospective attriters to the remaining members of the panel, but the wage differences were smaller for women than for men (MaCurdy et al., 1998). In summary, these authors concluded:

We present evidence suggesting that attrition from the NLSY is not a random process, but we have little support for contending that this process induces biases of any consequence. Indeed, our analyses show that the NLSY tracks the major features of the CPS trends for youth, a monumental feat given the vigorous evolution of these trends both over time and across ages. (p. 434)

Sample Description. Appendix A gives a complete description of the NLSY respondents beginning in 1984, five years later in 1989, and in 1994. These three years were selected because they roughly represent the time span for the analyses presented in subsequent chapters. Also, in 1985 a portion of the military sample was dropped from the sample, and in 1991 a portion of the supplemental sample was dropped from the survey. Comparing the demographic profiles for 1984 and 1994 will show how these changes to the sample affected its demographic composition.

The composition of the sample remained stable between 1984 and 1994 in terms of gender, ethnicity, and parental years of education, so we have profiled these data in the baseline year, 1984 (see Figures 3.1–3.3). The sample was about evenly split between males and females; approximately 6% of the sample was Hispanic, 14% was African American, and about 80% of

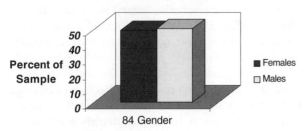

FIGURE 3.1. Gender.

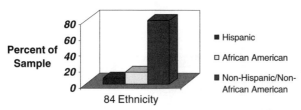

FIGURE 3.2. Ethnicity.

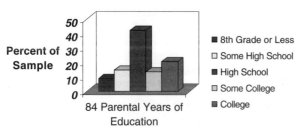

FIGURE 3.3. Parental education.

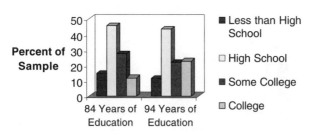

FIGURE 3.4. Education.

the respondents were of other ethnicities both in 1984 and in 1994. The parental years of education variable was measured as the highest of either parent's level of education, if information was available on both parents. This measure is often viewed as a proxy for the socioeconomic status (SES) of the family in which the respondent was raised. This characteristic also remained stable between the 1984 and 1994 survey years, with 23.4% of the respondents reporting a parent with less than a high school education, 42.3% reporting a high school education, and 20.6% reporting a parent with a college degree.

In contrast to the relative stability of the gender and ethnicity composition of the sample between 1984 and 1994, some of the respondent characteristics were more dynamic and resulted in a changing demographic profile during this time period. Figures 3.4–3.8 provide a snapshot of the changing demographic composition of the sample over this ten-year period

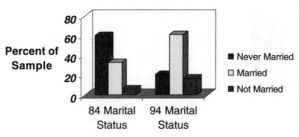

FIGURE 3.5. Marital status.

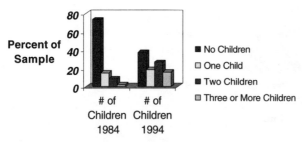

FIGURE 3.6. Number of children.

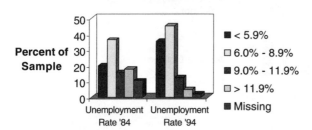

FIGURE 3.7. Unemployment rate.

in terms of education, marital status, number of children, the local unemployment rate, and age.

During the ten years from 1984 to 1994, the educational attainment of the respondents increased, with 22.8% reporting a college education in 1994 compared to only 11.8% in 1984 (see Figure 3.4). In 1984, 14.8% of respondents reported not having a high school diploma, whereas in 1994 this percentage fell to 11.7%. During this same time period, respondents also settled into marriage and started families (see Figures 3.5 and 3.6). In 1984, about one-third of the respondents were married, and 26.5% had one or more children. By 1994, 61.6% were married, and 62.5% had one or more children. The respondents were nineteen to twenty-seven years old in 1984 and twenty-nine to thirty-seven years old at the time of the 1994 interview (Figure 3.8a–b). During this ten-year period, there was also a large

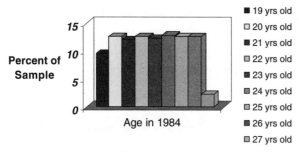

FIGURE 3.8a. Age in 1984.

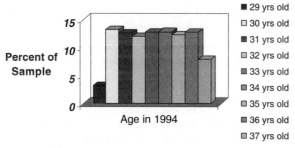

FIGURE 3.8b. Age in 1994.

fluctuation in economic conditions as measured by the unemployment rate (Figure 3.7). In general, the economic climate was less favorable in 1984, as reflected by higher unemployment, when compared to 1994. In 1984, approximately 20% of the respondents lived in areas with an unemployment rate below 6.0%, whereas in 1994, this figure was 35%. In 1984, about 18% of the respondents lived in areas with the worst economic conditions (unemployment rate above 12.0%), but in 1994, this figure had fallen to 5.0%. For a more complete description of NLSY respondents, see Appendix A.

Sample Weights. The NLSY selected civilian respondents using a multistage stratified area probability sample of dwelling units and group quarter units within the United States. The NLSY provides sample weights that can be used to combine the civilian samples to yield more accurate estimates of population values. The sample weights come with each release of the data and are intended to estimate how many individuals in the United States each respondent's answers represent. In general, weights for the baseline year (1979) were derived in order to accomplish the following five goals (NLSY79 Technical Sampling Report) (Frankel, Williams, & Spencer, 1983, p. 35):

1. Correction for differential probability of selection at the initial stage of household selection.

2. Correction for differential completion rates at the initial "screening phase" of data collection.
3. Correction for differential subsampling rates for Hispanic and African American cohort members prior to initial interview. Correction for differential completion rates among all cohort members at the first-year interview stage of data collection.
4. Proper combination of cases obtained in the primary and supplemental samples.
5. Adjustment of weighted cohort sizes to conform with outside, independent census estimates projected to January 1, 1979.

In subsequent years, these weights were modified to account for the panel's changing composition over time due to death and emigration (this effect had little influence on the weight adjustments) and to account for differential nonresponse among subgroups of respondents in subsequent interviews. Use of the sample weights depends on several factors, including whether the analyses are based on the entire sample (or subgroups) and what time frame is selected for use, that is, a single year versus a longitudinal record.

Analyzing data from a single year of the NLSY permits a straightforward application of the sampling weights to produce more accurate estimates of population values. When analyzing the survey data longitudinally, across multiple survey years, or when the analysis is restricted to respondents interviewed during the last year of interest, the NLSY recommends using the sampling weights from the last year (CHRR, 1999). When conducting regression analyses, fitting separate regressions to different sampling subgroups (e.g., by race or gender) or including indicator variables representing these groups is recommended. The optimal approach to weighting remains subject to debate. Some researchers have made specific suggestions for reconceptualizing sample weighting in the NLSY, including a proposal to add new weights for use with the subset of continuously interviewed respondents (see MaCurdy et al., 1998).

In our analyses, which are primarily longitudinal in nature, we used the sampling weight for the final year studied and included indicator variables representing membership in the various racial and gender groups. We also routinely tested interactions among these indicator variables in order to evaluate possible differential relationships within the racial and gender groups (Cochran, 1977; Potthoff, Woodbury, & Mantou, 1992). In most situations, we fit our regression models both with and without using the sampling weights and typically found no substantive inferential differences between the two approaches. Each subsequent chapter indicates whether or not the sampling weights were used in the analyses. The very large sample sizes of the NLSY provide ample statistical power, so the significance of observed effects tends to remain stable across alternative weighting schemes.

MEASURES

Measuring Underemployment

Official Measures. The Bureau of Labor Statistics provides the official U.S. unemployment rate based on data from the Current Population Surveys. This rate is often used as an indicator of labor market hardship, but it is deficient in that it ignores difficulties associated with inadequate employment for large numbers of employed individuals (Allan & Steffensmeier, 1989; Clogg, 1979; Jensen & Slack, in press; Lichter, 1989; National Commission on Employment and Unemployment Statistics, 1978; Sullivan, 1978). Whereas the official unemployment rate reflects the proportion of workers unemployed (the number wanting work relative to the labor force), it does not provide information about the quality of employment for the labor force. Nevertheless, the CPS-based unemployment rate serves as a widely accepted proxy for the overall health of the economy and can serve as a benchmark against which to check the NLSY's estimates of unemployment.

Efforts to measure the quality of employment have resulted in studies of economically inadequate employment. As noted in Chapter 1, the term "inadequate employment" is one form of "underemployment," although the two terms are often used synonymously. As will be discussed in the final chapter, the BLS has explored alternative labor force measures that go beyond unemployment to reflect other forms of underemployment, including some that are similar to the types of inadequate employment studied here. However, none of these alternatives has yet become a standard equivalent in stature to the unemployment rate. Consequently, we have had to adapt definitions of inadequate employment borrowed from other researchers.

Labor Utilization Framework. There is no universally agreed-upon method of defining or operationalizing underemployment. The literature has proposed several different but conceptually related methods (Clogg, 1979; Clogg & Sullivan, 1983; Clogg, Sullivan, & Mutchler, 1986; Gilroy, 1975; Glyde, 1977; Ham, 1982; Hauser, 1974; Jones, 1971; Sullivan, 1978; Tipps & Gordon, 1985; U.S. Commission on Civil Rights, 1982; Vietorisz, Mier, & Givlin, 1975). One frequently used measure of underemployment is the Labor Utilization Framework (LUF), as developed by Hauser (1974).

In its original form, the LUF consisted of six components called S, U, H, I, M, and A. The "S" component refers to "sub-unemployment," which is a measure of the discouraged-worker phenomenon. The "U" component refers to unemployment, and "H" to hours of work – that is, a measure of involuntary part-time work. The "I" component represents low-income full-time workers who make less than a poverty-level income. The "M" refers to a mismatch between level of education and occupation. Finally, "A" represents the residual of all other workers, who presumably enjoy adequate employment. There is a hierarchical ordering to the LUF components, S-U-H-I-M-A, reflecting a continuum of labor market hardship from severe, as represented by the discouraged-worker component (S), to none for the adequate employment or A category. The LUF components are also mutually exclusive – that is, workers can be assigned to only one category of underemployment. For example, if a worker had an involuntary part-time job (H) that paid a near-poverty-level wage (I), the worker would be categorized in the H category. The LUF can be used to produce prevalence measures for each of the S to A components, and it can also be used to produce a single prevalence measure of total "underemployment" by combining over the S–M components.

Sullivan (1978) derived measures of labor "underutilization" rates based on the LUF, using census data from 1960 and 1970. This author's summary measure of underutilization used unemployment, hours of work, level of income, and mismatch. These four components of underutilization are the same as their counterparts in the LUF as measured by U, H, I, and M. Much of the work in the present book is based on a similar characterization of underemployment, also derived from the original LUF, called "economic underemployment," as proposed by Clogg (1979), Clogg et al. (1986), and Tipps and Gordon (1985). We first describe how the NLSY characterizes employment status and then present the specific components of economic underemployment and the resulting categorization of employment status used in this research.

Employment Status and the NLSY. The NLSY collects detailed data representing the labor force status, transitions, and work histories of survey respondents. These data resemble but, in some cases, are richer than those from the Current Population Survey, which are used by the BLS to characterize the nation's economy. The NLSY uses this extensive data collection to create several key variables reflecting the labor force participation of respondents both during the survey week and since the past interview.

One of these variables, Employment Status Recode (ESR), captures the labor force activity of each respondent during the week preceding the interview and is available for each year of the survey. This variable describes the labor force activity of the respondent in a manner consistent with the CPS, using one of the following categories: (1) working, (2) with a job – not at work, (3) looking for work, (4) keeping house, (5) going to school, (6) unable to work, (7) other, (8) in the active armed forces. The NLSY also creates a collapsed version of this variable (ESR-Collapsed) for each survey year, which classifies respondents into one of the following four

TABLE 3.2. *Key labor force concepts*

Employed:
1. All civilians who, during the survey week, did any work at all as paid employees in their own business or profession, or on their own farm, or who worked fifteen hours or more as unpaid workers in an enterprise operated by a member of the family; and
2. All those who were not working but who had jobs or businesses from which they were temporarily absent because of illness, bad weather, vacation, labor-management disputes, or various personal reasons, whether they were paid for the time off or were seeking other jobs. Excluded are persons whose only activity consisted of work around the house (such as own-home housework, painting or repairing own home) or volunteer work for religious, charitable, and similar organizations.

Unemployed:
All civilians who, during the survey week, had no employment but were available for work and
1. had engaged in any specific job-seeking activity within the past four weeks, such as registering at a public or private employment office, meeting with employers, checking with friends or relatives, placing or answering advertisements, writing letters of application, or being on a union or professional register;
2. were waiting to be called back to a job from which they had been laid off; or
3. were waiting to report to a new wage or salary job within thirty days.

Not in the Labor Force:
All civilians fifteen years old and older who are not classified as employed or unemployed are defined as "not in the labor force." This group of persons who are neither employed nor seeking work includes persons engaged only in own-home housework, attending school, or unable to work because of long-term physical or mental illness; persons who are retired or too old to work; seasonal workers for whom the survey week fell in an off season; and the voluntarily idle. Persons doing only unpaid family work (less than fifteen hours during the survey week) are also classified as not in the labor force.

Source: Adapted from Center for Human Resource Research (1999, p. 214) and originally published by the U.S. Bureau of the Census (1987).

categories: (1) employed (working or with a job but not at work), (2) unemployed, (3) out of the labor force (keeping house, going to school, unable to work, or other), (4) in the active armed forces.

Table 3.2 defines important concepts used by the U.S. government prior to 1994 (i.e., during the period covered by our analyses) to characterize the labor force and employment status (U.S. Bureau of the Census, 1987). These definitions provide the basis for our characterization of the labor force activity of NLSY respondents.

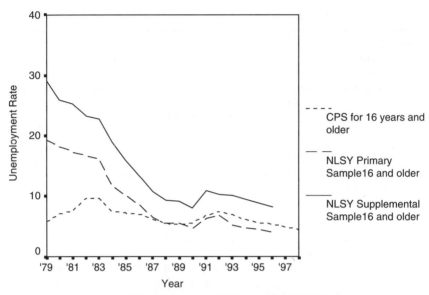

FIGURE 3.9. Current Population Survey (CPS) and NLSY unemployment rates.

In order to describe the economic climate experienced by NLSY respondents, we compared the unemployment rates derived from the NLSY
and the CPS for the 1979–98 time period. Figure 3.9 presents the "official"
BLS unemployment rate from the CPS, which is based on all individuals
sixteen years old and older and two unemployment rates from the NLSY for
individuals of this same age group – one for the primary sample and one for
the supplemental sample. Note that the CPS unemployment rate is much
lower than that of the total NLSY sample, for several reasons. First, the
NLSY sample is composed of a nationally representative primary sample
and a supplemental sample. The supplemental sample oversamples groups
typically underrepresented in large national surveys: African Americans,
Hispanics, and economically disadvantaged non-Hispanic, non–African
American youth. As shown in Figure 3.9, unemployment rates are higher
for the supplemental sample, with the nationally representative primary
sample more closely approximating the CPS.

Another reason for the difference in unemployment rates is the different
age compositions of the CPS and NLSY samples. The NLSY sample is
much younger than the CPS sample, which is selected to be representative
of the entire nation. Figure 3.10 shows the unemployment rate for youths
sixteen to nineteen years old and for adults twenty years old and older from
both the CPS and NLSY. Unemployment rates are higher among youth in
general, with youth rates from the CPS being lower than comparable rates
from the NLSY (note that beginning in 1985, the youngest respondent to
the NLSY was twenty years old). As was seen in Figure 3.9, unemployment

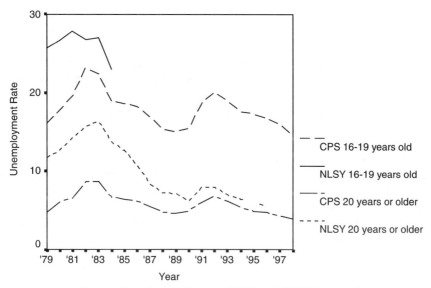

FIGURE 3.10. Current Population Survey (CPS) and NLSY unemployment rates by age.

rates for those twenty years old and older from the NLSY and CPS converge as the NLSY sample ages and begins to approximate more closely the age of the CPS sample.

Finally, differences in data collection between the NLSY and CPS offer another explanation for the disparity in unemployment rates estimated by these two surveys. Although NLSY interviewers are trained to collect information consistent with that of the CPS, they do not have the extensive experience of CPS interviewers (CHRR, 1999).

Definition of Employment Status for This Study. We adapted the NLSY employment status measures in order to assign respondents to the under-employment categories developed in the LUF and its variants. The NLSY categorizes the labor force activity of each respondent during the week prior to the interview as employed, unemployed, out of the labor force, or in the active armed forces. We extended this categorization to include the notion of "economic underemployment." Economic underemployment, as first proposed by Clogg (1979), includes unemployment, involuntary part-time employment, and employment with poverty wages. Tipps and Gordon (1985) and Clogg and colleagues (1986) proposed modifying this original characterization to include an additional category of "intermittent unemployment" that helps to reflect economic hardship in individuals who are employed during the week of the survey but have a recent history (past year) of unemployment.

In contrast to the original LUF, this characterization of "economic under-employment" differs by the addition of the "intermittent unemployment" category and the exclusion of the "mismatch" category. The mismatch (M) category was excluded on the grounds that there was no strictly economic basis for mismatch as a form of underemployment (Clogg, 1979). The LUF defines mismatch by evaluating the distribution of education within occu-pational groups as defined by the *Dictionary of Occupation Titles* (DOT) (U.S. Department of Labor, Employment, and Training Administration, 1977). One standard deviation is added to the mean educational level within each group to define the cutoff value. Workers with educational levels that exceed the cutoff value for their particular occupations are considered mis-matched. As a practical matter, defining "mismatch" using the NLSY data set is difficult, because occupational (DOT) codes were not available af-ter 1981. Consequently, the mismatch form of underemployment was not considered in this research.

We modified the original NLSY categorization of employment to include the categories of involuntary part-time employment, employment with poverty wages, and intermittent unemployment. Although these workers are typically counted among the employed, they often experience greater economic hardship relative to other employed workers.

Involuntary part-time work involves working fewer than thirty-five hours during the week prior to the survey for one of the following eco-nomic reasons: (1) slack work, (2) material shortages, (3) equipment or plant repair, (4) start of a new job or end of an old one, (5) inability to find full-time work. Poverty-wage work involves average weekly earnings less than 1.25 times the federal poverty level for unrelated individuals under sixty-five years old (Clogg & Sullivan, 1983). Poverty-wage employment was based on earnings during the previous calendar year divided by weeks worked, providing a weekly estimate. This estimate was compared to 1.25 times the U.S. poverty level (adjusted to a weekly basis) to charac-terize poverty-wage employment. We used 1.25 times the poverty level in order to be consistent with prior LUF practice. "The uniform standard of 1.25 × Poverty Threshold is low enough to isolate deficiency in earnings and to also isolate a fraction of the labor force with excessively high rates of unemployment" (Clogg & Sullivan, 1983, p. 144). The low-income people defined by this cutoff are also at higher risk of inadequate employment through involuntary part-time employment and discouragement.

In its original form, intermittent unemployment included workers who were employed at the time of the interview but who had been unem-ployed for fifteen or more weeks during the previous year, or who had three or more spells of unemployment during that time. We were unable to consistently classify spells of unemployment[3] among NLSY workers

[3] In earlier surveys (1979–87), the NLSY collected "gaps" in employment and, in the case of job loss, the reason for the job loss. These gaps represent "nonemployment," and because

and thus used fifteen or more weeks of unemployment during the previous year as the sole criterion for defining intermittent unemployment.

The NLSY defines persons "out of the labor force" (OLF) as persons who are not employed, unemployed (wanting and trying to find work), or in the active armed forces. This includes respondents who are engaged in own-home housework, in school, unable to work because of long-term physical or mental illness, or retired, and "discouraged workers," or those who have given up looking for work. A discouraged worker wants a regular job, either full-time or part-time, but is not seeking employment because he or she could not find work, had nowhere to look, or thought no work was available; felt lacking in the necessary skills; felt too young or too old; or had other handicaps in finding a job. We reassigned such "discouraged workers" from OLF to a separate category. Because this group tends to be too small for separate analysis, we usually combine it with the unemployed group as defined by the more usual CPS criteria.

In summary, we defined the following employment status categories using NLSY data: unemployed (including discouraged workers), inadequately employed (including involuntary part-time employment, poverty-wage employment, and intermittent unemployment), adequately employed (including those in the active armed forces), and OLF. Table 3.3 provides detailed definitions of the employment-status categories used in subsequent chapters.

Measuring Health and Well-Being

The NLSY, besides collecting data on labor force participation and other life events of the respondents at each interview, also gathers information on respondents' health and on their psychological and social functioning during selected years. This section provides a brief introduction to the NLSY measures of self-esteem, alcohol misuse, and depression. Each of these variables will be discussed further in later chapters devoted to the analysis of their relationship with underemployment (self-esteem in Chapter 5, alcohol misuse in Chapter 6, and depression in Chapter 7).

Self-esteem. Self-esteem was measured in 1980 and 1987 using the Rosenberg ten-item scale (1965). This scale has been shown to reflect global as opposed to situation-specific self-esteem (O'Brien, 1985). Each item has four responses, and the additive scoring method gives a possible range of 10 to 40, with high scores representing higher self-esteem. The items for the Rosenberg Self-Esteem Scale are shown in Table 3.4, and this scale is the focus of analysis in Chapter 5.

it was not entirely clear whether all such gaps were voluntary (e.g., people desiring to take time off between jobs) or involuntary, it was decided to use fifteen or more weeks of unemployment as the sole criterion for defining intermittent unemployment.

TABLE 3.3. *Employment status categories used in this study*

1. *Official Unemployment*: Civilians who, during the survey week, had no employment but were available for work and (1) had engaged in any specific job-seeking activity within the last four weeks or (2) were with a job but not at work and were "waiting to be called back to a job from which they had been laid off" or "were waiting to report to a new wage or salary job within thirty days." This is the standard definition used by the Bureau of Labor Statistics to define unemployment.

2. *Discouraged Worker*: A discouraged worker (U.S. National Commission on Employment and Unemployment Statistics, 1978) wants a regular job, either full or part-time, but is not looking because he or she believes that work is unavailable or cannot be found. Discouraged workers may feel that they lack necessary schooling, training, skills, or experience or that employers think they are too young or too old. Discouraged workers may also have other personal handicaps that preclude them from finding a job. Because these individuals have given up looking for work, they are considered "out of the labor force" by BLS standards and, as such, are not counted in labor force participation statistics. But in the present analyses, they are typically combined with the official unemployment group.

3. *Involuntary Part-time*: Involuntary part-time workers are defined as persons working fewer than thirty-five hours during the week prior to the survey and indicating one of the following economic reasons for their part-time work: (1) slack work, (2) material shortages, (3) equipment or plant repair, (4) start of a new job or end of an old one, or (5) inability to find full-time work. This is the standard definition used by the Bureau of Labor Statistics.

4. *Poverty-Wage*: Poverty-wage workers are employed during the survey week with average weekly earnings for the particular survey year (total yearly earnings from wages and salary divided by number of weeks worked) below 1.25 times the federal poverty-level weekly wage for unrelated individuals under sixty-five years old.

5. *Intermittent Unemployment*: Intermittent unemployment refers to individuals who were employed during the survey week but who were unemployed fifteen or more weeks during the previous year.

6. *Adequate Employment*: This category refers to employed workers not falling into the inadequate employment categories. Members of the active armed forces are considered adequately employed. In some analyses, the intermittently unemployed were found to be similar to the adequately employed and were combined with them for subsequent analyses.

7. *Out of the Labor Force (OLF)*: OLF refers to persons who are neither employed nor unemployed. It includes those engaged in own-home housework, in school, unable to work because of long-term physical or mental illness, or retired.

TABLE 3.4. *Items used in the Rosenberg Self-Esteem Scale*

---

1. I am a person of worth.
2. I have a number of good qualities.
3. I am inclined to feel I am a failure.
4. I am as capable as others.
5. I feel there is not much to be proud of.
6. I have a positive attitude.
7. I am satisfied with myself.
8. I wish I had more self-respect.
9. I feel useless at times.
10. At times, I think I'm no good at all.

Note: Response set is 1 = strongly disagree; 2 = disagree; 3 = agree; 4 = strongly agree. Items 3, 5, 8, 9, and 10 are reverse coded.
Source: Rosenberg (1965).

Alcohol Misuse. The NLSY collects detailed information on both alcohol consumption and symptoms of alcohol abuse during selected survey years (see Appendix B for a detailed list of all alcohol data collected by the NLSY). Alcohol abuse is generally characterized in two ways: the number of alcohol-related symptoms experienced by the respondent during the year preceding the interview, and heavy consumption or binge drinking during the thirty days preceding the interview. Common to both of these characterizations is the "nondrinker" category. The NLSY asks questions about alcohol consumption and symptoms only of respondents who report having had a drink during the thirty days preceding the interview. Therefore, respondents who report not having had a drink during the past thirty days are grouped into the nondrinking category for both the alcohol symptom measure and the binge drinking measure.

Characterizing the level of alcohol-related symptoms is complicated in the NLSY by its use of different items in different years. Thus, comparing respondents' symptom levels over different years requires some special procedures. Alcohol symptoms are coded into two categories: (1) nondrinker during the past thirty days, or drinker but no or low symptoms of alcohol abuse, and (2) presence of high alcohol symptoms. The latter category is created by using the number of symptoms defining the upper 10% of the distribution of alcohol symptoms. For some years, the symptom items are comparable to *Diagnostic and Statistical Manual* (DSM) abuse/dependence criteria, and the diagnostic categorization of respondents can be compared with the upper-10% criterion used for analysis across all years.

Binge drinking is defined using a question asking the respondent on how many occasions during the thirty days preceding the interview he or she has had six or more drinks. We used this variable to create the two

categories of the binge drinking measure: (1) nondrinker during the past
thirty days, or nonbinge drinker, and (2) binge drinker, defined as consumption of six or more drinks on a single occasion on six or more days
during the past thirty days (Dooley & Prause, 1998). This approach will be
used in Chapter 6, which focuses on alcohol misuse in the entire sample. A
less stringent definition of binge drinking is used in Chapter 8, which deals
only with women, for whom fewer binge episodes mark heavy drinking.
Table 3.5 summarizes the alcohol measures described in this section.

TABLE 3.5. *Summary of alcohol measures*

Measure	Definition
Bingeing	*Binge*: Six or more drinks on a single occasion during the thirty days preceding the interview.
	Frequency of Binge Drinking: The NLSY measures the frequency of binge drinking in the thirty days preceding the interview using the following eight categories: 1. Nondrinker in the thirty days preceding the interview 2. Never drank six or more drinks 3. One time 4. Two or three times 5. Four or five times 6. Six or seven times 7. Eight or nine times 8. Ten or more times.
	Binge Drinker: Defined using the approximate top 10% to 15% of the frequency distribution of binge drinking in the thirty days preceding the interview. Consequently, a different frequency of binge drinking was used to define a binge drinker depending on the particular sample being studied – e.g., for women on AFDC, one occurrence of bingeing defined a binge drinker, whereas for the group of inadequately employed, six or more occasions of binge drinking during the thirty days preceding the interview was used.
Alcohol symptoms[a]	*Low Symptoms*: Nondrinker in the thirty days preceding the interview, and drinkers who report no symptoms during the previous year or who report fewer symptoms than used to define the upper 10–15% of the symptom distribution.
	Symptoms: Cut-point determined using a value corresponding to the upper 10–15% of the symptom distribution. Symptoms are recalled over a one-year period preceding the interview.

[a] A complete list of alcohol symptoms from the NLSY by survey year is presented in
Appendix B.

Depression. Depression was measured using the Center for Epidemiologic Studies Depression Scale or CES-D (Radloff, 1977). The original scale consists of twenty items asking about the respondent's mood over the past week, using a four-point (0–3) scale. Although designed for general population surveys rather than for clinical diagnosis, the CES-D discriminates known psychiatric patients from people with low levels of depression and agrees well with clinical and other ratings of depression (Myers & Weissman, 1980; Roberts & Vernon, 1983; Weissman et al., 1977).

The full twenty-item scale was used in the 1992 survey, but a seven-item subset was used in the 1994 survey. Shortened versions of the CES-D have often been employed in an effort to conserve resources, including different seven-item (Reynolds, 1997), ten-item (Mirowsky & Ross, 1995), eleven-item (Umberson, Wortman, & Kessler, 1992), and sixteen-item variants (Craig & Van Natta, 1979). The 1994 NLSY seven-item set correlates well with the full twenty-item set used in 1992 (r = .90) and has reliability in 1994 of alpha = .81, compared to the full twenty-item set's reliability of alpha = .88 in 1992. The CES-D items used in 1992 and 1994 are shown in Table 3.6.

Contextual Variables

Control Variables. Multivariable statistical models can make adjustments for characteristics of the sample or environment that might account for the relationship between the key variables of interest (e.g., becoming underemployed) and the outcome variable (e.g., alcohol abuse). These variables, commonly referred to as "confounding" variables, might cause both of the key variables of interest and thus explain their association as spurious (Kleinbaum et al., 1998). Statistical control for such variables removes them as possible explanations, and such adjustment allows estimation of the magnitude of the nonspurious share of the association, if any.

We routinely checked several potential confounding variables in our statistical models. For example, an environmental variable such as the local unemployment rate should directly affect the risk of underemployment, because areas with high local unemployment may put individuals at greater risk for an adverse employment change. In addition, the local unemployment rate might also directly influence symptoms of all residents of the community through demoralization. In this way, aggregate unemployment could cause personal underemployment and symptoms of distress to move together even if underemployment did not directly cause symptoms (i.e., confounding). Other variables might also operate in this manner. The variable "parental years of education" was used to reflect the general socioeconomic status (SES) of the respondent. Higher parental educational attainment is associated with greater family resources that could allow offspring to acquire more education and training for higher-status

TABLE 3.6. *Center for Epidemiological Studies Depression Scale (CES-D)*

---

   1. I was bothered by things that usually don't bother me.
 *2. I did not feel like eating; my appetite was poor.
   3. I felt that I couldn't shake off the blues even with help from my family and
      friends.
   4. I felt that I was just as good as other people.
 *5. I had trouble keeping my mind on what I was doing.
 *6. I felt depressed.
 *7. I felt that everything I did was an effort.
   8. I felt hopeful about the future.
   9. I thought my life had been a failure.
  10. I felt fearful.
*11. My sleep was restless.
  12. I was happy.
  13. I talked less than usual.
  14. I felt lonely.
  15. People were unfriendly.
  16. I enjoyed life.
  17. I had crying spells.
*18. I felt sad.
  19. I felt that people dislike me.
*20. I could not get "going."

Note: The full twenty-item scale was used in the 1992 survey; in 1994, a subset of seven items was used (indicated with an asterisk). Coding is based on symptom frequency in the past week: 0 = rarely/none of the time/0–1 day; 1 = some/a little of the time/1–2 days; 2 = occasionally/moderate amount of time/3–4 days; 3 = most/all of the time/5–7 days. Items 4, 8, 12, and 16 are reverse coded.
Source: Radloff (1977).

occupations. More highly educated parents are also more likely to provide positive role models, leading to more stable and continuous work histories. Greater parental economic resources might help offspring to cope with stressors that would otherwise lead to symptoms.

Demographic characteristics such as age, sex, and race/ethnicity were also evaluated as potential confounding variables. Other studies have documented increased rates of underemployment for nonwhite groups (Borus, 1984; Clogg & Sullivan, 1983; Lichter, 1988; Pollard, 1984). Females are more likely than males to experience certain forms of underemployment – specifically, discouragement, low pay, and involuntary part-time employment (Leppel & Clain, 1988) – and to report higher levels of depression but lower levels of binge drinking.

Our statistical models also routinely evaluated marital status and personal educational attainment because of their relationship to employment and well-being. Research suggests that individuals who are married and more highly educated are more likely to be employed as opposed to unemployed, especially during youth (Borus, 1984). More highly educated individuals also tend to report fewer symptoms of depression and higher levels of self-esteem (Dooley & Prause, 1997a). Previous employment history – specifically, a history of unemployment – has been identified as important in predicting current employment status and also may pose a threat to well-being (Prause & Dooley, 1997). Additionally, youths with a history of unemployment experience more volatile employment patterns – specifically, a reduction in future employment (Pollard, 1984).

Explanatory Variables. Multivariable models can also test specific hypotheses about the relationships among variables – specifically, mediated and moderated relationships. In general terms, mediating variables help to clarify the mechanism by which a cause produces an effect (Barron & Kenny, 1986). A mediating variable intervenes in the causal path between the "cause" and the "effect." As an example, consider the link between becoming unemployed and increased levels of depression. A possible mechanism that might explain this link is loss of income, which is a consequence of becoming unemployed. If loss of income is associated with depression and our estimate of the effect of job loss on depression changes or disappears with statistical adjustment for loss of income, then loss of income would qualify as a mediating variable.

Multivariable models can also test for the presence of moderated relationships involving interactions between variables (Cohen & Cohen, 1983; Jaccard, Turrisi, & Wan, 1990). A moderating variable helps to clarify the circumstances under which the relationship between a key variable of interest and an outcome exists. In the job loss and depression example, gender might serve as a moderating variable. We may find a main effect for job loss where becoming unemployed is associated with higher levels of depression. But upon inspection of the interaction between job loss and gender, the relationship may appear to be much stronger for males than for females, indicating that gender moderates the relationship between job loss and depression.

The presence of a moderated relationship can be tested statistically by constructing a multiplicative interaction term, the product of the supposed causal variable of interest and the potential moderating variable. In our analyses, we construct conventional product-term interactions that are sensitive to "bilinear" forms of interaction.[4] Multivariable statistical models yield formal tests of significance for all terms in the model, making it possible to determine whether an interaction between the key variable of interest and the moderator is present. These tests are usually done in a hierarchical

---

[4] A bilinear interaction assumes that the slope of the line between the key variable of interest and outcome changes in a linear fashion over the levels of the moderator variable (Cohen & Cohen, 1983; Jaccard et al., 1990).

fashion, where the interaction term is evaluated in the presence of the constituent main effect terms. In our multivariable models, we fit potentially confounding variables first, then the key variable(s) of interest, followed by potential mediating variables, and finally by the interaction terms.

ANALYTIC MODELS

We use two general types of multivariable models: logistic regression and ordinary least squares (OLS) regression. Although both of these statistical techniques permit control of confounding variables and allow testing of complex relationships between variables (i.e., mediated, moderated relationships), the two techniques have several practical differences (Clogg & Shihadeh, 1994; Hosmer & Lemeshow, 2000; Kleinbaum et al., 1998; Long, 1997; Neter, Wasserman, & Kutner, 1990).

First, the mathematical basis used to estimate the regression coefficients in a logistic regression (a maximum likelihood estimation procedure) differs from that of an OLS regression (a least squares estimation procedure). As a consequence, these two statistical models make different distributional assumptions about the set of predictor variables. Specifically, logistic regression does not depend on prior assumptions of multivariate normality among the predictor variables. Second, logistic regression assumes that the outcome or dependent variable is dichotomous, ordinal, or categorical, while in OLS regression the outcome variable is typically assumed to have the properties of an interval scale. Finally, the regression coefficients, which are a reflection of the "effect size" or strength of the relationship between the variables, have different interpretations in the two models.

For further reading on the mathematical basis for estimating the regression coefficients using these models, readers should consult one of the references just cited. For readers unfamiliar with the statistical terms, the next sections review the interpretation of regression coefficients using the two models.

Logistic Regression

Types of Models. Two different multivariable logistic regression models are used in our analyses. One model, the traditional logistic regression model, assumes a dichotomous outcome variable – for example, adequately employed versus underemployed, ill versus healthy. In these models, the outcome variable is coded using the values zero and one, where a value of one is typically assigned to the group for whom the probability has the most interpretative interest – for example, the probability of underemployment relative to adequate employment, or the probability of disease relative to nondisease.

The other logistic regression model permits the outcome variable to have more than two values – that is, a nominal or categorical outcome variable – and is sometimes referred to as a "polytomous" or "multinomial" logistic regression model (Hosmer & Lemeshow, 2000). Common to both of these techniques is use of the "odds ratio" as an indicator of effect size or strength of the relationship between the predictor variables and the outcome.

Interpreting Coefficients. An odds ratio (OR) can be calculated using two different, but mathematically equivalent, methods. Typically, it is derived from a simple transformation (exponentiation) of the logistic regression coefficient. Alternatively, when evaluating the relationship between a categorical predictor variable and a dichotomous outcome, the OR can be calculated from a $2 \times k$ contingency table formed by the two-level outcome variable and the k-level categorical predictor variable. Because the OR is used as a measure of effect size throughout the chapters, a brief review of its calculation and interpretation is presented here.

The OR ranges between zero and infinity, with values greater than one reflecting a positive relationship between the outcome and predictor variables. An OR less than one indicates a negative relationship between the two variables. An OR equal to one indicates no association between the outcome and predictor variables. A dichotomous predictor variable, when coded zero/one, is considered a special case of an interval variable when interpreting the OR. The OR for an interval variable is interpreted as the increased (or decreased) risk of the outcome associated with a one-unit change in the predictor variable. For dichotomous predictor variables (when coded zero/one), the unit increase is from zero to one, providing a comparison of the risk between the group coded one and the group coded zero. In general terms, the OR reflects how much more likely (or less likely) it is for the outcome to be present among those with a value of one than among those with a value of zero on the predictor variable. Given this interpretation, it is important to clarify how both the predictor and outcome variables are coded when used in logistic regression analyses.

Table 3.7 presents a contingency table showing the relationship between gender, a dichotomous predictor variable (1 = male, 0 = female), and

TABLE 3.7. *Association between gender and employment status:*[a] *NLSY92*

Employment Status	Female	Male	Total
Employed	(A) 2,494	(B) 3,203	5,697
Underemployed	(C) 580	(D) 503	1,083
TOTAL	3,074	3,706	6,780

[a] "Employed" represents all adequately employed in 1992; "Underemployed" represents all involuntarily part-time employed, poverty-wage employed, and intermittently unemployed in 1992.

employment status, characterized as adequately employed or under-employed (a dichotomous outcome variable, 1 = underemployed, 0 = adequately employed). These are actual data from the NLSY and illustrate the cross-sectional association between gender and employment status among respondents in 1992. The four cells of the contingency table have been labeled A–D. The odds (sometimes referred to as the "simple" odds) of underemployment for females (designated by O-F) are calculated by dividing cell C by cell A, yielding, O-F = 580/2494 = .233, which indicates that for females the odds of being underemployed are .23 to 1. In a similar manner, we can calculate the simple odds of underemployment for males (O-M) by dividing cell D by cell B, yielding O-M = 503/3203 = .157. This indicates that the odds of a man being underemployed are just .157 to 1.

The odds ratio is the ratio of these two simple odds (OR = .157/.233), or alternatively, using the cell letters, it is calculated as: OR = (D/B)/(C/A). The odds ratio, also referred to as the "cross-product" ratio, can be calculated from a 2 × 2 contingency table by taking the ratio of the cross-products (in our example: OR = A × D/C × B). The OR is interpreted as the increased (or decreased, in this case) risk of underemployment for males (the value of the predictor variable is one) relative to females (the value of the predictor variable is zero). In the present example, OR equals .67. This indicates that underemployment is less likely in males than in females. Specifically, the odds of underemployment for males are just 67% of those for females, or 33% less than for females. Estimating the odds of underemployment from these same data using a logistic regression procedure yields a regression coefficient equal to −.393 for gender (coded as above: 1 = male, 0 = female). Exponentiation of this coefficient yields the odds ratio, OR = exp(−.393) = .67.

The odds ratio gives a point estimate of the population odds, but it is often useful to provide an interval estimate for the population odds ratio. This interval, called a confidence interval, gives a range of possible values that will include the unknown value of the population odds ratio at a given probability (typically, 95%). In this example, the 95% confidence interval for the population value of the odds ratio ranges from .59 to .77. When the 95% confidence interval contains the value one, the predictor variable is not statistically associated with the outcome variable. Since this interval does not include the value one, we infer that gender is associated with underemployment in the population at the $p = .05$ level of significance.

For categorical predictor variables with more than two levels (specifically, nominal level variables), the odds ratio is calculated using one of the levels of the predictor variable as the reference level. In this situation, the odds ratio represents the risk of experiencing underemployment associated with change between a given level and the referent level of the predictor variable.

The logistic regression model based on a dichotomous outcome is easily extended to allow for a multicategory outcome variable in "polytomous" or "multinomial" logistic regression models. As an example, it is possible to expand the model describing the association between gender and underemployment to include the three forms of inadequate employment: involuntary part-time employment, poverty-wage employment, and intermittent unemployment. In this example, employment status is cast as a four-level outcome variable to include adequate employment and the three forms of inadequate employment. When using the polytomous logistic regression model, it is necessary to designate one of the levels of the outcome variable as the reference level that serves as the basis of comparison for each of the other levels. Choosing to use the adequately employed group as the reference group would result in three sets of odds ratios (each relative to the adequately employed group) for each predictor variable: the odds of involuntary part-time employment, the odds of poverty-wage employment, and the odds of intermittent unemployment.

Although the example presented in this chapter included only a single predictor variable (gender), both the binary model (with a dichotomous outcome) and the polytomous model easily extend to more complex models including many predictor variables. These models are often referred to as multivariable logistic regression models. When many predictor variables are simultaneously included in the model, the effect of each individual predictor is statistically adjusted for the effects of other predictor variables included in the model. This feature allows for the control of potential confounding variables and is a major advantage of multivariable models over models that include only single predictors.

Ordinary Least Squares Regression

Ordinary least squares regression models were used to evaluate hypotheses about relationships between the predictor variables and the CES-D depression scale, which is generally assumed to approximate the properties of an interval scale. The unstandardized (b) and standardized (beta) regression coefficients both reflect the magnitude or strength of association between the predictor variables and depression.

The unstandardized regression coefficient (b) represents the change in the outcome variable for a one-unit increase in the predictor variable. The standardized regression coefficient (beta) reflects the standard deviation change in the outcome for a one-standard-deviation increase in the predictor variable. When many predictor variables are included in the model, the relative effects of the predictor variables are often assessed using the beta coefficients, because they are given in standard units that facilitate comparison among them. The ratio of the unstandardized regression coefficient to its standard error is distributed as a t-statistic and is used to determine the statistical significance of the association between the predictor and outcome variables as reflected by both the unstandardized and standardized regression coefficients.

When many predictor variables are simultaneously included in the OLS regression model, it is often referred to as a multiple regression model or, in general terms, a multivariable regression model. A major advantage of including multiple predictor variables is the statistical control of potential confounding variables. In these models, the regression coefficients are often referred to as "partial" regression coefficients, because the effect of each predictor variable is statistically adjusted or "partialled" for the effects of all other predictors included in the model. The adjusted multiple R^2 is used to reflect the relationship between the set of predictor variables and the outcome (usually CES-D, in our analyses). This summary statistic is interpreted as the percentage of variation in the CES-D scale attributable to the set of predictor variables as a whole.

The primary model-building strategy employed for all of our multivariable models (both the logistic and OLS models) was based on theory-driven, hierarchical orderings of the predictor variables. One general strategy was to cluster predictor variables into theoretically meaningful groups (e.g., demographic variables, psychological variables, environmental variables) and then to evaluate the association of each variable within a group to the outcome variable. The groups of predictor variables were then hierarchically screened for inclusion in the various statistical models. Generally, only predictor variables that were significantly associated with the outcome variable were retained in the final models. One exception was when a variable was hypothesized to have a possible mediating or moderating influence, in which case it was retained in order to allow a formal test of the hypothesized relationship.

4

Reverse Causation

Findings on the Selection Hypothesis

> ...it is doubtful if many of them could or would work full time for long
> together if they had the opportunity.... there will be found many of them
> who from shiftlessness, helplessness, idleness, or drink, are inevitably poor.
>
> Booth, 1892, pp. 42–43

INTRODUCTION

Background

A century of research has repeatedly found an association between adverse
employment change – usually unemployment – and indicators of ill health,
particularly behavioral and emotional disorders. However, the interpretation of this correlation has proved difficult. As noted in Chapter 2, at least
three different mechanisms could account for it, each intuitively plausible:
social causation, confounding, and selection.

Social causation views adverse employment change as the cause of ill
health. The remaining chapters of this book will focus on this mechanism,
with the others controlled. An ever-present rival explanation to both social
causation and selection involves confounding by other variables. When
the contributions of such confounding variables are removed, usually by
statistical control, the initial association may weaken or disappear. Any
prior variable that serves as a risk factor for both employment and health
change could function as a confounder. For example, growing up in poverty
may increase the risk of intermittent unemployment in adulthood because
of educational inadequacies. In addition, it may increase the risk of ill
health in adulthood as a result of inadequate health care in childhood or
the acquisition of poor health habits. As a result, employment status and
health status may not cause each other; their association may be due to
their common origin in childhood poverty.

In contrast to both social causation and confounding, the selection perspective sees prior illness as causing later employment change. In this view, employers improve their competitive position by eliminating workers with health limitations that reduce their efficiency or reliability. The rising cost of employer-paid health insurance premiums may further encourage shedding those workers who have the highest risk of consuming health benefits. Because of the seriousness of this rival explanation, tests of the social causation hypothesis need to control for selection, as is done in the following chapters. However, such reverse causation warrants attention in its own right, and the remainder of this chapter will focus on the selection path from health status to adverse employment change.

Our focus on health as a cause of adverse employment experience should be distinguished from other psychological factors that dispose people not to work. The conventional wisdom expects some unemployment from lack of motivation or ambition. Historical accounts have long noted the problem of the "work-shy" or lazy worker: "Mention unemployment to many a man with a business of his own, or who has what he fondly supposes to be a permanent job, or who has made a few or even one advantageous move in his lifetime. 'Some folks won't work,' he says placidly..." (Calkins, 1930, p. 7). Instead, we focus here on those worker characteristics that affect employability through dysfunction. For example, alcohol abuse has long been recognized as a factor in job loss: "...[of] men who lost their last regular work for unsatisfactory reasons, we find that these reasons are miscellaneous, though 'drink' heads the list" (Rowntree & Lasker, 1911, p. 185).

Why Study Selection?

The Selection versus Social Causation Debate. The relationship between adverse employment change and behavioral disorder can be located in the larger context of an earlier and still ongoing dispute about the causal direction between mental illness and poverty. As noted in Chapter 2, it has long been recognized that socioeconomic status is associated with an elevated prevalence of psychiatric disorders (Faris & Dunham, 1939; Jarvis, 1855/1971). Whether the stress of poverty produces mental illness (social causation) or mental illness leads to the descent into poverty (selection) has perplexed researchers for most of the last century.

Efforts to establish causal priority (selection versus social causation) in the poverty area have often been limited by reliance on cross-sectional data. In order to overcome this difficulty, some researchers have used the variable of ethnicity to produce differential tests of the competing hypotheses (Dohrenwend & Dohrenwend, 1969; Dohrenwend et al., 1992). Under the social causation hypothesis, the stress of membership in a disadvantaged ethnic group should add to the stress stemming from poverty in such a way that disadvantaged ethnic group members would have higher rates of psychiatric disorder at each socioeconomic level. Under the selection hypothesis, preexisting disorder accounts for shifts into poverty, but these shifts vary with the prejudice and discrimination that apply differently to different ethnic groups. Healthy members of disadvantaged ethnic groups are assumed to have more difficulty rising in socioeconomic status than do healthy members of advantaged groups. Thus, at each socioeconomic level, disadvantaged ethnic group members should have lower rates of disorder. A recent application of this approach found support for both causal directions. Selection operated more for schizophrenia, but social causation operated more for depression in women and for antisocial personality and substance abuse in men (Dohrenwend et al., 1992).

Another approach utilizes longitudinal data to control for prior economic or mental health status in assessing change over time in poverty and psychiatric functioning. One such approach has used multigenerational prospective data (e.g., Johnson et al., 1999; Miech et al., 1999; Timms, 1996). A similar longitudinal method uses shorter-term data to contrast these causal mechanisms within a panel (Moos, Cronkite, & Moos, 1998; Weich & Lewis, 1998). Together, these varying approaches have found evidence that both selection and social causation may operate, but differently for different types of disorder. For example, one study found that social causation was more important for anxiety, depression, and personality disorders, but that selection seemed stronger for substance abuse disorders (Johnson et al., 1999). Another study found no selection for anxiety and depression but strong evidence for selection for conduct disorder and attention deficit disorder; it also found social causation for anxiety and antisocial disorders but not for depression or attention deficit disorder (Miech et al., 1999).

The best interpretation of such findings is that selection and social causation are not mutually exclusive. Rather, they may both operate, but differently for different types of disorders. There may well be a sequential reciprocal process, perhaps even a cross-generational one. For example, parental socioeconomic status or change in status may influence children's risk of adult disorder and coping ability, which may in turn influence the child's later chances for rising or falling in occupational status (Timms, 1996). Generalizing from these findings on socioeconomic status, it seems plausible that both selection and social causation may operate in the employment change area, but differently depending on the indicator of psychological functioning and such moderators as gender.

However, it is important to remember that socioeconomic status differs significantly from employment change. The former is a status, a relatively enduring condition, usually operationalized by such indicators as occupational or educational attainment, which tend to remain fixed for much of an adult's life. By contrast, employment change is an event, a transition between employment statuses. Life events such as job loss can and do occur to members of different socioeconomic status groups. Such events may serve as the mediating mechanism by which socioeconomic status selection proceeds. For example, if schizophrenia causes an individual to fall to a lower status than his or her parents', the process of drifting down the occupational ladder may well consist of a sequence of job losses and rehires. Of course, such stressful life events may also serve as the stressors that impinge on individuals to produce elevated symptoms (Stueve, Dohrenwend, & Skodol, 1998). Thus, the present exploration of adverse employment change and well-being may help to illuminate the long-standing theoretical problem of selection versus causation in the socioeconomic status domain.

Policy Implications. Most research in the employment change area has concentrated on the social causation pathway. When selection has received attention, it has usually involved the need to statistically control for it as a rival hypothesis. Of course, the scarcity of selection findings may reflect a real absence of this mechanism in the employment change–well-being relationship. On the other hand, it could also reflect a bias on the part of some researchers who may wish to document the assumed social costs of job loss and underemployment. If there is such a bias, it may serve to balance the opposite kind of bias that "blames the victim." Classical economists assumed that everyone could have a job if willing to accept a low enough wage and that unemployment must stem from some defect of the worker, such as "work shyness" or dysfunction. Explicit attention to the selection mechanism may help to illuminate this area, around which assumptions and opinions so readily form.

Attributions for underemployment, whether to individual traits or to economic circumstances, have major implications for debates about such policies as those governing welfare. Do we see welfare recipients as unlucky players in the employment lottery, moochers who do not want to work, or fellow citizens too disabled by illness to take work? Our answer to this question may well affect the way we structure our welfare system. The social causation and selection processes of welfare transitions will be explored later (Chapter 8).

Deciding whether selection or social causation plays the preponderant role in the employment–well-being relationship will lead to different policy choices and thus warrants our attention for quite practical reasons. From a public health perspective, we should be interested in all explanatory factors for community well-being, including prior health. To the extent that employment provides psychological as well as economic benefits, helping people overcome barriers to getting good jobs may offer a useful tool for improving public health. From an economic perspective, the achievement of full employment may require us to understand the magnitude and distribution of the selection effect as a first step in mitigating health problems that hinder job placement and retention.

The usual research approach that finds social causation effects while controlling for selection does not imply the absence of selection effects. If there is a sequential reciprocal process, as implied by the poverty–psychiatric disorder literature, selection may well play a role in sustaining or amplifying social causation. Individuals who experience adverse employment change (e.g., those who are reduced to part-time work due to falling demand for labor) may become depressed or use increased drinking as a way to cope. These behavioral changes may in turn harm the worker's productivity and raise the risk of further reduction in hours or even termination. These latter events might further exacerbate the symptoms, making the worker less competitive in the search for a new job. To the extent that the social causation and selection processes operate together, each represents an intervention target for ameliorating the other. For example, in order to decrease the risks of job loss and its health effects, social interventions might target the individual's behaviors that contribute to layoff (selection). Thus, even those primarily interested in reducing the social costs of adverse employment change should be interested in the relative magnitude of the social causation and selection processes and the conditions under which one or the other may predominate.

Selection may prove just as complicated as social causation and may involve variations brought about by different mediating and moderating variables. As noted in Chapter 2, the preponderance of selection versus social causation may even swing back and forth, depending on such contextual variables as the community unemployment rate. During very low unemployment periods, it seems likely that only the most dysfunctional workers would fail to find jobs, but during high unemployment periods, many healthy and productive workers cannot find jobs. Moreover, aggregate economic conditions may influence the public perception of the extent of selection. People who think it is easy to find work will probably judge the jobless more harshly than will people who have their own employment difficulties.

Disability and the Uncovering Hypothesis. Our discussion of the relationship between worker functioning and labor market conditions must note the role of disability. The term "disability" is used here to refer to dysfunction sufficiently severe that it keeps people from competing for jobs at acceptable wages and qualifies them for transfer payments in lieu of earned income. People who are unable to work and who must rely on disability income are officially considered out of the labor force rather than unemployed, because, at least in principle, they are not seeking work. Someone whose illness or injury causes them to lose a job and go onto disability assistance seems an obvious case of selection. However, our concern here is not with such obvious cases but rather with the less certain selection effects of milder dysfunction that does not rise to the level of official disability. Thus, we will focus on symptoms that reflect potentially decreased ability to compete for adequate employment, as distinct from severe, unambiguous disability that shifts the worker completely out of the labor market. However, we must recognize that the distinction between official disability and less severe signs of dysfunction is hazy, and it is worth noting some of the ways in which disability complicates the analysis of selection versus social causation.

Although becoming severely disabled can and often does lead to job loss, not everyone with official disability automatically leaves the labor force. One of the purposes of the Americans with Disabilities Act was to help remove the barriers that keep disabled people from working. Although joblessness is certainly higher among the disabled than among the general population, many disabled people are employed, and still others seek employment (Burkhauser, Daly, & Houtenville, 2000).

Aside from the obvious selection effect of severe disability into joblessness, a more subtle mechanism may also operate. Some of the early aggregate time-series studies of the social causation hypothesis reported an association between employment rates and mental hospitalization rates (e.g., Brenner, 1973). The usual interpretation of this association was that adverse employment changes provoked increased incidence of mental disorder, resulting in increased rates of mental hospitalization. It is implausible that aggregate behavioral indicators such as mental hospitalization rates could cause aggregate economic indicators such as unemployment rates. But this logical rejection of selection may stem from the definition of terms and thus be less compelling than it seems. Someone who is hospitalized is, by definition, out of the labor force and cannot be counted among the unemployed in official statistics that derive from surveys of the noninstitutionalized population. However, selection may still operate in interaction with aggregate economic conditions, as predicted by what is called the uncovering hypothesis.

As employers adjust their production to varying market conditions, they will naturally lay off some workers during slack periods. Presumably, employers choose the least productive workers for such layoffs, and these workers may well be selected for those characteristics or symptoms that make them least reliable or agreeable. In this scenario, adverse employment change does not cause increased symptoms. Instead, surrounding economic conditions trigger the selection of more symptomatic people into underemployment. But when already dysfunctional people find themselves unable to get along economically, they may need to fall back onto disability assistance or to accept mental hospitalization or other institutionalization as a last resort. Thus an observed increase in mental hospitalizations or other forms of help-seeking behavior may reflect not the provocation of new disorder (social causation) but rather the uncovering or selection of existing disorder (Dooley & Catalano, 1984).

In this uncovering view, the status of being disabled or occupying the "sick" role of mental patient is a function not only of actual symptoms but also of how well those symptoms are tolerated by the local environment, especially the job environment. As the unemployment rate rises, competition for scarce jobs will drive down wages. Those individuals who have a viable claim to disability compensation will quite rationally make that claim when their expected wages fall below their reservation wage, or the benefit of not working (Burkhauser, 1986).

To test this uncovering hypothesis, one study measured the association between unemployment rates and disability caseloads over a period of 109 months in California, starting in September 1986 (Catalano & Kennedy, 1998). Consistent with the uncovering prediction, the unemployment rate predicted monthly differences in the prevalence of disability compensation with a seven-month lag. By contrast, another study monitored the national employment rates of people with and without disabilities during the period 1987 through 1998 (Burkhauser et al., 2000). Surprisingly, the employment rates of disabled men and women fell during the long expansion starting in 1992. For disabled men, employment rates fell from 41.6% in 1992 to 34.4% in 1998, and for disabled women, employment rates fell from 34.3% to 29.5% (Burkhauser et al., 2000, Table A6, p. 47). Given the rising demand for labor during this expansion and the rising employment levels of other workers, it is surprising that the disabled did not enjoy parallel gains. The explanation of this counterintuitive drop in employment remains unclear. Perhaps employers in the new economy require workers to perform a wider range of tasks or hesitate to take on workers with the new entitlements given by the Americans with Disabilities Act.

In sum, there is evidence that dysfunction can lead to adverse employment change and that during economic downturns, this selection process may well induce the most severely disabled workers to seek formal disability status or even the role of institutionalized patient as a means of economic survival. However, other evidence from the most recent expansion indicates that the expected increase in employment of disabled people did not occur. Perhaps the uncovering process, if it once existed, is now changing with new employment circumstances. In any event, it remains to be seen whether milder symptoms, below the threshold of disability, also predict adverse employment change, after controlling for prevailing economic conditions. The remainder of this chapter focuses on this question. Specifically, we will explore the selection effect of those psychological and behavioral indicators that will, in later chapters, serve as the outcome measures for the tests of the social causation hypothesis.

Prior Findings on Selection into Underemployment

Psychological and behavioral measures reflect potential assets or disadvantages with respect to finding and holding adequate employment. The establishment of personal characteristics that influence selection into or out of employment may well begin in childhood (Caspi et al., 1998). However, such psychosocial characteristics are just a few of many factors that help to determine a person's employment, including educational and vocational training, intellectual and physical capabilities, motivation, and opportunities such as the prevailing unemployment situation in the person's occupation, industry, and community. Thus any single behavioral indicator should only partially predict future employment status, especially if such other determinants are taken into account.

Moreover, the predictive power of any variable should decrease as the criterion of later employment moves further in time from the predictor. By its nature, the assessment of employment selection requires longitudinal data that provide not only prior indicators of any potential predictor but also employment status at both prior (as a control) and later (as the criterion) time points. Perhaps because of these difficulties, relatively few studies have reported employment selection effects for the kinds of indicators studied here, and most of those have focused on unemployment as distinct from other forms of inadequate employment. The following sections provide a brief overview of the research that has addressed selection by self-esteem, alcohol abuse, and depression.

Self-esteem. Self-esteem consists of a person's perception of being worthwhile and valuable (Rosenberg, 1965). Self-esteem is a self-appraisal that presumably derives in part from prior accomplishments (Schwalbe & Staples, 1991) and thus should enhance employability in several ways. People with high self-esteem may give the impression of competence and self-confidence, making them more attractive to potential employers, and they may appear more pleasant and personable, enhancing their network connections and job leads. To the extent that the self-esteem measure also reflects self-efficacy, it may predict greater persistence in seeking and holding jobs (Bandura, 1995).

Research on the relationship between self-esteem and employment status has concentrated largely on school-leavers. This approach begins with young people who are nearing the end of their secondary educational careers and follows them into the workforce. Studies of this sort have been reviewed elsewhere and typically concern themselves more with social causation than with selection (Dooley & Prause, 1997b; Winefield et al., 1993). However, a few of these studies have explored the prediction of later employment status by self-esteem measured while still in school, and the results of these studies appear to be mixed.

Several studies reported no difference in high school self-esteem between those who later differed in employment status (Bachman, O'Malley, & Johnston, 1978; Banks & Jackson, 1982; Donovan et al., 1986; Gurney, 1980a,b; Patton & Noller, 1984). One study that did find such a difference described a counterintuitive relationship, in which those with lower self-esteem in high school later had more success becoming employed (Patton & Noller, 1990). On the other hand, other studies found significant and intuitive selection results, in which those with higher self-esteem had better success becoming employed (e.g., Feather & O'Brien, 1986).

If there is a selection effect, it appears to be complex. One study that followed the same panel for most of a decade found the intuitively expected selection effect within one year of leaving school (Tiggemann & Winefield, 1984) and two years after leaving school (Winefield & Tiggemann, 1985). However, this relationship disappeared in later years, particularly after controlling for such background variables as socioeconomic status (Tiggemann & Winefield, 1989). Selection by self-esteem may vary not only by elapsed time but also by characteristics such as gender. For example, one study found that higher self-esteem predicted lower unemployment duration more for women than for men, and that it predicted lower duration of part-time work more for men than for women (Spenner & Otto, 1985).

Perhaps self-esteem does not have the same meaning for all subgroups as it relates to employment (Martinez & Dukes, 1991; Wade et al., 1989). For example, an adolescent's self-esteem may derive importantly from his or her development of a satisfactory gender identity (Hendry, 1987), which may in turn depend on the successful display of culturally prescribed gender-specific behaviors (Josephs, Markus, & Tafarodi, 1992). In particular, boys may derive their self-esteem more from stereotypically masculine or "agentic" traits – such as autonomy, assertiveness, rationality, and technical competence – that can lead to observable success in competition with others. By contrast, girls may base their self-esteem more on stereotypically feminine or "communal" traits such as connectedness, warmth, caring, and interpersonal responsiveness (Harter, 1990). Studies have also suggested racial differences in such self-esteem sources as perceived physical attractiveness (Wade et al., 1989). In addition, such racial differences in self-esteem sources may interact with gender (Martinez & Dukes, 1991). Thus, measures of self-esteem might predict future employment status differently for gender and racial subgroups.

Alcohol Abuse. In contrast to the school-leaver studies of self-esteem, research on alcohol abuse and employment status has focused mainly on adults. Excessive alcohol consumption seems intuitively likely to harm occupational performance, and the standard alcohol abuse symptom measures refer to dysfunction in social roles, including work. Research has documented the adverse effects of alcohol misuse, which include absenteeism from the job, industrial accidents, and inefficiency (Gill, 1994).

If alcohol abuse leads to significant declines in worker productivity, it seems likely that employers would select alcoholic workers for dismissal, especially during slack demand periods when some layoffs must occur. Some evidence for this selection has appeared with respect to unemployment. In one large-scale panel study, employed people who met the diagnostic criteria for alcohol abuse at the first interview were more likely to be unemployed (as measured by receipt of unemployment compensation) one year later, controlling for the prevailing aggregate unemployment rate (Dooley, Catalano, & Hough, 1992). However, the literature offers no evidence on selection by alcohol abuse into inadequate forms of employment.

Depression. Serious depression might also adversely affect workers' productivity and employment prospects. One study of over 6,000 employees found that those with depressive symptoms missed more work because of health problems and performed with reduced effectiveness when at work than those without depressive symptoms (Druss, Schlesinger, & Allen, 2001). Employees with poor attendance records or who appear dispirited or listless because of serious and recurring emotional problems may have a higher risk of selection into unemployment or inadequate employment. A few studies have noted such an association between prior measures of depression and later unemployment. One panel study of over 2,000 Norwegian workers found that psychological items reflecting anxiety and depression in 1989 predicted layoffs by 1993 (Mastekaasa, 1996). Another study of more than 1,000 Swedish young people found that depression measured during the last year of compulsory schooling predicted unemployment five years later (Hammarström & Janlert, 1997).

However, the few studies on this question have not reached consensus. One study of employed adults found that prior depression did not predict falling into unemployment a year later (Dooley et al., 1994). Perhaps only severe depression can disable a worker. Employees and their employers may tolerate moderate to low levels of depression as acceptable variations in performance. Alternatively, if depression represents subjective distress with one's employment situation, it may even operate as motivation to improve that situation. One study of unemployed workers found that those with elevated depression and anxiety were more, not less, likely to find jobs a year later (Kessler et al., 1988).

As with alcohol abuse and self-esteem, depression studies have concentrated on selection into unemployment and paid little or no attention to shifts into inadequate employment. Moreover, selection effects, if they exist, may operate more strongly for some groups than for others, but such moderating interactions remain largely unexplored.

METHODS

Samples

Not all of the psychological and behavioral measures used in the present analyses were asked on every NLSY annual survey. Testing the selection hypothesis requires at least a pair of surveys arranged so that a measure of the predictor appears in the first year of the pair and a measure of employment status appears in the second. Although the employment status data were available for every survey year, we chose the follow-up year for each predictor so as to parallel the social causation analyses described in the next three chapters.

Self-esteem was measured twice, in 1980 and 1987. In Chapter 5, 1987 self-esteem will serve as the outcome measure for the effects of employment transitions, controlling for 1980 self-esteem. Using the same two surveys, the present analysis will study the prediction of 1987 employment status by 1980 self-esteem. Because the focus was on the transition from high school into the workforce, this sample was limited to respondents who did not go on to college or other postsecondary education. The use of 1987 as the criterion year has the additional advantage of ensuring that the respondents, some of whom were in the early years of high school in 1980, had all left school and could have begun their entry into the workforce. Similarly, depression was measured twice, in 1992 and 1994. In Chapter 7, 1994 depression will serve as the outcome measure for the effects of employment transitions, controlling for 1992 depression. Using the same surveys, the present analysis will study the prediction of 1994 employment status by 1992 depression.

Alcohol abuse measures appeared in more NLSY waves and consisted of more widely varying items than did the measures of either self-esteem or depression. For simplicity, we have limited the alcohol measures to two types, symptoms and binge consumption, and have limited the years studied to two pairs, paralleling the analyses of Chapter 6. In that chapter, we will focus on the effects of employment change from 1984 to 1985 and from 1988 to 1989. In the present analyses, we use 1984 alcohol measures to predict 1985 employment and use 1988 alcohol measures to predict 1989 employment. Table 4.1 summarizes the years studied for each predictor and describes the sample sizes and average ages. Note that the mean age of the self-esteem sample in 1987 is similar to the mean age of the alcohol abuse sample two years earlier in 1985. This reflects the selection of a younger subsample for the self-esteem analyses, consisting of those who were in high school in 1980.

Table 4.2 provides a brief demographic profile of the four samples used in these analyses. All samples had a higher percentage of males (ranging from 51.3% to 58.8%) than females and were predominately

TABLE 4.1. *Predictors, sample characteristics, and studied years*

Predictor	Predictor Year	Sample Size	Mean Age in Outcome Year	Outcome Year
Self-esteem	1980	3,055	23.9	1987
Alcohol abuse	1984	4,286	24.2	1985
Alcohol abuse	1988	6,217	28.3	1989
Depression	1992	5,113	33.1	1994

TABLE 4.2. *Sample characteristics by year of predictor*

Characteristic	Self-Esteem 1980[a] (%) (n = 3,055)	Alcohol Abuse 1984 (%) (n = 4,286)	Alcohol Abuse 1988 (%) (n = 6,217)	Depression 1992 (%) (n = 5,113)
Percent male	51.3	57.0	58.8	57.6
Ethnicity				
Hispanic	8.1	5.5	5.5	6.0
African American	16.5	9.3	10.5	11.1
Other	75.5	85.2	84.0	82.9
Marital status				
Never married	49.9	56.0	36.3	23.5
Married	39.1	37.6	52.5	62.2
Not married	11.1	6.4	11.5	14.3
Education				
Less than high school	25.8	8.7	8.2	7.2
High school	74.2	49.6	43.3	40.3
Some college	–	24.9	23.1	24.0
College	–	16.8	25.4	28.4
Parental years of education				
Eighth grade or less	11.6	6.4	6.6	6.8
Less than high school	21.0	12.8	12.5	12.8
High school	49.3	45.1	43.4	42.9
Some college	11.0	14.7	14.6	14.5
College	7.1	21.0	22.9	23.0
Unemployment rate				
<5.9%	33.8	22.3	54.1	20.6
6–8.9%	34.1	37.4	30.0	53.1
9–11.9%	21.4	13.8	9.4	15.9
>11.9%	3.9	14.4	1.3	7.4
Missing	6.8	12.1	5.2	2.8

[a] Because members of this sample were enrolled in high school in 1980, marital status, years of education, and the unemployment rate are presented for the outcome year, 1987.

non-Hispanic/non–African American (from 75.5% to 85.2%). The largest differences were between the sample used to study the prediction of 1987 employment status from 1980 self-esteem (defined using non-college-bound respondents who were in high school in 1980 and had not completed any college as of 1987) and the remaining three samples, which were all composed of adequately employed respondents in the baseline year. About three-fourths of the former sample had completed high school (by definition, none went to college), and 39.1% were married as of 1987. By contrast, about 35% of the respondents in the other three samples had either some college or a college degree; in 1988, 52.5% were married, and in 1992, 62.2% were married. There were also differences in parental years of education between the non-college-bound sample and the other three samples. About one-third of the non-college-bound sample had parents with a high school education or less, compared to about 18% of the respondents in the other three samples. The surrounding economic climate was best in 1988, when 54.1% of the sample lived in areas with less than 5.9% unemployment, in contrast to only 20.6% of the sample in 1992.

Measures

Criterion Measures. The employment categories to be predicted in these analyses consist of adequate employment, inadequate employment, unemployment, and out of the labor force. The definitions of these categories follow the procedures spelled out in Chapter 3. Inadequate employment always includes involuntary part-time work and low-wage work for all of the analyses. However, based on earlier findings (Dooley & Prause, 1997b), an additional underemployment category was included in the self-esteem analyses only, that of intermittent unemployment (people currently working but reporting fifteen or more weeks of unemployment during the past year). Unemployment refers to people out of work but wanting work, including both those who have recently sought employment and those too discouraged to seek a job. Adequate employment consists of all other employment, and the remaining respondents are considered out of the labor force.

In order to control for prior employment status, we selected respondents who shared the same employment status during the first of each pair of years. In the case of self-esteem, the sample consisted of respondents who were still in high school as of the first year. For alcohol abuse and depression, the samples consisted of respondents who were adequately employed during the first year. Thus, for each pair of years, these analyses will predict whether respondents fall into adverse employment categories (inadequate employment or unemployment) or out of the labor force, relative to the more desirable category of adequate employment.

Predictor Measures. The measures of the predictors were introduced in Chapter 3 and need only brief review here. More detail on these measures can be found in later chapters (self-esteem in Chapter 5, alcohol abuse in Chapter 6, and depression in Chapter 7). Self-esteem was measured using the ten-item scale developed by Rosenberg (1965). It gives scores ranging from 10 to 40, where low scores represent low self-esteem. Respondents in 1980 were divided into two groups, using the cut-point of one standard deviation below the mean. Those scoring less than 28 were coded 0 for low self-esteem, and those scoring 28 or more were coded 1 for average or high self-esteem.

Depression was measured with the Center for Epidemiologic Studies Depression Scale or CES-D (Radloff, 1977). Each of the twenty items of this instrument is scaled from 0 to 3, yielding a possible total score ranging from 0 to 60. However, the CES-D is often dichotomized in order to identify respondents with depressive symptoms approaching the clinical level. We used the conventional cut-point of 16 or more for high depression (coded 1) and less than 16 for average to low depression (coded 0).

Alcohol abuse was measured in two ways – symptoms attributed to alcohol abuse over the past year and binge drinking over the past month. Following the NLSY procedure, a binge is defined as consuming six or more drinks in a single session. The 1984 and 1988 samples were divided into three groups based on the number of reported binges during the past month. The high-binge group consisted of approximately the top 10%, defined as six or more binges. The low-binge group served as the reference group and consisted of all others who reported some drinking but five or fewer binge episodes during the past month. The remaining group consisted of those who reported no drinking whatsoever during the past month.

In both 1984 and 1988, respondents who reported any drinking during the past month were asked eleven yes/no questions pertaining to their experience of alcohol-related symptoms during the past year. As with the binge variable, the samples were divided into three groups based on the number of such symptoms. The high-symptom group consisted of those people reporting three or more symptoms, or about the top 10% of the sample. The low-symptom group served as the reference group and consisted of those people who reported drinking during the past month but who reported two or fewer symptoms during the past year. The third group consisted of those who reported no drinking during the past month.

Because an association between prior symptoms (low self-esteem, high depression, alcohol abuse) and later employment status could be the result of confounding by other variables, a standard set of control variables was included in each analysis. Only those predictive relationships that survived such controls and reached statistical significance are discussed here.

Analysis

Each hypothesis was tested using polytomous logistic regression. The outcome variable consisted of an odds ratio. In each analysis, this ratio was defined as the odds at time two of being in the adverse employment category (such as unemployment) rather than in the category of adequate employment for the at-risk group (e.g., people with high depression at time one), relative to the odds for the reference group (e.g., those with low or moderate depression at time one).

This analytic approach provides an estimate of these odds ratios adjusted for all of the other predictors, including the control variables. Moreover, it permits the testing of potential moderators of the predictors. Prior symptoms might better predict later employment change for one population subgroup (e.g., females) than for another (e.g., males). We routinely checked the interactions between predictor and standard control variables in order to explore this possibility.

RESULTS

The findings for the selection hypotheses are summarized in Table 4.3. For each predictor or interaction during the initial year, significant associations for the adverse employment categories during the follow-up year appear in the adjoining columns. In each case, the relationship tested consisted of the odds of being unemployed or inadequately employed relative to being adequately employed for those high on the predictor variable compared

TABLE 4.3. *Selection results adjusted for controls: odds ratios for significant associations relative to adequate employment*

Predictor	Term (including Interactions)	Unemployed	Inadequately Employed
Self-esteem 1980–87	Main effect	.56**	
	× gender (male = 1)	.48**	.45***
	× ethnicity (black = 1)	3.90***	
Alcohol abuse 1984–85	Symptoms	1.55**	1.39*
	binge × education (≤12 years = 1)		3.33***
Alcohol abuse 1988–89	Symptoms	1.70**	1.81***
	× age	1.49***	
	× gender		2.55**
Depression 1992–94	Main effect	3.06**	
	× education (≥12 = 1)	.33*	

Employment Status spans Unemployed and Inadequately Employed columns.

$^*p < .10, ^{**}p < .05, ^{***}p < .01$

to those low on the predictor. All tests are adjusted for all other significant predictors.

Self-esteem

Higher self-esteem in 1980 (average to high coded 1, low coded 0) was associated with lower risk of unemployment but not with inadequate employment seven years later. This apparent selection into unemployment by lower self-esteem was moderated by two variables – gender and ethnicity. The magnitude of the main self-esteem effect was comparable to that of other important variables, such as educational level. The respondents with average to high self-esteem in 1980 enjoyed a decrease in the risk of being unemployed in 1987; their risk was only 56% of that for low self-esteem respondents. In comparison, being a high school graduate at any time up to 1987 reduced the risk of unemployment to 53% of that for people who had not graduated from high school. However, the interactions with gender and ethnicity indicate that the beneficial effect of higher self-esteem on later employment operated more for males than for females and more for whites than for blacks.

There was one interaction between self-esteem and gender in the prediction of inadequate employment that paralleled the one for unemployment. Higher self-esteem reduced the odds of inadequate employment for males but not for females. These selection effects appeared seven years after the initial measurement of self-esteem and after controls for a host of other significant predictors, including education, gender, ethnicity, marital status, the prevailing unemployment rate, and aptitude (see Dooley & Prause, 1997a).

Because the criterion measure of employment status was taken at just one point, seven years after the predictor measure, this analytic approach leaves open the question of how respondents fared during the intervening years. In analyses reported more fully elsewhere, a cumulative unemployment measure was also created (Dooley & Prause, 1997a). It consisted of total weeks unemployed between first leaving high school and the 1987 interview divided by total weeks unemployed plus total weeks employed (either adequate or inadequate). This gives the percentage of time each respondent was unemployed out of the total time spent in the labor force (excluding time spent out of the labor force, in such categories as full-time student, homemaker, or disabled). Using ordinary least squares regression for the smaller sample with complete data ($n = 1,905$), 1980 self-esteem again was a significant predictor ($b = -.109$, beta $= -.065, p \leq .003$). Unlike the logistic regression analyses reported earlier, there was no interaction with gender or ethnicity.

The later measure of self-esteem was also checked as a predictor of still later employment status in the depression analyses that follow. Higher self-esteem measured in 1987 appeared to be marginally associated with a decreased risk of shifting from adequate employment in 1992 to either unemployment or inadequate employment (defined as involuntary part-time or low-wage work) in 1994 (Dooley, Prause, & Ham-Rowbottom, 2000). This 1987–94 selection effect may well be mediated by depression, because earlier self-esteem (1987) is a significant predictor of later depression, which in turn, as will be seen, significantly predicts later employment status. For example, 1987 self-esteem predicted 1994 depression even after controls for 1992 depression and a host of other variables, including changes in employment status and marital status (Dooley et al., 2000).

Alcohol Abuse

Of the two different measures of alcohol misuse – binge consumption over the past month and symptoms over the past year – only the latter significantly predicted later employment status after adjusting for the various control variables. In general, respondents who reported more symptoms (relative to those who reported some drinking but few or no symptoms) had a higher risk of adverse employment change one year later. For the 1984–85 period, the increased risk was substantial (55% for unemployment, $p \leq .05$, and 39% for inadequate employment, $p \leq .07$). The same pattern appeared in slightly stronger form for the 1988–89 period, with the risk increasing by 70% and 81%, with both effects clearly significant.

These associations between earlier alcohol abuse and later employment status change survived controls for a number of potential confounding variables. In the 1984–85 analyses, statistically significant controls included ethnicity, gender, age, years of education, the unemployment rate in 1984, marital status in 1984, and change in marital status by 1985. For the 1988–89 analyses, the significant controls included ethnicity, gender, age, years of education, the unemployment rate in 1988, and marital status in 1988.

The associations between earlier alcohol misuse and adverse employment change one year later were checked for consistency across levels of the control variables, such as gender and years of education. For the 1984–85 period, the association between symptoms and later employment change was not moderated by any of these variables. Although there was no overall association between binge drinking and adverse employment change one year later, binge drinking did predict an approximately fourfold increase ($p < .005$) in the odds of inadequate employment for the group without a high school education. By contrast, binge drinking did not significantly predict increased odds of inadequate employment for the group with at least a high school education.

For the 1988–89 period, none of the control variables moderated the relationship between binge drinking and later adverse employment change. However, the association between symptoms of alcohol misuse and employment status change varied by gender for the inadequately employed ($p < .03$), and by age for the unemployed ($p < .001$). Although alcohol symptoms predicted increased odds of inadequate employment for males ($OR = 2.73$), there was no such relationship for females. In general (across all ages), alcohol symptoms were associated with increased odds of unemployment, but this relationship was more pronounced for older members of the sample than for younger members.

If alcohol abuse predicts adverse employment change for those currently in adequate employment, might it also predict employment change for those who are underemployed? This possibility was explored using another sample of NLSY respondents analyzed elsewhere (Dooley & Prause, 1997c). A total of 1,437 respondents who were either unemployed or inadequately employed in 1984 were reassessed for favorable employment change a year later in 1985 and five years later in 1989. Adjusting for employment change by 1985 and for other significant control variables, the count of alcohol symptoms in 1984 was positively associated with increased risk of both unemployment and inadequate employment in 1989. Thus for those having employment difficulties in 1984, elevated alcohol abuse symptoms appear to damage the chances of moving to adequate employment as much as five years later.

Depression

Respondents reporting higher depression in 1992 were much more likely to be unemployed in 1994, but this relationship appeared to be moderated by educational level. The adverse effects of depression appeared to be stronger for those with fewer years of education ($p \leq .059$). For respondents with less than twelve years of education, 50% of those who became unemployed by 1994 were from the high-depression group in 1992. By contrast, for those with twelve or more years of education who became unemployed, only about 21% were from the high-depression group. Depression failed to predict entry into inadequate employment.

The prediction of unemployment by prior depression persisted despite controls for a series of potential confounders. Significant control variables included gender, marital status in 1992, change in marital status by 1994, children in 1992, the unemployment rate in 1992, a history of unemployment, and 1992 income. The same general findings also appeared when CES-D was handled as a continuous rather than a dichotomous variable (Dooley et al., 2000).

Earlier research suggested that psychological distress might also predict reemployment for those who had been laid off (Mastekaasa, 1996). The possibility of selection out of underemployment by depression was explored in another study of NLSY respondents (Prause & Dooley, 2001). For those who were employed in inadequate jobs in 1992 ($n = 639$), depression had no main effect but did interact with gender to predict 1994 job status. At lower levels of depression, the chances of either adequate or inadequate employment (relative to unemployment) were substantially better for men than for women, but at higher levels of depression, this gender difference was reduced. For those who were unemployed in 1992 ($n = 521$), there was a significant main effect of depression that reduced the odds of either adequate or inadequate employment in 1994, relative to unemployment. For the unemployed in 1992, both ethnicity and marital status moderated the effects of earlier depression. The advantage in gaining adequate employment of non-Hispanic/non–African Americans over Hispanics and African Americans observed at low levels of depression decreased as the level of depression increased. People married with a spouse present had an advantage over people with no spouse in gaining inadequate employment (versus remaining unemployed) at higher levels of depression, but this advantage decreased with falling depression.

DISCUSSION

Summary and Limitations

Researchers who have occasionally explored selection into unemployment have rarely studied other forms of underemployment. The present analyses show that low self-esteem (especially for males) and elevated alcohol abuse symptoms can predict later shifts not only into unemployment but also into such forms of inadequate employment as involuntary part-time work and low-wage work. By contrast, depression predicted becoming unemployed but not later inadequate employment. Although these findings are suggestive, it is premature, with so few studies, to conclude that there is a general tendency for selection into inadequate employment by either low self-esteem or alcohol abuse.

The present findings of selection into unemployment agree with some prior research, but confidence in our findings is also limited by contrasting findings in other studies. As noted earlier, several school-leaver studies have reported no selection into later unemployment by low self-esteem (Bachman et al., 1978; Banks & Jackson, 1982; Donovan et al., 1986; Gurney, 1980a,b; Patton & Noller, 1984). And at least one prior study of adults found no selection into unemployment by depression (Dooley et al., 1994). While alcohol abuse seems intuitively likely to harm a worker's chances of keeping his or her job, selection into unemployment by alcohol symptoms is surprisingly little documented. Thus, the present evidence for selection into unemployment joins a sparse literature that is far from unanimous on this question.

Furthermore, the present study has its own mix of strengths and weaknesses. The present sample is quite representative of a particular generation of workers in one nation during one period of recent economic history. Whether the selection effects observed for this sample would hold for other countries or for the next generation of American workers in a changing economy remains to be seen. The interactions involving self-esteem with gender and race may also be subject to change as women and minorities increasingly assume roles in the American workforce similar to those traditionally held by white males. Some of the selection effects appear to be large in magnitude and might be expected to reappear in later replications. However, the large sample sizes studied here provide high statistical power that could make even modest selection effects appear to be significant. On the other hand, the failure of some earlier studies to find significant selection effects may well be due to the low power associated with smaller sample sizes.

Implications for Research and Theory

If prior psychosocial functioning predicts later employment change, it might do so by either of two mechanisms. The more intuitive mechanism might be labeled the asset/deficit model. From this perspective, one's mood or behavior might serve either as an asset in the competition for desirable jobs or as a deficit that undercuts one's efforts to find or retain employment. An alternative mechanism might be labeled the motivational distress model. In this view, indicators of well-being, such as depression and self-esteem, may reflect individuals' distress with their current situation, including their employment status. Individuals with greater distress may have more motivation to change those conditions and to compete more energetically for better employment. Some evidence for the motivational distress mechanism has been noted in a study of reemployment (Kessler et al., 1988), but the present findings all agree with the asset/deficit model. Higher self-esteem, less depression, and fewer symptoms of alcohol abuse all predicted better employment outcomes.

These findings do not mean that motivational distress never operates. The present analyses largely involve short-term employment transitions rather than long-term unemployment. Some individuals experiencing prolonged joblessness may cope with their lowered employment prospects by disconnecting their sense of self worth and well-being from employment. In this way, high self-esteem and lower depression might become associated with less rather than more energetic pursuit of reemployment. On the other hand, it is hard to imagine a scenario in which elevated drinking or more symptoms of alcohol abuse would ever be positively associated with favorable employment change. Indeed, some evidence suggests that actual or threatened job loss might lead to decreased drinking, as workers, knowing that their drinking is a deficit, make efforts to hold onto or regain their jobs (Catalano et al., 1993; Warr, 1987). More generally, perceived job insecurity might lead to more help-seeking behavior in workers with psychological symptoms (Catalano, Rook, & Dooley, 1986). In the competition for scarce jobs, workers seem to appreciate the need to appear sober, confident, and positive in their self-presentation to current and potential employers.

Although the asset/deficit model of employment status selection may have general validity, the present findings suggest some areas for further exploration. One such area involves the moderators of the selection effect. Several significant interactions point to differences in the degree to which self-esteem operates as an asset or depression as a deficit. Such findings from a single study require replication and explanation before we can rely on them for theoretical or policy guidance. Nevertheless, corroborating evidence has appeared for some of these interactions.

For example, why did self-esteem operate as an employment asset more for males than for females, and more for whites than for blacks, in these data? In a study of college students that involved setting more difficult goals in a laboratory task, researchers found that self-esteem was associated with ambition and that this ambition effect of self-esteem appeared to be stronger in males than in females (Levy & Baumgardner, 1991). Self-esteem may have a different meaning for males than for females, and a different meaning for blacks than for whites. A study of the relationship between self-esteem and self-reported instrumental (agentic achievement) activities found little association between them for black, inner-city male adolescents or for pregnant females but a strong association for white male college students (Malton, 1990). One explanation for this racial difference comes from a study showing that in blacks, the self-worth facet of self-esteem (as measured in this study and as distinct from the self-efficacy facet) derives more from relations with family and friends (Hughes & Demo, 1989). In contrast, the self-efficacy facet that is linked to future employment may be more closely aligned with the self-worth facet in whites, thus accounting for the stronger selection effect observed for them in this study. Such interactions invite further research to spell out the different mediating mechanisms by which self-esteem or other psychological attributes operate in employment selection.

For research on social causation, which is the primary focus of this book, these selection findings reemphasize the need to adjust for prior psychosocial functioning. If preexisting low self-esteem, depression, or alcohol abuse can select people into or out of adverse employment statuses, then the impact of these transitions can only be assessed after controlling for these characteristics. It follows that cross-sectional research, which can correlate only current employment and current psychosocial functioning, necessarily confounds the selection and social causation effects and must be checked by longitudinal methods, as used here.

Implications for Policy

The magnitudes of the selection effects observed in these samples appear to be large enough to warrant consideration by social policy makers. For example, young people with high or average self-esteem were only 56% as likely to be unemployed seven years later as were low self-esteem youth. This is comparable to the effects of education; high school graduates were 53% as likely to be unemployed as were nongraduates. Similarly, respondents with high levels of depression were three times as likely to be unemployed two years later as respondents with low and average depression levels. Again, this magnitude is comparable to that of income; people in poverty were 2.8 times as likely to be unemployed as people with incomes above the poverty line.

Of course, some of these selection effects were significantly moderated, suggesting that any policy applications need to take into account potentially complex interactions. For example, employment selection by self-esteem was stronger for whites than for blacks, and stronger for males than for females. Selection by depression was greater for those with less rather than more education. Programs aimed at decreasing the risk of later unemployment by increasing self-esteem might work for white males but not, according to these findings, for blacks or for females. Similarly, efforts to lower unemployment risks by targeting depression might work for those with less education but not for those with more education.

Allowing for such complexities, programs might try to reduce later underemployment by increasing such personal assets as self-esteem or by decreasing deficits such as alcohol abuse and depression. Whether programs exist that can modify such traits is one question. Whether such artificially manipulated traits (as opposed to "natural" self-esteem, for example) will operate according to the present findings is another question. Current programs that attempt to promote the job prospects of unemployed people might add modules for raising self-esteem or for reducing depression to see whether they add anything to standard skill training for job finding, job interviewing, and work performance. For example, one two-and-a-half-week program successfully used behavioral modeling to boost self-efficacy, job-search activity, and, among those with the least self-efficacy, actual reemployment (Eden & Aviram, 1993). Some evidence exists that such interventions can also help to inoculate unemployed workers against the depressive effects of later bouts of unemployment (Vinokur & Schul, 1997).

The present research suggests a symmetric relationship between these selectors and both adverse and favorable employment change. Self-esteem among high school students was negatively related to later unemployment but positively related to later adequate employment. For unemployed young adults, lower levels of depression predicted more favorable employment change two years later. The fact that such traits can select people out of unemployment as well as into it invites the inclusion of relevant interventions in programs for those already experiencing underemployment. If adverse job change has significant social costs, these adverse effects might, in turn, reduce the chances for reemployment. Thus, the cycle of adverse job change and adverse psychological change could, in principle, be broken by intervening either on the worker's employment status (e.g., placement in a job) or on the worker's behavior (e.g., reducing alcohol abuse).

5

Leaving School

Self-esteem in an Unwelcoming Economy

> A man's work is the primary base for his life in society. Through it he is 'plugged into' an occupational structure and a cultural, class and social matrix. Work is also of great psychological importance; it is a vehicle for the fulfillment or negation of central aspects of self.
>
> Levinson, 1978, p. 9

> In general, we obtain the same effects upon the personality of unemployed youth as upon that of unemployed adults, but because of the greater susceptibility of youth and because they are going through a transition period between childhood and maturity these effects are probably more lasting.
>
> Eisenberg & Lazarsfeld, 1938, p. 383

INTRODUCTION

This chapter explores the relationship between employment status and self-esteem in young people. Controlling for their self-esteem when the NLSY respondents were still in secondary school, does later self-esteem vary depending on whether the school-leaver is unemployed, inadequately employed, adequately employed, or out of the labor force?

Employment and Development

Work and Childhood. Child labor laws now encode the consensus that young children risk serious harm from most kinds of labor. This harm may be either physical (e.g., risk of injury) or psychological (e.g., denial of appropriate education). These laws do not allow young children to work except under unusual circumstances (e.g., child actors) and then only with careful monitoring to protect against exploitation and mitigate the risks (e.g., providing tutors on the movie set). Nevertheless, reports still surface from time to time of child labor being practiced under horrific circumstances.

We can imagine parents and communities tolerating this practice only when the health risks of allowing children to work appear certain to be exceeded by the health risks of going without the children's income (e.g., starvation).

At what age does paid employment stop being harmful and begin to prove beneficial for young people? In most countries, child labor laws are relaxed when young people reach middle to late adolescence, typically permitting youngsters to work at least part-time, subject to the mandatory educational requirements. Here the question of harm and benefit becomes less clear-cut. From an economic perspective, youth labor may supplement family income, to the special advantage of people living in or near poverty. From a psychological perspective, part-time labor may offer young people valuable training in the work habits necessary for future success in the job market. On the other hand, part-time work while in school, even when legal and physically safe, may distract young people from their primary mission of mastering their educational and other developmental tasks. Such academic learning and socialization may prove more valuable in the long run than students' part-time earnings, both for their later careers in the workforce and for their mental well-being (see Greenberger & Steinberg, 1986). Aside from affecting the well-being of young people, policies that influence the prevalence of youth employment (e.g., by providing for lower "entry-level" youth wages) might also affect the well-being and employment opportunities of those adults who must compete with young people for scarce jobs at higher adult minimum wages.

The role of employment in the lives of children who are still in school and the potentially moderating effects of increased income and of training for future employment on any adverse psychological effects in these children, while important, go beyond the scope of this study. Instead, we will focus on the transition of older adolescents from secondary school to early adulthood in the labor market, and on the effect of different employment statuses on the psychological rather than the economic well-being of young people.

Transition to Adulthood. Life-span perspectives on human development typically distinguish several stages at which individuals must face different age-specific challenges (e.g., the theories of Freud and Erikson). Success in resolving the challenge presented at each stage presumably strengthens the foundation for progress through later stages and, ultimately, increases the chances of happier adjustment in adulthood. On the other hand, failure to negotiate a developmental task may leave the individual feeling incomplete and unprepared for later challenges. Life-span theories vary in the number and characterization of their stages, with some emphasizing earlier and others later developmental crises.

With regard to the developmental impact of employment in modern industrial societies, one life stage seems especially critical. This is the phase during which people leave late adolescence and enter early adulthood, typically from the late teens to the early twenties (Bocknek, 1980). This transition takes the individual from being a full-time student, living at home and dependent on his or her parents, to being a self-supporting worker in the labor force and living away from home. Young adults typically want to become economically independent but, depending on the prevailing employment opportunities, may find themselves unable to participate in the labor force (Mortimer & Borman, 1988; Wittenberg, 1968). Society expects the young adult to make his or her own way but does not always provide the opportunity to meet this obligation. This psycho-economic bind can leave young adults feeling rejected and devalued precisely at the moment of their first attempt to achieve autonomy.

Self-esteem and Employment. From this life-span perspective, the school-leaver faces the challenge of establishing a meaningful occupational identity, a task for which finding a satisfactory job is crucial (Erikson, 1959; Hendry, 1987). Success at this task should result in such favorable psychological outcomes as an increased sense of autonomy, self-worth, and self-efficacy. But failure at this critical juncture could lead to increased self-doubt, dependency, and even self-loathing. Thus, the construct of self-esteem should serve as an especially apt marker for a young person's psychological passage through this transition.

Self-esteem scales reflect the perception of oneself as worthwhile and valuable. Such positive aspects of self-image should, in the course of normal psychological development, rise during the adolescent-to-early-adulthood transition (Rosenberg, 1965). Self-esteem is viewed as the product of the individual's history of successes and failures (Levy & Baumgardner, 1991). It is a self-appraisal based on observation of one's past accomplishments (Schwalbe & Staples, 1991). Thus, we should expect that performance in such a major test as the transition from school into the workforce would count heavily in a young person's assessment of his or her self-worth. Moreover, self-esteem appears to be linked to other outcomes, ranging from mental health to later success in the job market (e.g., selection into more and less adequate jobs, as reported in Chapter 4).

Prevalence of Youth Underemployment

Age Trap. The natural tendency of employers to try to get the best production (marginal rate of return) from their employees at the minimum possible wage tends to put young adults in an economic trap. When there is a reduced "entry" wage for young people or an apprenticeship system, adolescents may find work under special low-wage conditions. But when the young worker reaches the age at which full adult minimum wages should be paid or when the apprenticeship is complete, he or she may find it difficult to compete for scarce jobs (Burnett, 1994). Older adults can offer more advanced skills commensurate with adult wages, and younger workers may be able to perform the same work at the lower "entry" wage for which young adults no longer qualify.

As a result, a pattern of high unemployment among young adults has appeared in the industrial economies at least since the turn of the twentieth century and may have helped to motivate measures to increase the school-leaving age (Burnett, 1994). Keeping young people in school longer should help to reduce the substitution of youth labor for adult labor and could encourage young people to acquire more human capital through longer periods of educational investment. But raising the school-leaving age might only postpone the moment at which young people, finished with their schooling and ready for independence, enter the job market. And if the economy were unwelcoming, that cohort of school-leavers would still have to deal with the consequences of initial rejection. Extending below-minimum "entry" wages might help younger workers to get jobs, but these jobs would, by definition, be economically inadequate in terms of income and security.

Numerous anecdotal reports have described the emotional distress of young adults struggling to find steady work and to establish their identities in careers. Some have described their exploitation as child workers, after which their employers have discharged them to the frustrating task of looking unsuccessfully for adult-wage employment. Finding none, these young people begin to internalize the message of the job market, that they have little of value to offer (Burnett, 1994). Intensive qualitative studies have added further evidence to such anecdotal reports. One longitudinal study of men in the 35–45 age range followed ten subjects with little or no college experience (two had some college) who had gone into hourly-wage work in industry (Levinson, 1978). Of these, eight reported having had an occupational crisis when entering adulthood, and five reported that they had hit the "rock bottom" time in their lives. For these workers, there was "at least one period in which it seemed unlikely that they would ever get married and have a stable family or that they would find steady employment with reasonable prospects for interesting work and promotion" (Levinson, 1978, p. 81).

Youth Unemployment Levels. Even if some young adults have great difficulty making the transition into the world of work, youth unemployment may be a limited problem affecting only a small portion of any school-leaver cohort and thus warranting no special attention from policy makers. In fact, the level of youth unemployment has been recognized throughout the industrialized world as ominously high for at least the last several decades. Consider first the case of the United Kingdom, the origin of some of the earliest studies of the psychological effects of youth unemployment. There, unemployment rates for people under eighteen years old increased from 1% to 25% between 1951 and 1981, despite the government's special employment and youth training programs, without which the rates might have been twice as high (Burnett, 1994, p. 272). The next older age group fared little better. By 1985, the British unemployment rate for everyone under twenty-five was 21.5%, and the duration of unemployment was lengthening. The percentage of unemployed young people (under twenty-five) who had been jobless for more than a year increased from 7.5% in 1977 to 28% in 1985 (Burnett, 1994, p. 273).

Although industrialized countries exhibit widely varying unemployment rates in any given year, they have in common the fact that their young people experience joblessness at far higher levels than do other age groups. In 1993, the ratio of the unemployment rate of those under twenty-five to the unemployment rate of the general population ranged from 1.6 in the United Kingdom (where the youth unemployment rate was 17.3%) to 1.73 in the Netherlands (10.2%) to 2.24 in Spain (43.2%). These ratios were representative of the situations in other industrialized countries for earlier years extending back to the 1980s and 1970s (Winefield, 1997).

This pattern of elevated youth unemployment holds for the United States as well. However, in this multiracial society, the employment difficulties of youth are compounded by the difficulties of race and ethnicity even in good economic times. In 1999, the U.S. economy was performing very well, with an overall unemployment rate for everyone sixteen and over of just 4.2% (U.S. Bureau of Labor Statistics, 2000a). For those in the 16–19 age range, the unemployment rates were 12.6% and 11.3% for non-Hispanic/non–African American men and women, versus 30.9% and 25.1% for African American men and women. As described in Chapter 3, the NLSY respondents experienced higher rates of unemployment than the labor force as a whole, in part because of the youth of the NLSY panel and in part because it oversampled minority and poor young people.

BACKGROUND

School-Leaver Employment and Well-Being

Prior Research. Unlike cross-sectional studies of youth unemployment and mental health, longitudinal studies can rule out selection into employment status by prior psychological functioning. Most such longitudinal studies contrast employed with unemployed respondents in panels that are first measured before they leave secondary school. Although this research approach has the virtue of controlling for both prior mental status and prior employment status, it has generated relatively few studies. One review of the English-language literature before the present study began found just nine studies published in scholarly journals, all during the period from the late 1970s through the early 1990s (Dooley & Prause, 1997b).

Of these nine studies, five were based on samples from Australia, with only two each from the United Kingdom and the United States. Just four of the studies involved large samples of 800 or more respondents. However, all of these studies measured self-esteem or some related indicator of psychological well-being. These studies could assess selection into later employment status, and they provided mixed results on that question (see Chapter 4 for an analysis of school-leaver employment selection by self-esteem). This literature has focused primarily on the comparative impact of unemployment versus employment on self-esteem.

Representative of the general research strategy, but remarkable for its large initial sample and repeated follow-ups, was the Australian study by Anthony Winefield and his colleagues (1993). They began with an initial sample of 3,130 students in school in 1980 and followed this panel for a decade, with the final round of interviews conducted in 1989 (by which time the number of unemployed respondents available for reinterview had dwindled to just eight). In each follow-up year, the employed and unemployed school-leavers were contrasted on various criterion variables adjusted for measures collected when the sample was still in school. This study repeatedly found that those who were unemployed scored lower on various well-being indicators than those who were employed.

On the social causation issue, reviews of the literature find that most studies converge on the same conclusion, namely, that unemployed school-leavers report lower self-esteem (or report more symptoms on other psychological measures) than employed school-leavers (Dooley & Prause, 1997b; Winefield et al., 1993). Both the best early studies (e.g., Winefield et al., 1993) and the more recent studies tend to support this basic finding for young people leaving secondary school (e.g., Gore et al., 1997; Hammarström & Janlert, 1997; Schaufeli, 1997). Despite this apparent consensus, some issues invite further study. Among these, there is the usual need to replicate studies in different contexts in order to ensure the external validity or generalizability of the findings. For example, will a relationship documented in an Australian sample hold true for the culturally and racially more heterogeneous population of the United States? In addition, two substantive questions remain either unresolved or unexplored by the existing literature.

Mechanism. One of the unresolved questions involves the nature of the social causation effect, which could stem from different mechanisms. As indicated, most studies find that unemployed school-leavers report worse psychological status (e.g., lower self-esteem) than their employed counterparts. One process by which this difference could arise is through deterioration among the unemployed respondents from their prior level of functioning in secondary school. In adult unemployment studies, the deterioration that is observed following job loss is usually explained by the stressful effects of losing income, social status, social relations at the workplace, and other such benefits of employment (Jahoda, 1982). However, the "stress" explanation may not apply in the school-leaver case, because the respondents are not losing employment but instead are failing to gain it.

Another plausible mechanism for the observed social causation effect involves the employed making greater gains in psychological functioning (e.g., increased self-esteem) than their unemployed counterparts. In this scenario, those who cannot find jobs do not necessarily deteriorate from prior levels of well-being but rather are arrested in their normal development and thus delayed in their psychosocial maturation relative to their peers. This "arrested development" explanation does not require the respondents to have lost prior jobs and is consistent with the kinds of developmental-stage theories that emphasize the need of young adults to experience economic and occupational independence from their parents (Bocknek, 1980; Erikson, 1959; Levinson, 1978; Wittenberg, 1968).

Findings that the social causation effect results from a decrease in the unemployed school-leavers' well-being would favor the stress explanation. Such a pattern has appeared in some studies (Feather & O'Brien, 1986; Patton & Noller, 1984; Schaufeli, 1997). Findings that the effect results from the failure of the unemployed school-leavers' well-being to keep pace with the increase in the employed respondents' would favor the arrested development explanation. This pattern has appeared in somewhat more studies (Bachman et al., 1978; Donovan et al., 1986; Gore et al., 1997; Gurney, 1980a,b; Winefield et al., 1993). Of course, these two mechanisms are not mutually exclusive. The self-esteem gap between the employment status groups might widen both because the unemployed decline and because the employed improve rapidly. Results consistent with this dual-effect pattern have also appeared (Banks & Jackson, 1982; Patton & Noller, 1990).

Inadequate Employment. The unexplored question here involves the effect on school-leavers of falling into economically inadequate employment as distinct from both adequate employment and unemployment. As with other areas of research on employment status, the school-leaver literature has generally treated employment status as a dichotomy, contrasting employment and unemployment. Perhaps society takes for granted that young people will, if employed at all, have lower wages, fewer hours, and less job security than older workers. Laws permitting subminimum "entry-level" wages for young workers may seem logical extensions of traditional apprenticeship practices. From this perspective, the economic inadequacy of youth employment may seem both natural and beneficent, intended to help young people get a foot on the lowest rung of the employment ladder.

Perhaps young people feel gratitude for any employment at all and, therefore, make little distinction between jobs that are more and less economically adequate. However, some evidence suggests that school-leavers do distinguish among jobs, at least in terms of the subjective satisfaction that they provide. Using a single global item, Winefield and colleagues (1993) classified their Australian employed school-leavers into satisfied (about 90%) or dissatisfied (about 10%) subgroups. Analyses consistently found that the dissatisfied employed school-leavers more closely resembled the unemployed than the satisfied employed respondents on such criteria as self-esteem and depression.

Perhaps subjective job satisfaction serves as a proxy for a job's economic adequacy. Young people may derive their job satisfaction primarily from the objective economic parameters of wages and hours. In this case, the reported link between job satisfaction and well-being suggests the hypothesis that economically inadequate jobs will produce effects in school-leavers that more closely resemble those of unemployment than those of adequate employment. On the other hand, global subjective job satisfaction measures usually tap aspects of the job that go beyond wages and hours. These facets can include the intrinsic interest of the work and the quality of relationships with coworkers, among other important psychosocial features. Economically good jobs may involve boring tasks and hostile coworkers, and economically inadequate jobs may involve interesting work and friendly coworkers. Thus subjective global satisfaction and economic adequacy may have little or no association. Even in this case, the economic adequacy of employment may still influence the respondent's well-being, but the literature provides no evidence for this connection.

Hypotheses

Social Causation. The main hypothesis predicts that, controlling for self-esteem while still in secondary school, both unemployed and inadequately employed school-leavers will have lower self-esteem than their adequately employed counterparts. Based on the preponderance of prior findings, this relationship should have a pattern consistent with the arrested development mechanism. That is, the underemployed respondents, both unemployed and inadequately employed, should have little or no decrease in their self-esteem, but the adequately employed school-leavers should show a marked increase in their self-esteem.

Mediators and Moderators. In addition to testing this basic hypothesis, the present analyses permit study of the roles played by several other variables. One such variable is subjective job satisfaction as it relates to employment status and self-esteem. Prior research suggests that among the employed at follow-up, those reporting lower job satisfaction will also have lower self-esteem. Besides replicating this connection between job satisfaction and self-esteem, this study will also assess whether job satisfaction is associated with the economic adequacy of a job. If job satisfaction and economic adequacy are correlated, it is possible that one serves as the mediator between the other and self-esteem. For example, economic adequacy may serve as a cause of job satisfaction, which may in turn cause greater self-esteem. But even controlling for this indirect effect (by statistically adjusting for job satisfaction), the economic adequacy of a job may still have a direct effect on self-esteem.

Other variables might operate as moderators to influence the relationship between employment status and self-esteem. The meager school-leaver literature provides little guidance for predicting moderating effects. The present analyses explore the effect on self-esteem of interactions of the employment status variables with each of the following: gender, age, prior self-esteem, ethnicity, high school graduation status, and urban versus rural residence. The adult unemployment literature suggests another potential moderator – the community unemployment rate in the respondent's community (e.g., Cohn, 1978; Turner, 1995). The unemployment rate at reinterview should be inversely related to the actual opportunities for employment and thus to the perceived difficulty of gaining employment, which might in turn affect individual assessments of self-worth. Other research has pointed to the role of the individual's psychological commitment to being employed. Some studies have found that job loss has fewer adverse effects on people who are less work-involved (e.g., Stafford, Jackson, & Banks, 1980). Among unemployed school-leavers, perhaps those who place a higher value on working will assess their self-worth more harshly.

METHODS

Sample

The "Forgotten Half." The NLSY collected the criterion variable of self-esteem just twice, in 1980 and again in 1987. Therefore, the present analyses include those respondents who were surveyed in both of those years. In order to control time-one employment status, we limited the sample to those respondents who were in high school, less than twenty years of age, and not in the military during 1980. Some 4,852 respondents met these criteria.

The sample was reduced further by excluding any respondents who had completed one or more years of college by 1987 ($n = 1,448$). We wanted to focus on young people who were likely to face the challenge of finding work without the benefits of any college education. One of those benefits, of course, consists of the added human capital acquired through college courses and certified by diplomas. Another benefit consists simply in becoming older and gaining maturity and social experience in the shelter of a campus community rather than in the less nurturing environment of the job market. Aside from these advantages of going to college, college-bound young people on average have more family resources and intellectual ability than their non-college-bound peers. Those concerned about the widening income gap in America often point to the differential opportunities afforded young people who go to college versus those who do not. The latter have been termed the "forgotten half," because they seem to be left behind in the competition for good jobs and economic security (William T. Grant Foundation Commission on Work, Family, and Citizenship, 1988). Less mature and with fewer resources and skills when they enter the labor force, they will probably have more difficulty finding good jobs and developing a sense of self-worth at this critical developmental stage.

Characteristics. With the further loss of respondents providing incomplete data on the necessary measures, the sample size becomes 3,066. All high school students in 1980, this sample averaged 23.9 years of age by 1987, and over half of the sample was male (52.4%). For more details on the sample selection and characteristics, see Prause and Dooley (1997).

A brief demographic profile of these respondents is presented in Figures 5.1–5.5. About three-quarters of the sample was non-Hispanic/non–African American (17% were African American, and 8% were

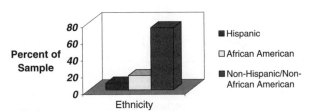

FIGURE 5.1. Ethnicity.

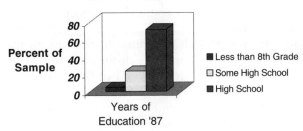

FIGURE 5.2. Education.

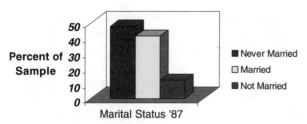

FIGURE 5.3. Marital status.

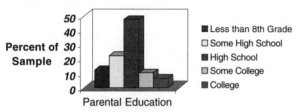

FIGURE 5.4. Parental education.

FIGURE 5.5. Unemployment rate.

Hispanic; see Figure 5.1). By 1987, just 72% had achieved high school graduation or the equivalent (Figure 5.2), and about 41% were married (Figure 5.3). More than one-third of the respondents had parents with less than a high school education (35.1%), while close to one-half of the respondents had a parent who had completed high school (47.6%) (see Figure 5.4). About one-third of the respondents lived in an area with an unemployment rate below 6.0% in 1987 (see Figure 5.5). The unemployment rate was between 6% and 9% in 1987 for an additional one-third of the respondents.

When these young people were still in high school in 1980, the official U.S. unemployment rate was 7.6%. It continued to rise during the recession of the early 1980s to a peak of nearly 10% during 1982 and 1983. The subsequent recovery continued through the end of the decade; by 1987, U.S. unemployment had fallen to 6.2%. As detailed in Chapter 3, the NLSY sample had a higher unemployment rate than the nation as a whole. This is due in part to the youth of the sample and in part to its inclusion of a supplement that overrepresents minority and poor white people.

Respondents in the present sample came from communities that experienced higher unemployment rates in 1987 than the nation as whole (mean = 7.4%, S.D. = 2.6).

Measures

Employment Status. Respondents were categorized by their 1987 employment status, using the framework detailed in Chapter 3. Respondents not working but wanting work were classified as unemployed ($n = 325$). These included 292 respondents who were actively seeking work and who would have met the official CPS criteria for unemployment. The additional thirty-three unemployed respondents were discouraged workers who said that they wanted work but had not recently looked for work because they believed none to be available to them. All other nonworking respondents were classified as out of the labor force or OLF ($n = 617$). The majority of these reported themselves as keeping house, but others fell into such categories as full-time student and disabled.

Inadequately employed workers fell into three categories, identified in the following hierarchical order.

1. Involuntary part-time workers had less than thirty-five hours of employment in the week before the interview, wanted to work more hours, but felt that additional hours were unavailable for economic reasons ($n = 63$).
2. Intermittent unemployment applied to currently employed people working full-time or voluntarily part-time who had experienced fifteen or more weeks of unemployment during the past year ($n = 161$).
3. Poverty-wage workers included those who were working full-time or voluntarily part-time and who had not experienced fifteen or more weeks of unemployment during the past year but whose job paid less than 1.25 times the federal poverty level for unrelated individuals under sixty-five ($5,910 in 1987).

This last group was sufficiently large ($n = 347$) to permit subcategorization by the number of weeks worked during the past year, either less than fifty ($n = 171$) or full year ($n = 176$). This distinction permits a comparison of two types of low-wage workers. The full-year employment group presumably has stronger attachment to the labor force and perhaps greater psychological investment or pride in being employed. Hypothetically, the workers who have weaker or more transient labor force attachment (less than fifty weeks worked) might feel less distressed by or better adapted to their low wages. All other workers were considered adequately employed ($n = 1,553$).

Self-esteem and Other Measures. The Rosenberg ten-item scale was used to measure self-esteem in 1980 and 1987 (Rosenberg, 1965). Self-esteem scales attempt to reflect the respondent's sense of self-worth. However, one's sense of self-worth may vary depending on the specific situation or domain (e.g., academic self-esteem). The Rosenberg scale attempts to represent an overall or global rather than a domain-specific type of self-esteem (Baker & Gallant, 1984/85; O'Brien, 1985). The scale yields scores ranging from 10 to 40, with high values indicating higher self-esteem, and it displayed adequate reliability in this study (Cronbach's alpha = .79).

The NLSY collected one job satisfaction item that asked respondents to rate their current job on a global four-point scale. All of the employed respondents were categorized either as satisfied with their job ("like it very much" or "like it somewhat") or unsatisfied ("dislike it very much" or "dislike it somewhat").

The standard control variables of gender, age, and ethnicity were included in the analyses along with several other background variables, such as whether the respondent had graduated from high school by 1987 (1 = yes, 0 = no). Parental years of education (higher level of either parent) served as a proxy for the respondent's family socioeconomic status. The Armed Forces Qualification Test (AFQT) estimated the respondent's verbal and mathematical aptitude in 1980. The work involvement construct was measured in the 1979 NLSY survey with an item asking whether the respondent would continue to work if he or she could live comfortably without working. Urban or rural residence and community unemployment rate in 1987 helped to characterize the respondent's work opportunities.

Analytic Approach

Because there were interactions between 1980 self-esteem (the primary covariate) and some of the employment status groups, ANCOVA analysis was inappropriate. Instead, ordinary least squares regression was used to model the effect of different 1987 employment statuses on 1987 self-esteem, controlling for 1980 self-esteem and other significant predictors, including pair-wise interactions between employment status and potential moderator variables such as 1980 self-esteem. The employment statuses were coded as dummy variables, and their effects were estimated relative to the reference group of adequate employment.

The association between subjective job satisfaction and the job's economic adequacy was assessed in a contingency table with chi-square statistics. A separate ordinary least squares regression model tested whether the employment status variables would still predict self-esteem after controlling for the potential mediation of job satisfaction.

RESULTS

Underemployment and Self-Esteem

Regression Model. In order to test the basic hypothesis that not only un-employment but also various types of inadequate employment might have adverse effects on school-leavers, 1987 self-esteem was regressed on 1980 self-esteem, various other background variables, and dummy variables representing various 1987 employment statuses. Table 5.1 gives the results for the main and interaction effects involving the employment status variables, controlling for all other significant predictors. These other predictors included age, ethnicity, parental years of education, AFQT aptitude, and 1980 self-esteem, as well as two interactions (graduation × parental edu-cation and ethnicity × aptitude). For additional details on this and related analyses, see Prause and Dooley (1997).

Compared to the self-esteem of the adequately employed respondents, all of the other employment status groups showed significant negative effects. The standardized regression coefficients imply that these effects were of similar magnitudes (betas ranging from −.032 to −.116), bracketing the effect for the unemployed respondents (beta = −.057). In fact, none of the differences among these employment status groups was significant, suggesting that the adverse effect of being unemployed did not exceed the adverse effect of falling into any of the inadequate employment groups.

Two interactions involved employment status groups. The gender-by-intermittent-unemployment interaction suggested that among the inter-mittently unemployed, women had lower self-esteem than males, while among other employment-status groups, there was no gender difference

TABLE 5.1. *Self-esteem and underemployment in 1987: ordinary least squares model*

Predictor	b	SE(b)	Beta
Unemployed	−.811**	.242	−.057
Involuntary part-time	−.908*	.465	−.032
Intermittent unemployment	−2.173***	.580	−.116
Poverty-wage (< 50 weeks)	−.816**	.292	−.046
Poverty-wage (50+ weeks)	−.623*	.294	−.035
Out of the labor force	−1.171***	.191	−.112
Intermittent unemployment × gender	1.937**	.677	.089
Poverty wages (< 50 weeks) × 1980 self-esteem	.220**	.083	.044

$^*p < .05$, $^{**}p < .01$, $^{***}p < .001$

Note: Overall model: R = .450, $R^2_{adj} = .199$, F = 59.49, df = 13, 3052, $p < .001$. The full model includes statistically significant effects for age, ethnicity, parental years of education, aptitude, 1980 self-esteem, and two additional interactions: ethnicity × aptitude and high school graduation × parental education.

Source: Based on Prause and Dooley (1997, p. 253, Table 3).

after controlling for prior self-esteem. The interaction between earlier self-esteem and full-year poverty-wage employment suggested that the adverse effect of such continuing low-wage employment was greater among those with lower than among those with higher initial self-esteem.

Mechanism. These results both confirm and extend the earlier research showing a social causation effect of unfavorable employment status on school-leavers' self-esteem. Both unemployment and economically inadequate employment appear to be linked to lower self-esteem. But is this effect caused by the stressful effects of undesirable employment status leading to a decline in self-esteem, or by the arrested development of normally increasing self-esteem? Figure 5.6 shows the plots of the mean levels of self-esteem for each of the employment-status groups (omitting the OLF group and combining the two poverty-wage subgroups, for clarity) over time.

All groups show rising self-esteem during the years from leaving high school to the mid-twenties. The differences in the intercepts for these lines reflect selection by early self-esteem into different employment statuses (see Chapter 4). Most importantly for the present question, the groups differed in the rates at which self-esteem rose. Those who were adequately employed in 1987 showed a markedly higher slope of rising self-esteem, whereas the several underemployed groups all had similar lower slopes. This pattern is consistent with the retarded development hypothesis.

Inadequate Employment and Job Satisfaction

Job Satisfaction and Self-esteem. Prior research reported that employed school-leavers' self-esteem depended on their level of job satisfaction (Winefield et al., 1993). We replicated this relationship in the NLSY (Dooley & Prause, 1995). Using the same 1980 and 1987 data points, the respondents who were employed but not satisfied (regardless of the economic adequacy of their jobs) appeared to be much more similar to their unemployed counterparts than to respondents who were satisfied with their jobs (see Dooley & Prause, 1995, Figure 1, p. 183). The unsatisfied employed showed an increase in mean self-esteem of 1.5 (from 30.4 to 31.9); the increase for the unemployed was 1.6 (from 30.1 to 31.7). By contrast, the satisfied employed reported an increase of 2 (from 31.1 to 33.1). The self-esteem change in the satisfied employed group was significantly different from that of the other two groups, and the difference between the unemployed group and the unsatisfied group was not significant.

Do Job Satisfaction and Economic Adequacy Measure the Same Thing? The similar effects on self-esteem of job satisfaction and economic adequacy might result if they were highly correlated reflections of the same

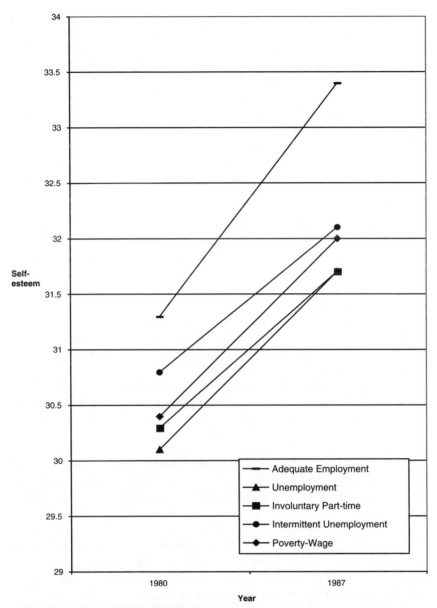

FIGURE 5.6. School-leaver self-esteem.

underlying construct. Perhaps most of the people in economically inadequate jobs are dissatisfied with their employment, and most of the people in adequate jobs are satisfied in their work. However intuitive, such a strong association did not appear in the NLSY.

The five categories of employed respondents (adequate, involuntary part-time, intermittent unemployed, full-year poverty-wage, and non-full-year poverty-wage) were cross-tabulated with the four levels of job satisfaction, and no significant association was found. When job satisfaction was dichotomized, the resulting five-by-two contingency table did yield a significant, but unexpected, association. Of the adequately employed respondents, 8.3% described themselves as disliking their jobs somewhat or very much. Although two of the inadequately employed groups reported higher job dissatisfaction rates (intermittently unemployed, 13.3%; non-full-year poverty-wage, 13.6%), two others reported lower rates (involuntary part-time, 7.8%; full-year poverty-wage, 5.5%). By large majorities, people in all types of economically inadequate employment report liking their jobs.

Job Satisfaction as a Mediating Variable. Although economic inadequacy of employment is not equivalent to job dissatisfaction, it remains plausible that the economic aspects of a job could contribute to overall satisfaction, along with other factors such as social and physical working conditions. From this perspective, economic adequacy of employment might affect self-esteem indirectly through the intervening variable of job satisfaction. The earlier reported analyses showing the connection between employment status and self-esteem would, in this case, include the indirect effect via job satisfaction, along with any additional direct effect remaining after job satisfaction is statistically controlled.

By considering only those respondents with measures of job satisfaction, it is possible to estimate whether there is any direct effect of inadequate versus adequate employment on self-esteem, controlling for the indirect effects via job satisfaction. For all those employed in 1987 (omitting the unemployed and the OLF respondents), 1987 self-esteem was regressed on 1980 self-esteem and other significant control variables, including job satisfaction. All of the inadequate-employment-status dummy variables were still negatively related to self-esteem. These associations were statistically significant, with one borderline exception. The exception was the involuntary part-time employment group, which was the smallest of the inadequate-employment categories and, therefore, the one with the least statistical power. Following are the beta coefficients and significance levels for each inadequate-employment group, controlling for job satisfaction: involuntary part-time (beta $= -.036$, $p = .07$), intermittently unemployed (beta $= -.048$, $p = .016$), full-year poverty-level workers (beta $= -.047$, $p = .021$), and non-full-year poverty-level workers (beta $= -.053$, $p = .009$). Thus, the effects of economically inadequate employment do not appear to operate through job dissatisfaction as a key mediating variable.

Job Satisfaction as an Additive Variable. Job dissatisfaction may operate less by passing along the adverse effect of a job's economic inadequacy and more by adding its own burden of occupational stress from noneconomic sources. In an analysis reported elsewhere, NLSY school-leavers were categorized into five groups by 1987 employment status: satisfied economically adequate, unsatisfied economically adequate, satisfied economically inadequate, unsatisfied economically inadequate, and unemployed (Dooley & Prause, 1997b). The odds of having low self-esteem (score ≤ 27) versus average to high self-esteem in 1987 were calculated for each group and compared to the odds for the adequately employed satisfied group.

The resulting odds ratios, based on weighted data, ranged from 1.57 for the adequately employed unsatisfied group to 1.66 for the satisfied inadequately employed, 2.26 for the unemployed, and 2.49 for the unsatisfied inadequately employed (Dooley & Prause, 1997b, Table 2, p. 105). These cross-sectional odds ratios were all statistically significant, but not significantly different from each other. A similar pattern of associations appeared in the longitudinal analyses, with controls for prior self-esteem and other potential confounding variables (Dooley & Prause, 1997b, Table 4, p. 107). The one exception to this pattern in the longitudinal analyses involved the adverse effect on self-esteem of the inadequately employed unsatisfied group, which did not reach significance, probably due to the low power of the test, which stemmed from its small sample size. Although both economic and noneconomic job factors may play a role in the relationship between employment and well-being, they are not functionally equivalent. Economic underemployment affects well-being independent of self-reported job satisfaction.

DISCUSSION

Conclusions

Similarity of Unemployment and Inadequate Employment. These findings add inadequate employment to unemployment as a risk factor for lowered self-esteem in young people. The adverse effect of unemployment on self-esteem in the NLSY panel appears to be consistent with the bulk of earlier findings in the school-leaver literature. However, the evidence that several different forms of economically inadequate employment can produce effects similar in magnitude to those of unemployment invites an expanded approach to studies of employment status. Inadequate employment appears to be functionally equivalent to unemployment in relation to the development of self-esteem in the transition from school to the workforce.

The several different categories of inadequate employment seemed to operate in the same way, at least for self-esteem. For example, the two low-wage subcategories (< 50 weeks vs. full-year employment) differed little from each other in their relationship to self-esteem. The large number of near-poverty workers in this youth sample made it possible to separate these two groups. However, as the panel ages and gains more employment success, the number of respondents in each of the inadequate employment categories will shrink, requiring their consolidation for analytic purposes in later chapters. For the smallest category, involuntary part-time workers, combination with other inadequate employment types may be essential in order to provide sufficient statistical power.

Of the various types of inadequate employment, the most surprising was intermittent unemployment, which might have been expected to resemble adequate employment more than the other types of inadequate employment. After all, respondents in that category have jobs for which they could feel some relief, if not gratitude, given their recent bouts of unemployment. Some job-finding interventions assume that reemployment serves as an antidote to the harm done by job loss, perhaps by elevating one's mood or reducing substance abuse. Studies of alcohol abuse and depression tend to support this assumption (see Chapters 6 and 7 for analyses of favorable employment change). However, self-esteem differs from these other indicators in that it is a cumulative assessment of self-worth over time rather than a momentary feeling or behavior. Apparently, the impact of substantial or repeated experiences of unemployment is not suddenly nullified by current employment. Rather, such experiences appear to leave residual doubts about one's value.

Mechanisms. On average, all of the employment-status groups showed increases in their self-esteem between 1980 and 1987. The social causation effect resulted from a greater increase in the adequate employment group than in the other groups. This pattern can be thought of as one of relatively delayed development for those in the underemployment categories and agrees with similar findings for unemployment from several earlier studies (Bachman et al., 1978; Donovan et al., 1986; Gore et al., 1997; Gurney, 1980a,b; Winefield et al., 1993).

How underemployment might retard the normal acquisition of self-esteem in young adults is a question that goes beyond the data available in this study. A different approach to this finding might ask, not why the underemployed had so little growth in self-esteem, but why they had as much as they did. The adequately employed had obvious reasons for gaining in self-esteem, including the sense of self-efficacy that comes with getting and holding a full-time, reasonably well-paid job. The fact that respondents in the other employment categories also showed rising self-esteem, albeit at a slower pace, implies that they were finding other ways to make positive assessments or to avoid negative assessments of their worth. Everyone in this sample of non-college-bound young people had in common one non-labor-force transition – leaving school, with its academic assessments and demands. To the extent that respondents' negative classroom performance was restraining the growth of their self-esteem, going from high school to an environment with different kinds of evaluations should help to promote gains in self-esteem.

The analyses of job satisfaction show that this variable does not account for the effects on self-esteem of the economic adequacy of jobs. Job satisfaction is clearly linked to self-esteem, and inadequate employment probably makes some contribution to a worker's overall sense of job satisfaction. However, the latter does not explain, as a mediator, the relationship between the former and self-esteem.

Several other potential causal or moderator variables failed to reach significance in these analyses. For example, the state of the surrounding economy seemed a plausible candidate to affect self-esteem, either directly or in interaction with personal employment status. At least one prior study had indicated that workers might suffer less self-esteem loss from unemployment if others in their community were also dealing with a high unemployment rate (Cohn, 1978). By contrast, other research has suggested that a high community unemployment rate might exacerbate the adverse effects of personal unemployment (Turner, 1995). Contrary to both of those studies, the present analyses found no interaction of aggregate unemployment with any of the personal underemployment statuses. Other research had suggested that the community economic climate might operate directly on employed workers, perhaps by giving them a sense of greater opportunities and bargaining power (Tausig & Fenwick, 1999). However, no direct effect of the community unemployment rate appeared in these data. Thus the surrounding economic climate appears to operate indirectly on the self-esteem of young workers through its influence on personal employment status (Dooley & Prause, 1997b).

Another potential moderator of the adverse effects of underemployment, particularly unemployment, is the individual's psychological involvement in work. This measure was collected in 1979, one year before the first self-esteem measure, at which time the great majority (almost 84%) of the respondents said they would continue to work even if they did not need to work in order to live comfortably. However, work involvement did not interact with unemployment in affecting 1987 self-esteem in the NLSY sample.

Implications

Interventions. From a developmental point of view, self-esteem provides a useful marker for overall emotional well-being, especially in young people making the transition into early adulthood (Rosenberg, 1965). However, the apparent harm that underemployment has on young people's self-esteem, lamentable as it may be, does not automatically justify economic interventions designed to raise self-esteem. One may regard self-esteem as merely a desirable psychological trait, a luxury rather than an essential ingredient for healthy functioning. If self-esteem is not crucial to public health, then policies aimed at raising self-esteem have low priority at best and are unwise at worst (Dawes, 1994).

On the other hand, self-esteem appears to play an important role both economically and psychologically. As described in Chapter 4, self-esteem measured in 1980 helped to predict employment status in 1987. Those concerned about the undesirable societal correlates of high youth under-employment should be interested in factors, such as increased self-esteem, that might help to reduce such problems. In addition, self-esteem appears to be linked to other psychological conditions that have clearer public health significance, such as depression. In the NLSY, 1987 self-esteem was inversely related to 1994 depression, even after controlling for 1992 depression and other factors, such as employment status (see Chapter 7). Thus, self-esteem may warrant public policy attention not for its own sake, as a pleasing psychological state, but rather for its instrumental role in other, more socially consequential outcomes.

Even if self-esteem warrants interventions to promote it, it does not follow that those interventions must come in the employment realm. Other factors that contribute to self-esteem invite exploration as intervention targets. In these analyses, by far the best predictor of 1987 self-esteem was 1980 self-esteem, which must have emerged from processes occurring largely prior to employment. Other early variables also predicted 1987 self-esteem, including ethnicity, parental years of education, and academic aptitude, among others. Unfortunately, some of these factors either offer little opportunity for social intervention or require that the interventions commence quite early.

By the time that non-college-bound young people have reached high school, it may well be that effective vocational training and placement programs offer the best way to promote their self-esteem. Employment-based efforts to increase self-esteem would help the young person to get and hold a meaningful job, from which the natural feedback (from boss, coworkers, friends) would communicate that the worker has value. One approach to improving the transition from school to work focuses on changing the high school curriculum in order to orient students better to future careers (Gore, Kadish, & Aseltine, in press).

The alternative to such job-based self-esteem promotion is short-term cognitive and behavioral training that tries to raise self-esteem through repeated messages of praise in a clinical setting. Will increases in self-esteem produced by such techniques persist and generalize to natural social environments? A brief (two-and-a-half-week) behavioral modeling workshop for an unemployed group succeeded in raising self-efficacy, job search activity, and, among those with the lowest initial self-efficacy, actual reemployment (Eden & Aviram, 1993). A related concern is that such clinical interventions may change the clients without creating new jobs. Even if effective in raising self-esteem, such interventions may only modify the competition among young people for scarce jobs, not increase the total number with good jobs.

Research. This research shows that forms of underemployment other than complete joblessness are negatively associated with self-esteem in young people. This invites an expansion of the usual employment-versus-unemployment research paradigm to include the links between various inadequate employment statuses and various psychological and behavioral outcomes. The next two chapters will study the relationship of alcohol abuse and depression, respectively, to inadequate employment in older age groups, as the NLSY panel moves through the twenties and enters the thirties.

However, the present results have implications not just for increased research on inadequate employment but also for improved methodology for the continued study of unemployment. Traditionally, the unemployment effect is measured by the reported gap in some health outcome measure between those who are unemployed and all those who are employed. These analyses demonstrate that the total of all employed workers includes a mix of the adequately employed, with relatively higher levels of well-being, and the inadequately employed, with relatively lower levels of well-being. A single reference group produced by combining these two types of employment will necessarily have a mean level of well-being that falls below that of the adequately employed respondents. In contrast to this lowered, combined score, the mean for the unemployed respondents will seem less adverse.

The degree to which combining all employed respondents into a single group will narrow the gap with unemployed respondents depends on two factors. One is the ratio of adequately to inadequately employed respondents. If inadequate employment is defined narrowly, so that this ratio is large, the small number of inadequately employed will have little effect on the overall well-being level, dominated by the more numerous adequately employed. The other factor is the size of the gap between adequately and inadequately employed respondents. If the outcome measure is one for which the inadequately employed seem more similar to the adequately employed than to the unemployed, the merger of the two types of employment will have little impact.

In the present case of school-leavers' self-esteem, in 1987 there were 1,732 respondents in adequate employment versus 538 in the various forms of inadequate employment, or a ratio of over 3. The 1987 mean self-esteem scores (unweighted and unadjusted for covariates) were 33.4 for the adequately employed, 32.0 for the inadequately employed (all types combined), and 31.7 for the unemployed. Combining the adequately and inadequately employed respondents would result in a reference group mean for all employed of 33.1. The gap between the adequately employed and the unemployed ($33.4 - 31.7 = 1.7$) would exceed the gap between all employed and the unemployed ($33.1 - 31.7 = 1.4$) by .3, or a drop of 18% resulting from a shift of comparison groups from the adequately employed to all employed.

Given the large samples available for analysis in the NLSY, an effect size drop of this magnitude will usually have little impact on the significance tests. However, in studies with smaller samples, such a difference in effect size might lead to different conclusions. And if the future brings a falling ratio of adequate to inadequate jobs or a rising well-being gap between adequate and inadequate jobs, the decision to lump all jobs together may undermine efforts to study the adverse effects of unemployment.

6

Early Adulthood

Alcohol Misuse and Underemployment

Give strong drink unto him that is ready to perish, and wine unto those that be of heavy hearts. Let him drink, and forget his poverty, and remember his misery no more.

Proverbs 31:4

... we often wonder if those of us who are apt to stand apart and judge thrift-less drunkards with but little sympathy would, under similar conditions, have done better than they!... living in a poor house and dingy street, and returning to it night by night after nine or ten hours of unskilled work, which rouses neither interest nor ambition... what wonder if, in their effort to in-troduce some colour into the drab monotony of their lives, they fall victims to the allurements of the bookmaker or publican, or lose heart and join the ranks of those who have ceased to strive?

Rowntree & Lasker, 1911, pp. 185–186

INTRODUCTION

Alcohol Misuse, Stress, and Employment

Alcohol Disorder and Its Causes. Alcohol misuse can be defined in var-ious ways, including heavy consumption (i.e., binge drinking) and symp-toms reflecting abuse (adverse personal and social consequences) or dependence (difficulty stopping drinking). One national survey estimated lifetime prevalence for alcohol abuse as 13.8% and found it much higher for men (23.8%) than for women (4.6%) (Helzer, Burnam, & McEvoy, 1991). Alcohol disorder not only has high prevalence, but it can also result in se-vere outcomes both to the individual and to his or her loved ones, such as family disruption, psychological distress, and death by cirrhosis or au-tomobile accident. Perhaps no behavioral disorder causes more social and economic harm than substance abuse, especially alcoholism. The annual cost of alcohol misuse has been estimated at up to 100,000 deaths and $100 billion in economic costs (Rice, 1993).

The prevailing explanation for many forms of behavioral disorder, including substance abuse, draws on the diathesis-stress perspective. Diathesis refers to a predisposition, vulnerability, or weakness, and stress refers to some environmental dislocation or adaptation-requiring challenge. In the case of alcohol disorder, the diathesis consists of the traitlike vulnerability of the individual to misuse alcohol. Presumably, this diathesis appears by late adolescence or early adulthood and derives from some combination of genetic inheritance, early child-rearing patterns, and adolescent experiences that shape lifestyle (Jang, Livesley, & Vernon, 1995; Koopmans & Boomsma, 1996). That alcoholism has a significant genetic or physiologic component is generally accepted. A review of family, twin, and adoption studies found an overall alcoholism heritability rate exceeding 60%, but the study also suggested that this disorder is polygenic and multifactorial (Schuckit, 1987). That is, the genetically influenced biological vulnerability or diathesis is not the result of a single dominant gene, and it interacts with environmental experiences and stressors.

Assuming that the diathesis for alcohol misuse remains fixed after being established, the changing exposure to stress helps to explain the spatial and temporal variability in the incidence or reoccurrence of alcoholism. Different cultures (McCord, McCord & Gudeman, 1960) and different occupations (Manello & Seaman, 1979) exhibit widely different rates of alcohol misuse. According to one epidemiologic study, only about one-quarter of the lifetime cases of alcohol disorder reported an alcohol problem during the past thirty days (Helzer et al., 1991). In other words, alcohol disorder presents discontinuously, with periods of remission and relapse, presumably in response to some environmental variables.

Stressful Events as a Cause of Alcohol Abuse. Given a constant distribution in the population of the predisposition for substance abuse disorder, why do more individuals become abusers at one time than at another? Norstrom's reservoir analogy offers one plausible explanation (1987). At any point in time, there are individuals in the population at varying stages of alcoholic disorder: some with the diathesis but not yet drinking, some drinking but not heavily, others drinking heavily but still functioning adequately in their work and social roles, and still others close to physical dependence or even death by cirrhosis (Llangenbucher & Chung, 1995).

Stressful life events impinge on the individuals in these reservoirs, with some events appearing randomly and others predictably from the social ecological context. In response to these events, some individuals will increase their alcohol consumption by way of maladaptive coping and, in rising numbers, cross the threshold to the next level of disorder or reservoir. Coping through alcohol consumption may be viewed as a conditioned response, reducing tension by altering cognition and perception in reinforcing ways (Steele & Josephs, 1988). For those most vulnerable to alcohol abuse and disposed to coping by self-medication with alcohol, more severe stressors will likely trigger increasingly heavy consumption and/or severe symptoms.

Employment Change Events and Alcohol Misuse. The disposition to abuse alcohol can be regarded as a probable trajectory that can change, for better or worse, as a function of changing circumstances. Losing a job or falling into less adequate employment may produce sufficient stress to affect adversely this trajectory and, thus, to function as a risk factor for alcohol abuse. If employment change were a significant risk factor for alcohol misuse, it would be a ripe target for intervention, because, at the aggregate level, it can be measured, predicted, and modified by political/economic policy makers.

Job loss or transition into inadequate work warrants special attention at the individual level because it appears to be one of the more powerful events among those occurring relatively frequently in the general population. As detailed in the opening chapters, employment has both manifest and latent functions. The manifest function is that of income generation, and its loss exposes the unemployed person to a host of threats associated with a declining style of life. But as Jahoda (1982) has articulated, employment also provides such latent functions as time structure, activity, social contacts, status, and collective purpose. Research has documented the association among unemployment, stress, and these latent functions. For example, Isaksson (1989) studied 100 young male welfare clients (20–35 years old) in Stockholm and found that the latent functions were diminished in the unemployed as compared to the employed men. Moreover, among the unemployed, those with lower ratings on the latent functions reported more symptoms of psychological distress.

Whether such subjective distress translates into increased alcohol or other substance abuse is an unresolved question. After surveying the state of the literature on this question, two researchers concluded that "few relevant findings on the dynamic relationships between drug use and employment history have yet to be reported and established" (Johnson & Herring, 1989, p. 4). As they point out, when researchers do address this topic, they often arrive at different answers. This issue has proved difficult to resolve in part because asking whether unemployment adversely affects substance abuse requires careful methodological controls for the possible selection of people with drug problems into the ranks of the unemployed. Whether alcohol abuse selects workers into underemployment was explored in Chapter 4. Here we will focus on the social causation of alcohol misuse by employment changes.

Past Studies of Employment Change and Alcohol Misuse

Job Loss. Various types of research design and measurement have yielded associations between indicators of unemployment and alcohol abuse (for a review of this literature, see Catalano et al., 1993). This literature can be divided into four major types, according to the design (cross-sectional versus longitudinal) and the level of analysis (individual versus aggregate). One of the few examples of the aggregate, cross-sectional approach found a sharp increase in the sale of alcohol in three northwestern towns after their lumber mills closed (Weeks & Drengacz, 1982). Unfortunately, such aggregate studies risk the ecological fallacy. In this case, the study does not indicate which residents increased their alcohol consumption – those laid off, or those still employed but perhaps made insecure by their colleagues' layoffs.

Individual-level cross-sectional studies tend to agree in finding an association between being unemployed and elevated alcohol misuse. For example, among a random sample of 2,349 British adults, the unemployed were more likely than the employed to binge drink and to drink amounts sufficient to produce adverse consequences (Crawford et al., 1987). Although not vulnerable to the ecological fallacy, this cross-sectional type of research cannot demonstrate that unemployment causes alcohol disorder because of the plausible rival explanation that alcohol abuse caused unemployment.

Longitudinal, aggregate studies typically correlate rates of unemployment and substance abuse disorder over time for some spatial unit, such as the state or the nation. For example, Harvey Brenner (1975) used time-series analysis to relate the U.S. unemployment rate to national indicators of alcohol sales, admissions to mental health facilities for alcohol-related disorders, alcohol-related arrests, and number of deaths by cirrhosis. He found positive relationships that must be interpreted cautiously, for two reasons. First, the aggregate nature of these data precludes their interpretation at the individual level because of the threat of the ecological fallacy. Second, time-series methodology has proved controversial in this field, and alternative statistical approaches may yield different results (Catalano et al., 1983, 1985).

Of the four types of research, the longitudinal, individual-level or panel approach can provide the most convincing support for the causation of alcohol abuse by unemployment. This type of research measures individuals both before and after their job loss. One meta-analytic review found that becoming unemployed was positively related to alcohol consumption among young males but negatively related for older males and for younger females, although none of these summary relationships reached statistical significance (Temple et al., 1991).

Longitudinal studies dealing with more severe alcohol abuse outcomes also have yielded mixed results. One negative study (Giesbrecht, Markele, & MacDonald, 1982) investigated striking mine workers, whose financial support from their union and solidarity and activity with their fellow strikers make them dissimilar to the involuntarily unemployed. Another negative study (Iversen & Klausen, 1986) took place in Denmark, where the high level of unemployment compensation (70% of original income) and counseling may have cushioned the impact of job loss. A third negative study started with 2,000 young Norwegians (17 to 20 years old) and found no increase in alcohol consumption in those experiencing unemployment both two and four years later (Hammer, 1992).

Other studies have provided positive findings for the unemployment–alcohol symptoms relationship, but often with sample limitations (e.g., Buss & Redburn, 1983; Kasl & Cobb, 1982; Leventman, 1981; Mittag & Schwarzer, 1993; Plant, 1979). Panel studies of unemployment have difficulty in capturing a sample of unemployed that is both large and representative. One either needs a very large sample of the general population in order to obtain a modest number of subsequent job losers, or one must have advance knowledge of a plant closing, which may not provide a representative sample. Nevertheless, these studies tend to support the thesis that the stress of unemployment increases the risk of alcohol disorder. For example, Kasl and Cobb (1982) found that pre-unemployment heavy drinkers were most likely to increase alcohol consumption in response to job loss, consistent with the above-noted reservoir model (Norstrom, 1987) and social learning (Steele & Josephs, 1988) perspectives.

More support for the adverse effect of unemployment on alcohol abuse comes from a report based on the Epidemiologic Catchment Area (ECA) study (Dooley et al., 1992). The ECA collected data from a very large panel, using the Diagnostic Interview Schedule to categorize respondents according to the DSM-III criteria for alcohol disorder. After removing all respondents who were currently alcoholic or unemployed and statistically controlling for lifetime diagnosis at first interview, it was possible to associate subsequent unemployment with alcohol disorder at reinterview. Based on almost 4,000 respondents from three sites, those becoming unemployed were over nine times more likely to become alcoholically disordered than those not becoming unemployed. Unfortunately, no measures of underemployment were available in the ECA data.

Overall, studies on unemployment and alcohol misuse tend to find an adverse social causation effect (Hammarström, 1994; Wilson & Walker, 1993). However, the substantial variation in results warrants caution in drawing conclusions. One example of this variation involves the outcome measure of alcohol consumption. A few studies have suggested that job loss may affect alcohol consumption in two offsetting ways, leading to either binge drinking or abstinence (Catalano et al., 1993; Lee et al., 1990; Warr, 1987). Some workers may respond to unemployment by medicating their increased stress with heavier drinking. Others may appraise their job loss as a challenge for increased responsibility, effort, and sobriety. Such a bimodal pattern of alcohol consumption could help to explain some of the inconsistency in findings in this area. A study of binge drinking might show increased drinking, whereas a study of average consumption might not, because increases in abstaining could cancel increases in heavy drinking. Perhaps illustrating this complexity, a Finnish study found employment status to be unrelated to drinking frequency in men or in women but found that unemployment was related to increased drinking-related health problems in men but not in women (Lahelma, Kangas, & Manderbacka, 1995).

Inadequate Employment. Studies on unemployment and alcohol misuse generally appear to be consistent with the stress model, in which job loss operates as a challenge that is met by more or less adaptive coping. For individuals with the disposition for substance abuse, unemployment may trigger increased alcohol misuse. By this line of reasoning, other adverse employment changes might also provoke increased alcohol consumption and, in turn, elevated symptoms of alcohol disorder (consistent with the negative association between underemployment and self-esteem reported in Chapter 5).

Unfortunately, other researchers have not tested the connection between shifts into inadequate employment (using the LUF definitions presented in Chapter 3) and alcohol or other substance abuse. Such an association might appear if prior heavy drinking or symptoms of alcoholism selected workers into unemployment or less adequate employment (as explored in Chapter 4). Thus, it is crucial to estimate the effect of adverse employment change on alcohol misuse only after controlling for prior alcohol consumption and symptoms.

Favorable Employment. If adverse employment change leads to elevated symptoms of distress, such as alcohol misuse, then favorable employment change might be expected to produce the opposite effect and lead to decreased alcohol misuse. Conventional wisdom holds that getting a job will cure the ills of unemployment, and some research has shown that interventions that aid in reemployment do reduce some affective problems such as depression (Vinokur, Price, & Caplan, 1991). Surveys that have followed unemployed workers who regained employment have reported improvements in their emotional well-being (Kessler et al., 1988).

However, such studies have not checked the restorative effects of reemployment on alcohol or other substance abuse. The stress process may operate differently for affective responses such as depression than for addictive responses such as substance abuse. Reemployment may have little effect in changing alcohol misuse that has become rooted by physiological dependence. The increased discretionary income brought by a new job might even lead to increased alcohol consumption.

Hypotheses

Adverse Employment Change. Prior research provides ample evidence that job loss can lead to increased symptoms of alcohol misuse. However, we know virtually nothing about the effect on alcohol misuse symptoms of other kinds of adverse employment, including becoming or remaining inadequately employed. The first hypothesis predicts that among people working at first interview, each of three conditions at reinterview (job loss, becoming inadequately employed, and remaining inadequately employed) will be associated with increased symptoms of alcohol abuse, controlling for prior symptoms.

Intuitively, we expect that high levels of alcohol abuse symptoms should be associated with high levels of consumption (Caetano & Tam, 1995). On the other hand, a person might drink heavily but, in the context of his or her culture or peers, feel that this level of consumption is appropriate and harmless. The literature has called our attention to an important distinction in the way psychosocial symptoms of alcohol misuse and alcohol consumption may respond to economic stress. Some studies have suggested that, unlike its generally adverse effect on symptoms, economic stress can produce both increased and decreased drinking as individuals respond differently to changes in employment status (Lee et al., 1990). Because symptoms of alcohol-related dysfunction and alcohol consumption do not necessarily parallel each other, we need to check the effect of adverse employment change on heavy drinking (binge drinking as distinct from average consumption) as well as on symptoms. The second hypothesis predicts that among people working at first interview, each of three conditions at reinterview (job loss, becoming inadequately employed, and remaining inadequately employed) will be associated with increased heavy drinking, controlling for prior heavy drinking.

We will test both of these first two hypotheses initially on the 1984–85 pair of years, when the respondents were in their mid-twenties. The 1988–89 pair of years, when the respondents were in their late twenties, will permit a replication of any findings in the service of a third hypothesis concerned with possible developmental changes.

The prevalence of alcohol disorder varies with age. It rises in early adulthood, with the appearance of abuse symptoms by twenty-three years old and dependence symptoms by twenty-five, on average (Llangenbucher & Chung, 1995). But it then declines in older adults, resulting in an overall negative correlation between alcohol disorder prevalence and age

(Caetano & Tam, 1995). The developmental period of the mid-twenties corresponds not only to the emergence of alcohol disorders but also to the end of schooling, entry into the labor force, and creation of new family units via marriage and children. The relationship between adverse employment change and alcohol disorder (measured either as symptoms or as heavy consumption) might vary in response to these developmental changes. The third hypothesis predicts that the association of employment status with alcohol symptoms and consumption found in the 1984–85 data (hypotheses 1 and 2) will differ from that found in replications using the 1988–89 data. Absent prior research on the age moderation of these relationships, this hypothesis is frankly exploratory.

Favorable Employment Change. If adverse employment change produces increased alcohol misuse, will favorable employment change lead to a symmetric decrease in alcohol misuse? Such a beneficial effect might arise by either of two mechanisms with different implications for preventive interventions. One possibility is that everyone, regardless of prior alcohol misuse, will enjoy decreased risk of later alcohol misuse as a result of favorable employment change. From this perspective, the increased economic opportunities and sense of self-worth brought about by favorable employment change could help to "inoculate" workers against other risk factors leading to alcohol misuse. This prevention mechanism would appear as a main effect of favorable employment change.

Alternatively, perhaps only those individuals already experiencing alcohol problems will benefit from favorable employment change. In this view, just those underemployed workers who had responded to adverse employment change with increased alcohol misuse would react with decreased alcohol misuse to any upturn in their employment status. In other words, favorable employment change would serve a restorative rather than a preventive function. Such a restorative mechanism would appear as an interaction effect in which favorable employment change would produce decreases in alcohol misuse only for those with prior signs of misuse.

Both the main (preventive) and interaction (restorative) effects of favorable employment change can be checked using the same analytic models. However, for the reasons described earlier, it will be desirable to run separate analyses for symptoms and consumption. These analyses will be based on a sample of workers who were underemployed at first interview in 1984 – either unemployed or inadequately employed – and who had experienced any one of three types of favorable change one year later in 1985 (unemployment to inadequate employment, unemployment to adequate employment, or inadequate employment to adequate employment). Hypothesis four predicts that favorable employment change will be associated with either a main or interaction effect of decreasing symptoms of alcohol misuse, controlling for prior symptoms. Hypothesis five predicts that favorable employment change will be associated with either a main or interaction effect of decreasing heavy drinking, controlling for prior heavy drinking.

If there is a preventive or restorative effect of favorable employment change in the short term, it will be helpful to know whether this effect persists over a longer term. The final hypothesis predicts that favorable employment change between 1984 and 1985 will produce beneficial effects on alcohol misuse (either symptoms or consumption) that persist at the five-year follow-up in 1989.

METHODS

Samples

Controlling for Reverse Causation. The threat of reverse causation makes it essential to adjust statistically for prior alcohol misuse in assessing the impact of employment status change on later alcohol misuse. Fortunately, the NLSY provides repeated measures of both alcohol consumption and alcohol-related symptoms in two pairs of consecutive years: 1984–85 and 1988–89. Although some alcohol consumption items were collected in other years (e.g., 1982, 1992), the omission of symptom items in those years limited the analytic possibilities for these years.

As detailed in Chapter 3, the NLSY began with an initial sample of 12,686 respondents fourteen to twenty-two years old in 1979 and has maintained a remarkable retention rate (reported as 91.4% in 1989 – Center for Human Resource Research, 1995). In order to test the present hypotheses, we selected subsamples based on employment status in the first year of each pair of years.

Selection of Subsamples. For the first three hypotheses on the effects of adverse employment change, the samples consisted of respondents who were employed in the first year of each pair of years. Employment was divided into adequate and inadequate categories, the latter defined as involuntary part-time or poverty-wage employment. Preliminary analyses revealed that respondents with adequate employment after recent unemployment (i.e., the intermittently unemployed) resembled the continuing adequately employed in their alcohol symptoms, and they were grouped with them for analysis. This finding for alcohol abuse differs from the finding for self-esteem in recent school-leavers (Chapter 5), in which the intermittently unemployed resembled involuntary part-time and low-wage workers more than the continuing adequately employed.

In order to check the effects of developmental change (hypothesis 3) as distinct from sampling changes, we defined a core sample of respondents for whom we had complete data in both pairs of years and who were employed in the first of each pair of years ($n = 2{,}441$). Although this core sample keeps the respondents constant over the time period studied, it does have two disadvantages. First, its smaller size reduces the statistical power of the analyses. Second, it introduces sample bias favoring the inclusion of respondents more likely to be employed and to be consistently available over time. As a check on these problems, we also defined two larger samples consisting of all respondents who were available for one pair of years but not necessarily for the other pair. After losses due to missing data on alcohol or control measures, this enlarged sample size for the 1984–85 analyses was 4,183. For the 1988–89 analyses, the enlarged sample size was 3,926.

In order to test the last three hypotheses on favorable employment change, we used samples consisting of respondents who were either unemployed or inadequately employed in 1984. The unemployed included both nonworking people who were actively seeking work and "discouraged workers." The inadequately employed included both involuntary part-time and poverty-wage workers. The intermittently unemployed were grouped with the adequately employed on the grounds that they had already experienced a favorable employment change by becoming reemployed. After excluding respondents with missing values, the sample size for the 1984–85 favorable change analyses was 1,659. For the 1989 follow-up, the sample size fell to 1,437.

Sample Characteristics. Table 6.1 describes the core sample of 2,441 respondents who were employed in both 1984 and 1988 and the sample of

TABLE 6.1. *Sample characteristics for employed and underemployed in 1984*

Characteristic	Core Sample: Employed in Both 1984 and 1988 ($n = 2{,}441$)			Underemployed in 1984 ($n = 1{,}659$)		
	M	%	SD	M	%	SD
Ethnicity						
Hispanic		4.9			5.9	
African American		7.7			15.6	
Other		87.4			78.5	
Male		64.6			49.7	
Married 1985		31.1			22.9	
Children in household						
1984		40.5			24.2	
Years of education 1985	13.3		2.0	12.7		2.1
Aptitude: Armed Forces						
Qualification Test	57.5		27.0	44.9		28.9
Unemployment rate 1985	7.8		1.9	8.6		3.2
Age 1985	23.8		2.3	22.9		2.3

1,659 respondents who were underemployed in 1984. The core sample was used to test the effect of adverse change in employment on heavy drinking and on alcohol symptoms. The underemployed sample was used to test the effect of favorable change in employment status on these same outcomes. In general, the demographic profiles of these two samples were quite different, with about 65% of the core sample of employed respondents being male, compared to 50% of the underemployed sample. About eight percent of the core sample was African American, as compared to 15.6% of the underemployed sample. About one-third of the core sample was married, and 40.5% had one or more children in the household, as compared to 22.9% married for the underemployed sample, of whom 24.2% had children. Average years of education and aptitude, as measured by the Armed Forces Qualification Test, were higher in the core sample (13.3 years and 57.5, respectively) when compared to the underemployed sample (12.7 years and 44.9, respectively). The unemployment rate was slightly higher for the underemployed sample (8.6%), and they were somewhat younger (22.9 years) when compared to the core sample (7.8% and 23.8 years, respectively).

Developmental Stage. Maturational change might affect drinking behavior both generally and in interaction with employment changes. For this reason, the sample ages are noteworthy. For the adverse-change sample, the mean age was 23.8 years in 1985 and 28.2 years in 1989. This developmental transition appears clearly in marriage and family formation. For the core sample, the percentage never married fell from 61.6% in 1985 to 36.9% in 1989, and households with children rose from 20.1% in 1984 to 40.5% in 1988 (for more details, see Dooley & Prause, 1998).

For the favorable-change sample, the mean age was 22.9 in 1985 and 27.4 in 1989. The percentage never married fell from 69.6% in 1985 to 44.1% in 1989. Households with children rose from 24.2% in 1984 to 45.1% in 1989 (for more details, see Dooley & Prause, 1997a).

Economic Climate. Workers experience employment transitions in the context of the prevailing economic climate. The perceived value of a job may well depend not only on the characteristics of the job (e.g., hours, pay) but also on the scarcity of jobs as reflected by rising or falling unemployment rates. In the early 1980s, the United States experienced a recession, with unemployment rates reaching 9.7% in 1982 and 9.6% in 1983. By the beginning of the period studied here, the recession was relenting. The national unemployment rate fell to 7.5% in 1984 and 7.2% in 1985. The economy improved steadily, and unemployment rates fell to 5.5% in 1988 and 5.3% in 1989.

National unemployment rates combine all of the varying local unemployment rates and do not necessarily describe the experience of the respondents in any given survey such as the NLSY. However, the economic environments in which the present NLSY respondents lived did closely parallel the national experience. For the core sample used in the adverse employment change analyses, respondents lived in communities with an average unemployment level of 7.8% in 1984 and 5.2% in 1988. In contrast to these respondents, those selected for the favorable employment change analyses (i.e., those experiencing some form of underemployment in 1984) lived in communities with generally higher average unemployment levels (8.6% in 1985 and 5.6% in 1989).

Measuring Alcohol Misuse

Symptoms. In the NLSY, only those respondents who report having had a drink during the past thirty days are asked about their alcohol-related symptoms, and the recall period for these symptoms includes the past year. The symptom items cover signs of abuse (psychosocial dysfunction) and dependence (tolerance, inability to stop drinking) similar to those defined in the official diagnostic criteria of the DSM (e.g., American Psychiatric Association, 1994). Although not designed to provide a clinical diagnosis of alcohol disorder, these symptom items have been validated against other standard epidemiological instruments (Harford & Grant, 1994).

The NLSY used two different sets of symptom items during the study period. One set of eleven dichotomous symptoms was used in the 1984, 1985, and 1988 waves. A different set of twenty-three four-level items was used in the 1989 wave. The shorter alcohol scale yielded alpha reliability coefficients between .74 and .77 in the 1984, 1985, and 1988 surveys. The longer scale, as would be expected, had a higher alpha reliability of .87 in 1989. Test-retest reliability for the number of reported symptoms ranged from .57 for the 1984–85 period to .48 for the 1988–89 period. Because of their extreme skew (most respondents reported no symptoms) and the differences between the short and long scales, the symptom measures were all dichotomized to identify approximately the top 10–15% of the sample. This cut-point is consistent with the estimate of 14% for one-year prevalence of alcohol abuse disorder in young adults (Harford & Grant, 1994). High-symptom respondents were those with three or more symptoms on the eleven-item scale and eight or more symptoms on the twenty-three-item scale.

Consumption. In addition to symptoms of alcohol misuse, this study focuses on heavy or excessive drinking as a possible maladaptive effect of employment change. Episodes of binge drinking may be associated with levels of inebriation that lead to other adverse consequences such as drunk driving accidents. The NLSY defines a drink as one six-ounce serving of wine, one can of beer, or one ounce of distilled spirits, and it defines a binge as consuming six or more drinks on a single occasion during the past month. Absent any official standard for a binge episode, the NLSY criterion of six drinks falls in the middle of the range of definitions that have appeared in the literature. For example, a British study defined heavy drinking as eight drinks in a row (Lee et al., 1990), and a U.S. study defined a binge as five drinks for males and four drinks for females (Wechsler et al., 1995). As with the symptom variable, the NLSY consumption measure was highly skewed and was dichotomized in order to distinguish the heaviest drinkers. A cut-point of six or more binges (defined as six or more drinks on an occasion) during the past month identified the top 13% in the study.

We considered the possibility that the two measures of heavy drinking and high symptoms might be redundant. However, analyses showed only partial overlap between them (kappa = .25, p < .001). Only 5% of the respondents fell into both the high-consumption and high-symptom categories. About 10% of the respondents were heavy drinkers but low on symptoms, and 9% were high on symptoms but low on heavy drinking. Although some of this discrepancy may reflect unreliability, some probably involves the timing of the two measures. The consumption item reflects the past month's drinking behavior, but the symptom items can reflect experiences going back a whole year. A respondent who had recently reduced his drinking might accurately report both high symptoms from six months earlier and no binge drinking over the past month. Alternatively, a respondent who was participating actively in a local culture of heavy drinking (e.g., a college fraternity) might report heavy drinking but perceive no adverse psychosocial symptoms of that drinking.

Analytic Framework

Logistic Regression. Because the outcome variables for these analyses are dichotomous, we used logistic regression to build separate models for symptoms and consumption for each pair of years. That is, the outcome variable in the later year (e.g., symptoms in 1985) was regressed on a sequence of possible predictors, including that same variable in the prior year (in this case, symptoms in 1984). After entering various potential control variables, the employment change terms were entered.

Change in employment status consisted of a set of dummy variables. For the adverse-change hypotheses, the reference status was adequate employment at time two (from either adequate or inadequate employment at time one). Contrasted to this group were four other conditions (percentage of 1984–85 core sample in parentheses): (1) any employment to unemployment (2.9%), (2) adequate employment to inadequate employment (6.1%), (3) inadequate employment at both time one and time two (6.6%), and (4) any employment to being out of the labor force (3.2%).

For the favorable-change hypotheses, the reference group consisted of those remaining underemployed (either unemployed or inadequately employed at both times) or experiencing adverse change from inadequate employment to unemployment. Contrasted to this group were four other conditions (percentage for 1984–85 sample in parentheses): (1) unemployment to inadequate employment (6.3%), (2) unemployment to adequate employment (14.8%), (3) inadequate employment to adequate employment (26.5%), (4) unemployment or inadequate employment to being out of the labor force (12.9%).

Main and Interaction Effects. Along with time one alcohol misuse and the employment-change dummy variables, each model includes a variety of other terms. Some of these terms provide controls against possible confounding, such as gender, age, and ethnicity, which might cause change in both employment status and alcohol misuse.

Other terms represent multiplicative combinations of other variables and serve to check possible interaction effects. Thus the same model might include a main effect for one or more of the employment-change dummy variables as well as an interaction with one or more of the dummy variables. The distinction between main and interaction effects will prove helpful in discriminating between the preventive (main effect of favorable change) and restorative (interaction between favorable change and prior alcohol misuse) hypotheses. In general, the final model consists of just the statistically significant terms, but whenever significant interactions appear, all of their constituent main effects are retained, whether significant or not.

RESULTS

Adverse Employment Change

Effect on Symptoms of Alcohol Misuse. Did respondents who experienced adverse employment change between 1984 and 1985 have an increased risk of alcohol symptoms compared to employed respondents who remained in or moved to adequate employment (hypothesis 1)? Table 6.2 summarizes the answer to this question for the core sample. Change from any employment to unemployment more than doubled the risk of a high level of alcohol symptoms (odds ratio = 2.21, $p < .05$). The continuing inadequately employed also had an increased risk of a high level of alcohol symptoms (odds ratio = 1.83, $p < .05$). The adverse effect on symptoms of shifting from adequate to inadequate employment fell just short of statistical significance (odds ratio = 1.55, $p = .08$). The change from adequate employment to each subcategory of inadequate employment – involuntary part-time ($n = 52$) and poverty-wage employment ($n = 97$) – was associated

TABLE 6.2. *Elevated 1985 alcohol symptoms predicted by adverse employment change 1984–85 and prior alcohol symptoms: logistic regression for all employed in 1984 (n = 2,441)*

Predictor	B	S.E.	Odds Ratio
Alcohol symptoms 1984	.58**	.04	1.79
Age (years)	−.11**	.03	.90
Gender (1 = male)	.39**	.16	1.47
Aptitude (AFQT)	−.002**	.00	.98
Region (relative to South)**			
Northeast	−.32	.20	.72
North Central	.05	.18	1.05
West	−.54**	.22	.58
Ever illicit drug use	.58**	.22	1.79
Life problems with alcohol	.49**	.21	1.64
Illicit drug use in past thirty days	.58**	.19	1.81
Adverse employment change (relative to adequate employment in 1985)***			
Job loss	.79**	.30	2.21
Adequate to inadequate job	.44*	.26	1.55
Continuing inadequate job	.60**	.25	1.83
Left labor force	.43	.37	1.54
Constant	−.09	.76	

$*p < .10, **p < .05, ***p < .01.$

Note: Alcohol symptoms are dichotomously coded where 1 = three or more symptoms and 0 = two or fewer symptoms during the year leading up to the interview.

Source: Adapted from Dooley & Prause (1998, Table 2, p. 676).

with an increased risk of alcohol symptoms, although neither reached the $p = .05$ level of significance.

The core sample is limited to individuals employed in both 1984 and 1988 and might not be representative of all NLSY respondents. Repeating the test of hypothesis 1 on the larger sample that included respondents who were available in 1984–85 but not necessarily in 1988–89 ($n = 4,183$) yielded results quite similar to those from the core sample analyses. Change from employment to unemployment and continuing inadequate employment increased the risk of high-level alcohol symptoms by about 86% and 50%, respectively. As in the core sample, the change from adequate employment to inadequate employment was associated with a borderline significant increase in alcohol symptoms ($p \leq .08$). Even in this larger sample, with its increased statistical power, there were no statistically significant interactions of the background variables with change in employment status.

Effect on Heavy Drinking. Was adverse employment change between 1984 and 1985 associated with elevated binge drinking in 1985 compared to

TABLE 6.3. *Heavy drinking predicted by adverse employment change and prior heavy drinking: odds ratios for interactions from a logistic regression model (n = 2,441)*

Employment Status Change and 1984 Drinking	Odds Ratio of 1985 High Binge Drinking	95% Confidence Interval
Adequate employment 1984 to inadequate employment 1985**		
Low binge drinking	.73	.36–1.47
High binge drinking	4.27	1.65–11.06
Continuing inadequate employment 1984–85*		
Low binge drinking	.64	.33–1.27
High binge drinking	3.10	1.03–9.35

$^*p < .05$, $^{**}p < .01$.
Note: High binge drinking is defined as six or more episodes of six or more drinks on a single occasion, and low binge drinking as fewer than six such episodes over the past thirty days. The odds of high versus low binge drinking for each subgroup are relative to the odds for the comparable group that was adequately employed in 1985. These results are adjusted for the main effects of each employment change group (all nonsignificant) and all the statistically significant controls, including the main effect of heavy drinking in 1984, gender, aptitude, region, and illicit drug use in the past thirty days.
Source: Adapted from Dooley & Prause (1998, Table 3b, p. 677).

remaining in or moving to adequate employment (hypothesis 2)? The core sample for 1984–85 revealed no statistically significant main effect for any change in employment status on heavy drinking. However, two types of employment change did affect later heavy drinking in interaction with prior heavy drinking (see Table 6.3). Change from adequate employment to inadequate employment more than quadrupled the risk of heavy drinking (relative to adequate employment in 1985) among those who were heavy drinkers in 1984, while there was no increased risk among those who were not heavy drinkers in 1984 ($p \leq .005$). Continuing inadequate employment more than tripled the risk of heavy drinking among prior heavy drinkers, while there was no increased risk among those who were not heavy drinkers in 1984 ($p \leq .05$).

These findings were partially replicated in the enlarged 1984–85 sample. There was no main effect of adverse employment on heavy drinking, and there was an interaction between prior heavy drinking and continuing inadequate employment. However, the interaction between prior heavy drinking and change from adequate to inadequate employment was not replicated.

One might expect measures of heavy and average drinking to move together as a function of employment status. If heavy drinking increases for a group of respondents, such as those continuing in inadequate employment, such increased consumption might be expected to increase average drink-ing in this group. But in this study, there was no association of mean drinks per drinking day with employment status, paralleling the finding for heavy drinking. In order to explain this paradox, we compared the proportion of respondents who had stopped drinking between 1984 and 1985 in the ad-equately employed group with that of all other respondents. Of those who drank in 1984, 10.9% of those adequately employed in 1985 had stopped drinking, but 16.1% of all others had stopped drinking by 1985 ($p < .0001$). These results suggest that adverse employment produces two offsetting reactions – both elevated heavy drinking among those who already drink heavily and increased abstinence.

Developmental Change. Did the same pattern of adverse employment change effects appear in the 1988–89 data as in the 1984–85 data (hypothe-sis 3)? Using the core sample for both pairs of years ensures that the same respondents are being compared at two different points in their lives. In general, analyses of the 1988–89 data revealed rather different results from those for 1984–85. For alcohol symptoms, there was no significant main effect of adverse employment status, but employment status did interact with the number of prior (1988) alcohol symptoms. Among respondents with many prior symptoms, change from employment to unemployment increased the risk of elevated alcohol symptoms in 1989 about six times ($p \leq .05$). By contrast, for those with no or few prior symptoms, job loss was not associated with an increased risk of elevated alcohol problems in 1989. For alcohol consumption, no statistically significant effects of employment status appeared for the years 1988–89 in the core sample.

Replication in the enlarged 1988–89 sample ($n = 3,926$) gave results similar to those from the core sample – that is, no main effect of employ-ment status on either alcohol symptoms or heavy drinking. However, the enlarged sample produced some significant interactions that did not ap-pear in the core sample. For example, continuing inadequate employment was associated with an increased risk of high alcohol symptoms among married respondents but not among unmarried respondents, and with an increased risk of heavy drinking among females but not among males (both $p \leq .05$). Despite such occasional interactions in the enlarged sample, the association between employment status and alcohol abuse appears to be weaker in 1988–89 than in 1984–85. For more details on the adverse change hypothesis tests, see Dooley and Prause (1998).

Favorable Employment Change

Effect on Symptoms of Alcohol Misuse. Was favorable employment change between 1984 and 1985 associated with decreased alcohol symp-toms (hypothesis 4)? After controlling for prior alcohol symptoms (1984)

TABLE 6.4. *Heavy drinking predicted by favorable employment change and prior heavy drinking: odds ratios for interactions from a logistic regression model* (n = 1,659)

Employment Status Change and 1984 Drinking	Odds Ratio of 1985 High Binge Drinking	95% Confidence Interval
Unemployment 1984 to inadequate employment 1985*		
Low binge drinking	1.19	.45–3.12
High binge drinking	.09	.05–.20
Unemployment 1984 to adequate employment 1985**		
Low binge drinking	1.33	.64–2.77
High binge drinking	.13	.05–.36
Inadequate employment 1984 to adequate employment 1985		
Low binge drinking	.91	.46–1.81
High binge drinking	.29	.14–.64

$*p < .05, **p < .001$.

Note: High binge drinking is defined as six or more episodes of six or more drinks on a single occasion, and low binge drinking as fewer than six such episodes over the past thirty days. The odds of high versus low binge drinking for each subgroup are relative to the odds for the comparable group that experienced no favorable change (remained underemployed or lost a job). These results are adjusted for the main effects of each employment change group (all nonsignificant) and all the statistically significant controls, including the main effect of heavy drinking in 1984, gender, education, marital status, age, lifetime problems with alcohol, ever used illicit drugs, and illicit drug use in the past thirty days.

Source: Adapted from Dooley & Prause (1997a, Table 3, p. 799).

and various potential confounding variables, the favorable employment change groups showed no significant main or interaction effects.

Effect on Heavy Drinking. Was favorable employment change between 1984 and 1985 associated with decreased binge drinking (hypothesis 5)? After controlling for prior binge drinking (1984) and such significant background variables as gender, education, marital status, age, and prior drug use, none of the favorable-change groups showed main effects. However, each of the three favorable employment change groups interacted significantly with 1984 heavy drinking. Table 6.4 describes the nature of these interactions.

The three favorable-change groups consisted of those moving from unemployment to inadequate employment, from unemployment to adequate employment, and from inadequate employment to adequate employment. For each of these groups, respondents who did not report high binge drinking in 1984 showed no change in the risk of high binge drinking by 1985. But for all of these favorable employment change groups, respondents who did report high binge drinking in 1984 showed a significant decrease in the risk of high binge drinking by 1985, relative to respondents remaining underemployed or changing from inadequate employment to unemployment. Compared to this reference group, the favorable-change groups had significantly decreased odds (ranging from 9% to 29%) of high binge drinking. These findings appear to be consistent with the restorative model, in which favorable employment change primarily helps those underemployed respondents who are already misusing alcohol.

Five-year Follow-up. Was favorable employment change between 1984 and 1985 associated with beneficial effects on alcohol misuse in 1989 (hypothesis 6)? There was no direct link between 1984–85 employment change and either symptoms or consumption in 1989. However, we considered the possibility that prior employment changes would indirectly influence 1989 alcohol misuse through intervening 1989 employment status.

In the same sample of respondents who were underemployed in 1984, employment status in 1989 was associated with 1989 high binge drinking (but not with high alcohol symptoms), controlling for 1984 alcohol misuse and other significant background variables. Specifically, inadequate employment (but not unemployment) in 1989 was associated with increased binge drinking during that year. Did favorable employment change between 1984 and 1985 influence the risk of being inadequately employed in 1989? Using polytomous logistic regression, we modeled the odds of being unemployed, inadequately employed, or out of the labor force in 1989 relative to the odds of being adequately employed. Controlling for alcohol symptoms and binge drinking in 1984, along with other significant background variables, all three favorable employment change groups in 1984 had decreased odds of being inadequately employed in 1989. Of these, two were significant: moving to adequate employment in 1985 from either unemployment (OR = .33) or inadequate employment (OR = .39) in 1984. These associations appear to be consistent with an indirect causal path in which favorable employment change (1984–85) reduces the risk of inadequate employment five years later, which in turn is associated with increased binge drinking (1989). For more details on the favorable change hypothesis tests, see Dooley and Prause (1997a).

DISCUSSION

Summary of Findings

Adverse Employment Change. The relationship between adverse employment change and alcohol misuse varied with the years studied. In 1984–85, when the respondents were approaching their mid-twenties, both job loss and continuing inadequate employment were associated with increased symptoms of alcohol abuse. During the same survey period, becoming and remaining inadequately employed were both associated with increased binge drinking among those who already were heavy drinkers. These findings extend the existing literature that has repeatedly found connections between job loss and increased levels of alcohol disorder. The present results add inadequate employment to unemployment as a risk factor for alcohol-related problems.

By the 1988–89 survey period, these associations either had disappeared or appeared to be much weaker. Several possible explanations might account for the change in this relationship over time. Although these data can shed light on some of these factors, they cannot settle the issue (see Dooley & Prause, 1998). For example, one difference between the two study periods involves the economic climate; the prevailing unemployment rate fell between 1984–85 and 1988–89. Other research has pointed to the effect of aggregate employment conditions not only on those who lose jobs but also on those who remain employed, perhaps by influencing the quality of employment in ways beyond those measured here. Workers in good economic times may perceive themselves as having more job security, or they may feel less pressure to remain in unhappy job situations (Fenwick & Tausig, 1994). Because the samples for each year represented many communities, the respondents experienced a wide range of economic climates, some with low unemployment and some with high (standard deviation of respondents' 1988 local unemployment rates = 1.8). If more favorable economic environments buffer the reaction to adverse personal employment change, this would appear as an interaction effect (adverse employment change by prevailing unemployment rate). However, tests for such interactions proved negative.

Another possible explanation for the declining association involves developmental change among the respondents. In the years between these two pairs of surveys, the NLSY respondents not only aged but also took on added responsibilities. Entering their late twenties, they were more likely to have married and to have had children, and previous research has linked long-term marriage with decreased drinking (Harford, Hanna, & Faden, 1994). The phase of formal education would have given way to that of developing a career. People who are trying to perform well in their jobs in order to care for their families might well cope with adverse employment change in more adaptive ways than by increased drinking.

Favorable Employment Change. Analyses of favorable employment change revealed some evidence for a short-term beneficial effect. Those who were heavy drinkers in 1984 decreased their drinking after their employment improved in 1985, consistent with the restorative model. However, no support appeared either for a main effect of favorable change (preventive model) or for beneficial effects on short-term (one-year) symptom change. These results offer some empirical support for a symmetrical pattern in the association between employment change and alcohol outcomes, in which favorable and unfavorable employment change produce opposite effects.

In the longer term, favorable employment change in 1984–85 showed no direct effect on 1989 indicators of alcohol abuse (controlling for 1984 indicators). However, alcohol abuse commonly presents as an episodic disorder, with misuse first remitting and then recurring in response to more proximal events. These data give some support to an indirect link between earlier favorable employment change and longer-term benefits. Change to adequate employment between 1984 and 1985 predicted decreased risk of inadequate employment status in 1989, which in turn was associated with heightened risk of heavy drinking in 1989.

Implications of Findings

Research and Theory. These findings seem to be consistent with stress theories of alcohol abuse. Life events that challenge existing coping repertoires may elicit a maladaptive response such as increased alcohol consumption, which in turn can move individuals to more advanced stages of alcohol abuse and dependence. Previous research had documented this relationship for job loss. The present research now invites alcoholism researchers to add inadequate employment (including involuntary part-time and low-wage work) to unemployment as likely triggers of alcohol misuse.

This research used two different indicators of alcohol misuse – symptoms of abuse and heavy consumption. The fact that different sets of symptoms appeared in different survey waves posed some difficulties. The first three waves (1984, 1985, 1988) used a short set of symptoms that was not designed to reflect the official diagnostic criteria for alcohol abuse or dependence. Although the last of the studied waves (1989) did include a larger symptom set, we used a dichotomous high-symptom-count variable for comparability across the different survey waves. However, for better comparison with clinical case-finding studies, future research on employment stress and alcoholism would benefit from using better proxies for official alcohol abuse/dependence diagnoses.

The other measure, heavy drinking, does not appear as part of the official diagnostic criteria for alcohol abuse. However, the present findings suggest that consumption measures can help to illuminate the nature of the response to employment change and should continue to be included in future research. First, this study found evidence suggesting that drinkers respond in two offsetting ways to employment stress. Although some turn to more heavy drinking, others may actually stop drinking. As noted elsewhere, this suggests that under conditions of employment stress, some drinkers may cope by reducing their consumption in order to compete more effectively in an insecure economic environment (see, e.g., Catalano et al., 1993; Lee et al., 1990; Warr, 1987). For this reason, measures of average consumption, which allow increased and decreased consumption to cancel out, might miss important employment-change effects.

Second, responses to both adverse and favorable employment change appeared in interaction with prior heavy drinking. Without a binge variable available to check for such moderating influence, opposite effects in heavy- and light-drinking subgroups might be overlooked in main effects models. As with the symptom measures, future research on alcohol consumption might explore alternative definitions of binge drinking behavior. These analyses used the NLSY criterion of six drinks in a session for both men and women. However, researchers interested in college drinking have suggested less stringent criteria that take into account gender differences in weight-related sensitivity to alcohol (Wechsler et al., 1995). Future studies might usefully compare alternative definitions of binge drinking in response to employment change across different gender, age, and cultural subgroups.

Finally, the difference in adverse employment effects between the 1984–85 data and the 1988–89 data raises questions about the stability of these relationships over time. Such repeated hypothesis tests might be judged as replications. From this perspective, differences could be attributed not to changes in the basic causal structure but rather to statistical anomalies having to do with variations in measurement reliability (possible attenuation effect) and analytic power (type I or type II error). However, the large sample sizes used here and the adequate measurement reliability at each time point suggests looking rather at developmental change in the studied panel. This study compared two adjacent periods in early adulthood. Later research could usefully check these relationships over a wider span of the life cycle, taking into account the possibly moderating effects of relevant life circumstances (e.g., family formation, career development).

Interventions and Policy. Our finding that there are alcohol effects of adverse employment change adds weight to existing studies that have already pointed to policies that minimize unemployment. However, the results for inadequate employment suggest that economic policy makers broaden their concern to include the social costs of low-paying and involuntary part-time work. At the clinical level, these findings call the attention of those who treat alcohol disorder to employment transitions as a consideration in planning their interventions.

The results for the benefits of favorable employment change seem to support the restorative model, in which job improvements help to reduce drinking primarily among those already engaged in binge drinking behavior. For workers without preexisting heavy drinking, favorable change does not seem to operate as a primary prevention tool. Other programs that target young people before they have begun their drinking careers may offer more hope for such primary prevention (Pentz et al., 1989).

As noted earlier, workers' age seems to buffer the effect of adverse change, and if there are long-term effects of favorable change on alcohol misuse, they appear to operate indirectly through intervening employment status. These results suggest that the effectiveness of employment-related interventions for alcohol problems may not hold for later age groups or be sustainable over long periods of time. Nevertheless, these findings do invite two expansions of existing programs in order to take into account the connection between interventions to improve employment status (e.g., Vinokur et al., 1991) and interventions to reduce alcohol abuse (e.g., Project MATCH Research Group, 1997). One is to include efforts to avoid or minimize not just unemployment but also inadequate employment. The other is to add measures of alcohol misuse to the usual outcome indicators, such as depression and reemployment.

7

Settling Down

Psychological Depression and Underemployment

> We have slowly come to realize that periodical idleness as well as the pay-
> ment of wages insufficient for maintenance of the manual worker in full
> industrial and domestic efficiency stand economically on the same footing
> with the 'sweated' industries, the overwork of women, and employment of
> children. But of all the aspects of social misery nothing is so heart-breaking
> as unemployment, . . .
>
> Jane Addams, 1910, pp. 220–221

INTRODUCTION

Background

Depression and Stress. According to the Diagnostic and Statistical Manual of the American Psychiatric Association (1994) (DSM-IV), major depressive disorder is characterized by at least one two-week long episode
of depressed mood accompanied by at least four additional symptoms,
such as feelings of worthlessness and recurrent thoughts of death or suicide. Psychological depression is a major public mental health problem
affecting approximately 17 million Americans each year (Jacobs, Kopans,
& Reizes, 1995). The lifetime prevalence of major depression has been estimated in the range of 10% to 25% for women and 5% to 12% for men, with
the point prevalence estimated in the range of 5% to 9% for women and
2% to 3% for men (American Psychiatric Association, 1994).

This disorder can appear at any age, but the average age at onset is the
mid-twenties, near the beginning of the age range of the NLSY respondents
in 1992. This is a recurring disorder, with half or more of those individuals
with major depressive disorder expected to have a second episode. There
is evidence for a familial pattern to depression and a clear physiological
basis for other mood disorders, such as bipolar disorder, but psychosocial
events also appear to play a significant role in precipitating the first one or

two major depressive episodes. Stress appears to combine or interact with a vulnerability or diathesis to produce the depressive reaction. The diathesis for depression appears to be sufficiently widespread that stressful events must be regarded as an important factor in the timing and distribution of this disorder (Monroe & Simons, 1991).

According to the diathesis-stress model, when a person with a vulnerable personality experiences a serious life event, the risk of becoming depressed rises. One possible diathesis for becoming depressed is personality type, particularly the dependent or self-critical personality type (Coyne & Whiffen, 1995). According to the psychodynamic perspective, women are more likely to develop a dependent personality, and this may explain the greater prevalence of depression in women than in men (Coyne & Whiffen, 1995). Whatever the vulnerability factors for depression, the literature consistently finds that depressed patients experience a larger number of stressful events in the months prior to onset than do normal controls, and that the risk of depression rises as much as fivefold during the six months following such an event (Lloyd, 1980). Unfortunately, much of this research relies on retrospective methods and tends to mix stressors rather than to focus on a particular type of event.

As developed in Chapter 4, a major problem in establishing the causal connection between any life event and illness is ruling out reverse causation. Even after controlling for possible confounding variables, cross-sectional studies leave the possibility that preexisting depression causes the life events with which it correlates. In order to address this problem, various researchers have conducted panel studies of life events and depression. Although not focusing on job loss, these studies have established that simultaneous or prior life events correlate with symptoms of depression, controlling for prior symptoms. These results have appeared consistently in studies based on two interviews (Billings & Moos, 1982; Solomon et al., 1987; Turner & Noh, 1988), three interviews (Ensel & Lin, 1991), and four interviews (Aneshensel & Frerichs, 1982), with between-interview lag periods ranging from four months to four years.

Certain kinds of events have especially high potential to produce depression – those involving loss and disappointment and threatening long-term consequences (Brown & Harris, 1978). Of such events, adverse employment change – especially job loss – is one of those most commonly implicated in the literature. Past research has typically found a correlation between unemployment and symptoms of depression, but, as just noted, the causal nature of this linkage is difficult to establish.

Job Loss and Depression. Of special interest here is evidence on the link between depression and job loss and the causal direction of any observed association. Unfortunately, most of the research on this question uses cross-sectional designs that cannot establish causal sequence. For example, some studies have compared unemployed people with matched controls who have jobs. Such studies typically find elevated symptom counts among the unemployed, whether men (Melville et al., 1985) or women (Hall & Johnson, 1988). Another variation on the cross-sectional design relies on a random community sample and typically finds that symptoms of depression correlate with unemployment, controlling for other variables (Dressler, 1986).

Retrospective reports of the timing and nature of job loss both clarify the nature of the unemployment (job loser versus new job seeker entering the labor force) and partially address the reverse causation problem in cross-sectional research. For example, one survey of stably employed, unemployed, and previously unemployed people included items designed to distinguish those who might have caused their own unemployment from those who had not contributed to their own job loss (Kessler et al., 1988). The results indicated that even controlling for voluntariness of unemployment, job loss was associated with more symptoms of depression.

Prospective designs would provide better evidence on this question. Unfortunately, the few recent panel studies in this area typically begin with people who have lost a job and follow them to reemployment. Such studies find that the continuing unemployed have more symptoms of depression than those who find work (Bolton & Oatley, 1987; Kessler, Turner, & House, 1989; Shamir, 1986). This longitudinal association might reflect a situation in which the most depressed job losers fail to seek reemployment. However, one such study found that the unemployed respondents who were more depressed were more, not less, likely to find reemployment than their less-depressed counterparts (Kessler et al., 1989). Thus, reemployment may serve to reduce the psychological depression caused by job loss. One prospective panel study started with employed persons and followed them for two years (Hamilton et al., 1993). That study found that losing a job was related to prior frequency of symptoms of depression and that symptoms of depression decreased when employment outcomes (either obtaining a wanted job, losing a disliked job, or remaining willfully unemployed) matched desires.

One panel study on job loss and depression analyzed data from the Epidemiologic Catchment Area (ECA) study of several U.S. communities (Dooley et al., 1994). Respondents were selected for study if, at the first interview, they were employed and were not clinically depressed, as determined by the Diagnostic Interview Schedule. Respondents who had become unemployed (defined as receiving unemployment compensation) by the second interview reported significantly elevated symptoms of depression compared to those respondents who were still employed, controlling for time-one symptoms. Unfortunately, the ECA data did not measure the adequacy of employment at either time point and thus could not fully assess the effect of becoming inadequately employed. Moreover, the measure of unemployment – receiving unemployment compensation – missed those job losers who did not qualify for such compensation or who may have used up their eligibility.

Another large panel study of unemployment used data from the National Child Development Study that followed a 1958 British birth cohort (Montgomery et al., 1999). Preexisting depression measured at age twenty-three, prior to unemployment, served as the covariate controlling for selection. The onset of depression or anxiety symptoms severe enough to result in a medical consultation during the years between twenty-four and thirty-three served as the outcome variable. Compared to respondents who were not unemployed, those who had been unemployed during the prior year had over twice the risk of developing symptoms warranting clinical attention. Although these panel studies support the causal sequence from unemployment to depressive symptoms, they do not address the impact of becoming inadequately employed. Clarification of the impact of other forms of underemployment on depression will require additional research.

Employment Change

Inadequate Employment and Depression. Prior to the present program of research, the literature offered no report that assessed the impact of becoming inadequately employed (as defined here) on psychological depression. However, the studies linking inadequate employment to such outcomes as decreased self-esteem and increased alcohol abuse (detailed in earlier chapters) support the suspicion of a similar link between inadequate employment and depression. If the loss of income in shifting from employment to unemployment can cause depression, so might the loss of income in shifting from above-poverty wages to below-poverty wages. If the loss of time structure, social engagement, or status in shifting from employment to unemployment can act as a stressful life event, so might shifting from full-time employment to involuntary part-time employment (Jahoda, 1982).

Finally, such employment transitions take place in the context of other factors, both environmental (e.g., the surrounding economic climate) and personal (e.g., gender). Research has shown that such contextual factors can interact with job loss. For example, various studies have found that the prevailing unemployment rate can moderate the effects of unemployment (Cohn, 1978), exacerbate such effects (Turner, 1995), or have no influence on such effects (Dooley et al., 1988; Dooley et al., 1994). Not surprisingly, the moderation of inadequate employment's effects on depression has received even less attention than has its main effects. Extrapolating from research on job loss, it seems likely that a host of contextual variables might interact with shifts into and out of inadequate employment. These include such characteristics as the respondent's history of depression, socioeconomic status (as indexed by educational level), gender, ethnicity, marital status, and the community unemployment level.

Favorable Employment and Depression. If adverse employment change helps to cause depression, can favorable employment change help to alleviate or prevent depression? A symmetrical association, in which employment gains and losses produce equal but opposite types of emotional effects, however intuitive, cannot be assumed (Lieberson, 1985). Conventional wisdom suggests that getting a job is the best cure for the ailments of unemployment, but the effects of adverse employment change may linger even after reemployment. For example, an unemployed worker, in order to cope with lost wages, may have to deplete savings or forgo important expenditures, such as tuition for a child's college education. Even after reemployment, these financial sacrifices may leave a residue of lasting worry and interpersonal distress. When workers do find new jobs, they may be inferior in wages, security, or personal satisfaction to their old jobs. On the other hand, moving from unemployment to any job or from an economically inadequate job to an adequate one could be the basis for a renewed optimism that erases all lingering depression.

The literature on reemployment consists of far fewer studies than the literature on job loss, and studies of the transition from less to more adequate jobs are quite rare. One study of the emotional functioning of previously employed workers reported that reemployment largely reversed their symptoms, including those of depression (Kessler et al., 1988). However, not all reemployment is equal. Another study found that individuals moving into less satisfactory jobs reported no mental health benefits, while those moving into satisfactory employment showed increased mental health (Wanberg, 1995). As detailed in the prior chapter, research on economically inadequate employment has linked favorable employment change with decreased binge drinking in those who had been heavy drinkers during the prior interview period. The effect on depression of favorable transitions either to or from inadequate employment has not been studied.

Questions remain as to whether such favorable employment effects will appear, if at all, as main effects (i.e., benefiting all equally, including those not experiencing elevated depression initially) or as interactions (i.e., providing restorative benefits mainly to those with elevated depression prior to their transition to more adequate employment). Does the prior status of underemployment matter, or only the end state? (For example, if one is underemployed, does it matter whether one has moved up from unemployment or merely held onto an inadequate job?) If only the end state matters, are there differences among the possible outcomes? (For example, does an inadequate job more closely resemble an adequate job or joblessness?)

Hypotheses

Adverse Change. Does falling from adequate to inadequate employment result in increased depression? If so, how does this increase compare with that associated with job loss? In order to answer these questions, we first fitted a main effects model that began with respondents in adequate employment at first interview. We then tested the hypothesis that respondents who were unemployed or inadequately employed at reinterview would have higher levels of depression than those still in adequate employment, controlling for initial depression and other potential confounding variables.

Other models can illuminate other aspects of the relationship between adverse employment change and depression. For example, some people may show a greater depressive response to adverse employment change than others. We checked the various contextual variables as potential moderators of the effect. Similarly, some variables might help to explain the mechanism by which adverse change produces increased depression. Therefore, we checked such variables as potential mediators of the effect.

Favorable Change. Does a favorable change in employment result in decreased depression? In order to explore this question, we began with respondents who were either unemployed or in inadequate employment at time one. We then tested the hypothesis that respondents who had gained adequate employment or who had gained inadequate employment would report lower depression than those who had remained unemployed, controlling for prior depression and employment status.

As with adverse change, these models explored potential moderator variables such as prior functioning. A simple main effect of employment status would suggest that favorable employment change operates as general primary prevention, that is, equally for all respondents, including those with few or no symptoms. On the other hand, the beneficial effects of favorable employment might appear more for those with high rather than low levels of prior depression. Such a finding would suggest a restorative effect consistent with secondary prevention and reaffirm finding a job as a sound early intervention for those coping with unemployment.

METHODS

Samples

Economic Climate. The respondents for these hypothesis tests were drawn from those interviewed in both NLSY surveys of 1992 and 1994, the only waves to include measures of psychological depression. This period saw the end of the recession of the early 1990s and the beginning of the next economic expansion. The national average unemployment rate had steadily

risen from 5.3% in 1989 to 5.6% in 1990 and to 6.8% in 1991, before reaching the recession's peak of 7.5% in 1992. Concern with high unemployment
became a major political issue in the 1992 presidential campaign. The subsequent recovery was uneven, with slower expansion in some areas (notably
California) than others. The national unemployment rate showed a slight
improvement to 6.9% in 1993, and then a more noticeable drop to 6.1% by
1994. Unknown to the respondents in 1994, this expansion would continue
on into the next millennium, becoming one of the longest in U.S. economic
history.

Official labor statistics revealed a massive loss of jobs during this recession. Over 9 million workers were displaced between January 1991 and
December 1992, of whom over 4.5 million had three or more years' tenure
in their jobs. Moreover, the recession had a lasting effect on the employment of these displaced workers. Of the long-tenured displaced group,
many were still unemployed (19.1%) or had given up and left the work
force (13.1%) by February 1994, despite the beginning of the economic recovery. But for many of those finding reemployment, the economic stress
remained. Of the previously long-tenured, full-time workers, 2.8 million
had found reemployment by February 1994, but of these, only 34% had
found full-time jobs at equal or better pay. Over 37% had full-time jobs at
lower pay than their lost job, and another 11% were working part-time,
with the rest being self-employed or unpaid family workers (U.S. Bureau
of Labor Statistics, 1996).

Two samples of NLSY respondents were selected for these analyses,
based on the definitions of adequate and inadequate employment described earlier (Chapter 3). Members of the adequately employed sample
in 1992 ($n = 5,113$) came from communities with an average unemployment rate of 7.8%, which was close to the official level for the nation in that
year. By contrast, members of the sample in inadequate employment or unemployment in 1992 ($n = 1,160$) resided in communities with an average
unemployment rate of 8.2%. Figure 7.1 compares the unemployment rate
between the adequately employed and underemployed samples in 1992.
In general, members of the underemployed sample lived in less favorable

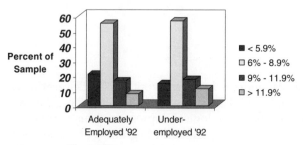

FIGURE 7.1. Unemployment rate.

economic environments than those in the adequately employed sample, with 29.8% of the latter living in areas with less than 5.9% unemployment, compared to 14.7% of the underemployed sample. Although some communities no doubt experienced an increase in joblessness as a function of local conditions such as plant closings, the country enjoyed a decrease in the overall unemployment rate between 1992 and 1994. As would be expected, therefore, only a small proportion of members of these samples lived in communities experiencing increased unemployment during this period. Just 11.5% of the 1992 adequately employed and 10.9% of the 1992 underemployed lived in communities that experienced increased unemployment between 1992 and 1994. In sum, workers in the present samples were experiencing a recession in 1992 that had begun to show signs of relenting by the 1994 survey.

Developmental Stage. In 1992, the NLSY respondents had reached their late twenties and early thirties. The adequately employed sample averaged 31.1 years of age in 1992 (SD = 2.3), and the underemployed sample was about two years older (M = 33.2, SD = 2.3). Most of these young adults had established marital bonds. Of the adequately employed, 61.1% were married with a spouse present. Of the older, underemployed sample, 52.1% were married with a spouse present, and another 18.9% had been married but were divorced, separated, or widowed (Figure 7.2). Most also had children by 1992 – 71.9% of the older, underemployed group and 59.3% of the younger, adequately employed group. These childbearing differences may also be related to the gender makeup of the two samples. The adequately employed sample had a majority of males (56.9%), whereas the underemployed group had more females (60%) (Figure 7.3). The ethnic make-up of the two samples was also different, in that 20.0% of the underemployed sample was African American versus 11.6% of the adequately employed sample (Figure 7.4).

Formal education is usually completed by this stage. Although older, the underemployed sample reported fewer years of education than their adequately employed counterparts in 1992 – 12.5 years versus 13.6 years.

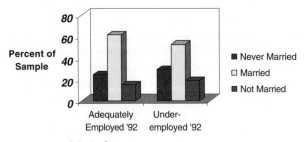

FIGURE 7.2. Marital status.

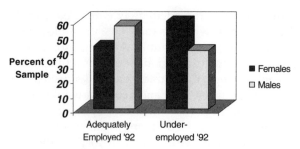

FIGURE 7.3. Gender.

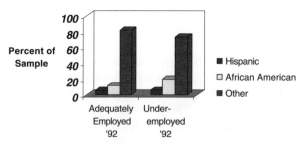

FIGURE 7.4. Ethnicity.

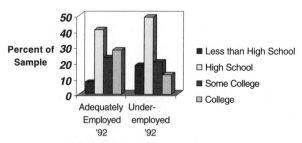

FIGURE 7.5. Education.

As shown in Figure 7.5, 7.9% of the adequately employed sample had less than a high school education, as compared to 18.1% of the underemployed sample. While 28.1% of the adequately employed sample had a college education, only 12.4% of the underemployed sample had a college education. The disparity in education between the two samples may by related to differences in the employment status of the two groups. Moreover, it may also be related to the socioeconomic status of the respondents' parents. The number of years of education of the more-educated parent was 12.8 for the adequately employed versus 11.9 for the underemployed. As shown in Figure 7.6, about one-third of the underemployed had parents with less than a high school education versus 21.5% of the adequately

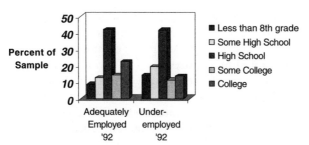

FIGURE 7.6. Parental years of education.

employed sample. Similarly, about 22.4% of the adequately employed sample had parents with a college education, compared to 13.6% of the underemployed sample.

Measuring Depression

CES-D. The NLSY used different versions of the Center for Epidemiologic Studies Depression Scale (CES-D) to measure depressed mood in the 1992 and 1994 survey waves. The original CES-D was used in 1992 and consists of twenty items (Markush & Favero, 1974; Radloff, 1977). Each item asks about a mood or experience during the past week (e.g., felt tearful) and receives a score based on the number of days that it was present, ranging from 0 (no days) to 3 (five to seven days). Thus the total score can range from 0 (no sign of depression) to 60. The CES-D was designed for and has been widely used in general population epidemiological studies. It has good psychometric properties and correlates well with other self-report measures of nonspecific psychological distress (Vernon & Roberts, 1981). It has been found to be associated with unemployment in aggregate time-series analyses (Catalano & Dooley, 1977).

A seven-item subset of the CES-D was used in the 1994 survey. Abbreviated versions of the CES-D have frequently been employed in an effort to save survey resources, including different seven-item (Reynolds, 1997), ten-item (Mirowsky & Ross, 1995), eleven-item (Umberson et al., 1992), and sixteen-item (Craig & Van Natta, 1979) sets. The 1994 NLSY seven-item set correlates well with the full twenty-item set used in 1992 ($r = .90$) and has good inter-item reliability in 1994 (Cronbach's alpha = .81) compared to the full twenty-item set's reliability in 1992 (Cronbach's alpha = .88). The CES-D can change over time reflecting shifts in mood, as indicated by the modest test-retest correlations of the seven-item 1994 measure with both the 1992 seven-item and twenty-item versions ($r = .42$).

What Is Being Measured? What aspect of depression does the CES-D reflect – transient mood or major clinical depression? It was designed for general population surveys and epidemiologic uses rather than for clinical diagnoses of individuals. Thus it does not match the criteria of the DSM-IV (American Psychiatric Association, 1994) and cannot identify persons with major depression for clinical purposes. However, research has shown that this scale can discriminate known psychiatric patients from people with low levels of depression and that it agrees well with clinical and other ratings of depression. Thus high scores on the CES-D commonly serve as proxies for clinically high levels of depression in epidemiological analyses. The most widely used cut-point for this purpose is ≥ 16 (on the 0 to 60 scale).

Using this conventional cut-point approach, the CES-D has repeatedly shown the ability to detect elevated depressive symptoms among the general population (Myers & Weissman, 1980; Roberts & Vernon, 1983; Weissman et al., 1977). One general population survey using the CES-D estimated community depression prevalence at 19.1% (Frerichs, Aneshensel, & Clark, 1981). This estimate exceeds the point prevalence for major depressive disorder as reported in the DSM-IV (American Psychiatric Association, 1994), based on case-finding community surveys (5–9% for women and 2–3% for men). However, the CES-D estimates of greater prevalence of depression among females than males and among young adults than older adults agree with the accepted epidemiologic findings.

Continuity Question. A related issue for the use of the CES-D arises from the debate about the "continuity" of depression. That is, do mild versus moderate-to-high depressive symptoms (as reflected in low versus medium-to-high scores on continuous scales such as the CES-D) differ quantitatively (by degree) or qualitatively (in kind)? If they differ qualitatively, one should categorize respondents based on various cut-points and avoid analyzing the scale as a continuous variable. But if depressive symptoms differ quantitatively, research can proceed with the analysis of continuous scale scores rather than of a small number of arbitrary categories. The resolution of this issue goes beyond our scope, but one review has provided support for the continuity hypothesis (Flett, Vredenburg, & Krames, 1997).

One advantage of using continuous analytic procedures such as ordinary least squares is that they offer more statistical power to detect significant effects than do categorical methods such as logistic regression. On the other hand, public policy makers may have a greater interest in the incidence of serious depressive disorder, as estimated by high CES-D scores, than in variations in the mean symptom levels in the low range. In this case, categorical methods such as logistic regression offer the advantage of estimating the increased risk of high (quasi-clinical) depression. Thus, as a practical matter, it will be useful to approach these depression measures from both continuous and categorical perspectives. Unfortunately, the seven-item version of CES-D used in 1994 has no conventional cut-point (such as $\geq$ 16 for the twenty-item version). For the present study, a cut-point was chosen that identified a group with an arbitrarily high level of depression – those falling in approximately the top 15% of the studied sample.

RESULTS

Unfavorable Employment Change

Cross-sectional and Bivariate Longitudinal Relationships. Many studies have used cross-sectional methods to relate employment status to measures of well-being, such as depression. We replicated this approach with the data for 1992. For all respondents in the workforce, we found the expected employment-status gradient for depression. Average CES-D scores (twenty-item scale) were lowest for the adequately employed (M = 8.3, $n = 5,113$), intermediate for the inadequately employed (M = 9.8, $n = 669$), and highest for the unemployed, including discouraged workers (M = 13.3, $n = 640$). The same pattern held when depression was analyzed as a dichotomous variable. The percentages with high levels of depression ($\geq$ 16) ranged from 15.5% for the adequately employed to 23% for the inadequately employed to 33.5% for the unemployed.

Of course, these data are equally consistent with several explanations, including social causation (employment status causes depression) and selection (depression causes employment status). In order to clarify this, we replicated this relationship after controlling for earlier employment status by removing those in underemployment in 1992. This allowed us to focus on adverse employment change among those who had in common an adequate level of prior employment. Even during the early stages of an economic expansion, some workers lose jobs or slide into economically less favorable employment. Table 7.1 describes the magnitude of such adverse employment change for just the NLSY respondents who were adequately employed in 1992 and displays their depression scores by 1994 employment status ($n = 5,113$).

Now we can see the extent to which the adequately employed in 1992 either continued in adequate employment or fell into some form of underemployment by 1994. Of these respondents, 170 (3%) became unemployed, and most of these met the criteria for unemployment of the Current Population Survey definition, in that they reported recent efforts to find work ($n = 153$). Only seventeen respondents said they wanted work but were too discouraged to keep looking. Because these discouraged workers were too few for separate study, they were grouped with the other unemployed for the remaining analyses. Another 227 (4.2%) respondents became inadequately employed during 1994, including 169 with poverty wages and 58 in

TABLE 7.1. *CES-Depression by 1994 employment status for 1992 adequately employed (n = 5,113)*

1994 Employment Status	1992 % ≥ 16[a]	1992 M (SD)	1994 M (SD)
Adequately employed (*n* = 4,437)	14.9	8.1 (7.6)	3.0 (3.5)
Unemployed (*n* = 170)	25.7	11.2 (10.4)	4.6 (4.9)
CPS unemployed (*n* = 153)	23.4	11.2 (10.6)	4.7 (5.0)
Discouraged workers (*n* = 17)	42.9	10.7 (9.1)	3.9 (4.3)
Inadequately employed (*n* = 227)	17.1	8.8 (7.9)	4.3 (4.5)
Involuntary part-time (*n* = 58)	30.6	11.5 (8.4)	4.5 (4.4)
Poverty-wage (*n* = 169)	13.0	8.0 (7.6)	4.2 (4.5)
OLF (*n* = 279)	18.8	9.4 (8.9)	4.8 (4.7)
TOTAL (*n* = 5,113)	15.5	8.3 (7.8)	3.2 (3.7)

[a] Percent of people with 1992 CES-D ≥ 16 within each of the 1994 employment groups.
Note: CES-D depression in 1994 is based on a seven-item subset of the original twenty items. CES-D depression in 1992 is based on the full set of twenty items.
Source: Adapted from Dooley et al. (2000, Table 1).

involuntary part-time work. Because of the small numbers, particularly for involuntary part-time work, and because of their similar depression levels in 1994, these two groups were combined in subsequent analyses.

As in the 1992 cross-sectional analysis, the 1994 depression levels showed a clear gradient tracking employment status. Based on the seven-item scale, depression was highest for the unemployed (M = 4.6), intermediate for the inadequately employed (M = 4.3), and lowest for the continuing adequately employed (M = 3.0). Note that those individuals who left the labor force entirely (OLF) also displayed elevated depression in 1994 (M = 4.8, *n* = 279). Those becoming OLF included the disabled, those in early retirement, on welfare, and in other such nonworking employment statuses that are not the focus of this analysis. Of these, the respondents entering welfare are of special policy interest and are considered in Chapter 8.

Do these findings demonstrate the effect of adverse employment change on depression? No, because as Table 7.1 shows, those people who were adequately employed in 1992 included subgroups with quite varying depression levels. Consistent with the selection hypothesis, those who had become unemployed by 1994 reported higher depression in 1992 than those who remained adequately employed in 1994 (see Chapter 4 on reverse causation). By contrast, those who were to become inadequately employed (particularly those destined for poverty wages) had 1992 depression levels only slightly higher than those of respondents who remained adequately employed. These data demonstrate the necessity for conducting longitudinal analyses that control not only for prior employment status but also for prior depression and other potential confounding variables.

Longitudinal Multiple Regression. To provide such controls, we next fit a series of ordinary least squares regression models based on the respondents who were adequately employed in 1992. The continuous measure of 1994 depression (seven-item CES-D) was adjusted for 1992 depression and for a series of potential control variables, mediating variables, and moderator variables. Table 7.2 summarizes the results of these analyses.

The first model controls for earlier depression and several significant control variables, including dissatisfaction with one's job in 1992, gender, education, presence of children in the household, 1987 self-esteem, and geographic region. Becoming unemployed, inadequately employed, and OLF were each associated with increased depression when compared to remaining adequately employed, after controlling for these variables (see Model 1). Depression at second interview was higher for females, the less educated, those with lower self-esteem, those with children, and those who were less satisfied with their jobs in 1992. Neither family poverty status nor marital status in 1992 was significantly associated with later depression, but they were retained in the model so that change in both variables could be evaluated as possible mediators.

The second model explored potential mediators that help to explain the mechanism by which adverse job change produced increased depression. Such variables should involve other changes occurring between 1992 and 1994 that might be produced by job change and in turn affect mood. If such variables fully explained the effect of adverse job change, the dummy variables for unemployment or inadequate employment, which were significant in the initial model, should fall below significance. Two variables were explored – adverse change in marital status (losing a spouse through divorce, separation, or widowhood) and adverse change in family income (falling below the poverty line for total family income, adjusted for number of family members). Losing a spouse was significantly associated with later depression, but change in family poverty status was not (see Model 2). Even after controlling for these potential mediators, becoming unemployed, inadequately employed, and OLF each remained significantly associated with increased depression.

One potential mediating variable not included in Model 2 is change in job satisfaction, because this could be tested only in respondents for whom job satisfaction measures were available – that is, those who were still employed in 1994. In a follow-up analysis, we checked this potential mediator in the subsample of respondents working in 1994 using two job satisfaction indicators: (1) job dissatisfaction in 1992 (a four-level ordinal scale) and (2) change in job satisfaction (1 = change from a satisfying job in 1992 to a dissatisfying job in 1994; 0 = no change in job satisfaction, or change from a less satisfying to a more satisfying job). Both higher job dissatisfaction in 1992 and change to a less satisfying job by 1994 were associated with increased 1994 depression. But after controlling for these variables,

TABLE 7.2. *1994 CES-Depression: ordinary least squares regression for the 1992 adequately employed (n = 5,113)*

Predictor	Model 1 b	Model 1 beta	Model 2 b	Model 2 beta	Model 3 b	Model 3 beta
CES-Depression (1992)	.15**	.33	.15**	.32	.15**	.32
Job dissatisfaction (1992)[a]	.17*	.02	.17*	.03	.12+	.02
Gender (1 = male; 0 = female)	−.95**	−.13	−.93**	−.13	−.96**	−.13
Years of education (1992)[b]	−.09**	−.06	−.08**	−.05	−.09**	−.06
Marital status (1992) (1 = spouse present; 0 = other)	−.11	−.01	−.28**	−.04	−.18	−.02
Children in household (1 = yes; 0 = no)	.22*	.03	.24*	.03	.24*	.03
Self-esteem[c] (1987)	−.07**	−.07	−.07**	−.07	−.07**	−.08
Geographic region (1992) (1 = North Central; 0 = other)	.24*	.03	.25*	.03	.23*	.03
Family poverty status 1992[d]						
Yes	.11	.006	.08	.004	.02	.001
Missing	.03	.002	−.04	−.004	.03	.003
Employment status in 1994[e]						
Unemployment (U)	.84*	.04	.81*	.04	−.86	−.04
Inadequate employment (I)	.67*	.04	.71*	.04	1.59**	.09
Out of the labor force	1.15**	.07	1.14**	.07	1.13**	.07
Change in marital status (1992–94) (1 = loss of spouse; 0 = other)			1.94**	.11	1.94**	.11
Change in family poverty status (1992–94) (1 = change to poverty; 0 = other)			.03	.007	.03	.008
U × Years of Education 1992					.24*	.03
U × Marital Status 1992					−1.46**	−.04
U × Job Satisfaction 1992					1.43**	.12
I × Marital Status 1992					−1.56**	−.06
Constant	4.19		4.16		4.25	
R^2_{adj}	.185		.196		.201	

** $p < .001$, * $p = .05$, + $p < .10$.
[a] Job satisfaction measured on a four-point scale, 1 = like job very much to 4 = dislike job very much.
[b] Years of education was centered to reduce correlation between main effect and interaction term (Cohen & Cohen, 1983).
[c] The Rosenberg Self-Esteem Scale, where higher values indicate higher levels of self-esteem.
[d] Reference group is family poverty status in 1992 = no.
[e] Reference group is the continuing adequately employed.
Source: Adapted from Dooley et al. (2000, Table 3).

depression at second interview was still significantly higher in the inadequately employed group when compared to the adequately employed group (b = .49, beta = .03, $p < .03$).

The third model checked possible moderators of the adverse employment effect. Variables that either exacerbate or buffer this effect should appear in significant interactions with unemployment or inadequate employment. Tests of the two-way interactions involving each 1992 contextual variable with each 1994 employment dummy variable revealed four significant interactions. These included inadequate employment with marital status, unemployment with marital status, unemployment with education, and unemployment with job dissatisfaction (see Model 3). Marital status appeared to buffer the effects of both types of adverse employment change. Among those with no spouse present, becoming either unemployed or inadequately employed was associated with large increases in depression, whereas for those with a spouse present, the increases in depression were smaller in magnitude. The significant interaction between unemployment and years of education suggests that education exacerbates the adverse effect of becoming unemployed. Finally, job dissatisfaction appears to exacerbate the adverse effect of becoming unemployed.

One background variable that did not appear as a main or interaction term in Model 3 was age, contrary to previous research that has linked depression with age (Mirowsky & Ross, 1992). The absence of this effect might be due to the narrow age range of the NLSY sample, raising the possibility that the present findings are unique to this particular age group. To assess the degree to which the findings presented here generalize to more age-heterogeneous samples, the relationship among age, employment status, and depression was analyzed in data from a different survey that represented all Californians in 1996 (California Work and Health Survey, 1999). As reported elsewhere (Dooley et al., 2000), older respondents in this survey reported significantly lower levels of depression, controlling for standard demographic variables (marital status, gender, children, education, and race). But there were no interaction effects between age and employment status on depression.

Longitudinal Logistic Regression. As mentioned earlier in regard to the "continuity question," a debate persists as to whether high depression scores reflect a qualitative or a quantitative difference from lower scores. One interpretation of the OLS findings just discussed is that the adverse employment effect, although statistically significant, consists only of a socially insignificant worsening of average mood. Perhaps many people react to their adverse employment change by feeling a little sadder, without crossing the threshold to clinical-level depression. While this effect would be regrettable, it might be regarded as an emotional inconvenience rather than as a guide for public mental health policy. Alternatively, the observed rise in CES-D scores for the underemployed may reflect increases throughout the range of symptoms, including the high end. If so, these results could have important implications for the incidence of serious mood disorder.

Unfortunately, the CES-D was not designed to diagnose clinical-level major depression. Moreover, the conventional cut-off score used with the CES-D as a proxy for serious depression was based on the full twenty-item instrument. In order to explore this issue, we identified an ad hoc cut-point for the seven-item CES-D used in 1994. The conventional cut-off point for the twenty-item CES-D scale of $\geq$ 16 identifies approximately the top 15% of the respondents who were adequately employed in 1992. The cut-off point for the seven-item scale that also identifies approximately 15% of the sample is $\geq$ 7.

Using this cut-point, the respondents in 1994 were dichotomized into high versus low-to-moderate depression groups. This variable became the outcome for a logistic regression analysis that controlled for 1992 depression and other variables implicated by the prior analysis. As before, the key predictors include dummy variables for each of the 1994 employment statuses. The null hypothesis is that becoming either unemployed or inadequately employed would not increase the odds of falling into the high-depression group rather than the low-depression group, relative to the odds for those remaining adequately employed. The results appear in Table 7.3.

TABLE 7.3. *Elevated depression by employment status in 1994: logistic regression for adequately employed in 1992 (n = 5,113)*

Predictor	B	S.E.	Odds Ratio
CES-D 1992	.075***	.005	1.078
Self-esteem 1987	−.050***	.011	.952
Gender (1 = male)	−.610***	.088	.543
Education 1992	−.086***	.020	.918
Marital status 1992	−.106	.091	.899
Marital change (1 = spouse 1992 to no spouse 1994)	1.033***	.165	2.810
Job dissatisfaction 1992	.146***	.061	1.157
Employment status 1994 (relative to continuing adequate employment)			
Unemployed	.260	.220	1.298
Inadequately employed	.548**	.179	1.729
Out of the labor force	.695***	.159	2.004
Constant	.699	.434	

Model chi-square = 579.47*** (df = 12).
*p < .05, **p < .01, ***p < .001.
Note: The model includes nonsignificant controls for family poverty in 1992 (income adjusted for family size).

Adverse job change was associated with elevated odds of high depression. This effect was statistically significant for becoming inadequately employed, but not for becoming unemployed. Even controlling for the potential mediating variable of marital change (becoming divorced, separated, or widowed) did not suppress the inadequate employment effect. The risk of being in the top 15% on the depression scale in 1994 was about 73% higher for the inadequately employed, but just 30% higher for the unemployed. Why did the unemployment effect fail to reach significance, as did the inadequate employment effect? These data cannot give a definitive answer to that question, but we speculate that it has to do with selection and the differential depression levels of those who later were to become unemployed versus those who were to become inadequately employed.

Favorable Employment Change

Effects of Prior Depression and Employment Status. Of the NLSY respondents who were unemployed ($n = 521$) or inadequately employed ($n = 639$) in 1992, 1,160 provided complete data on the CES-D and other variables at both the 1992 and 1994 interviews. Of the initially unemployed, 208 became adequately employed, 76 became inadequately employed, 117 remained unemployed, and 120 left the workforce (OLF). Of the initially inadequately employed, 293 became adequately employed, 221 remained inadequately employed, 54 became unemployed, and 71 became OLF. As with the adverse employment change analyses, prior depression might influence favorable employment change and thus account for any association between such change and later depression. Indeed, 1992 depression was significantly associated with later employment status in a complex manner that involved interactions with both prior employment status and other variables (see Chapter 4 for more details). Thus it is essential to control for prior depression in modeling the association between later favorable employment and depression.

Does prior employment status influence the association between later employment status and depression? The first approach to this question consisted of a 2×4 analysis of covariance (employment status in 1992 $\times$ employment status in 1994, using the seven-item version of the 1992 CES-D as the covariate and the seven-item 1994 CES-D as the outcome variable). There was a significant main effect for 1994 employment status ($F = 3.5$, d.f. $= 3, 1147, p = .015$). Pairwise comparisons showed that the adequately employed had significantly lower levels of depression when compared to both the unemployed and OLF groups in 1994 (Bonferroni adjusted $p = .008$). There was neither a main effect for 1992 employment status ($F = 1.7$, d.f. $= 1, 1147, p = .197$) nor an interaction between 1992 and 1994 employment status ($F = 2.1$, d.f. $= 3, 1147, p = .093$), and treatment-by-covariate interactions were not statistically significant. This finding was checked in multivariate regressions that included either 1992 employment status (unemployed versus inadequately employed) or 1993 employment status (unemployed, inadequately employed, adequately employed, or OLF). In no case did prior employment status add to 1994 employment in explaining 1994 depression (for more details, see Prause & Dooley, 2001).

Effects of Later Employment Status. As a result of these preliminary analyses, we used ordinary least squares regression to model the relationship of later employment status to depression, controlling for prior depression and any significant contextual variables. The results indicate that both adequate employment and inadequate employment in 1994 were significantly associated with reduced levels of depression, relative to unemployment (see Table 7.4). The difference between the two employed categories was

TABLE 7.4. *Relationship of 1994 employment status to 1994 CES-Depression: OLS regression for the underemployed in 1992 (n = 1,160)[a]*

Variable	b	se(b)	Beta
CES-Depression 1992	.147*	.012	.340
Self-esteem[b] in 1987	−.097*	.030	−.087
Gender (1 = male; 0 = female)	−.893*	.253	−.098
Children in 1994 (1 = yes; 0 = no)	.331*	.096	.097
Marital status 1994[c]			
Never married	1.019*	.325	.101
Spouse no longer present	.593	.340	.055
Change in marital status 1992–94[d]			
Never/not married to spouse present	.406	.552	.019
Spouse present to no spouse present	1.406*	.576	.069
Percent time unemployed 1979–91[e]	.016*	.005	.084
Employment status 1994 ($p < .001$)[f]			
Adequate employment	−1.588*	.354	−.176
Inadequate employment	−1.561*	.384	−.152
Out of the labor force	−.745	.412	−.062
Intercept	6.065	1.133	

* $p < .05$.

[a] In 1992, there were 1,160 NLSY respondents who were unemployed or underemployed who had provided complete data on variables used in the multiple regression analyses.

[b] Rosenberg Self-Esteem Scale, ranging from 10 to 40, with higher values indicating higher levels of self-esteem.

[c] Reference group is married with spouse present.

[d] Reference group is no change in marital status – continuing not married or continuing married with spouse present.

[e] Number of years unemployed divided by number of years in the labor force (unemployed or employed).

[f] Reference group is the unemployed, including discouraged workers.

Note: $R^2_{adj} = .265$; $F = 35.736$ (df = 12, 1147), $p < .001$.

not significant, suggesting comparable reductions in depression regardless of job adequacy. Those leaving the labor force (OLF) did not differ in 1994 CES-D from the unemployed.

For this sample of underemployed respondents in 1992, higher depression in 1994 was associated with lower self-esteem (measured in 1987), being female, and having children. Depression was higher for both the never-married and not-currently-married groups when compared to the married-with-a-spouse-present group. More time unemployed during the twelve years prior to 1992 was also significantly associated with increased levels of depression in 1994.

The association of 1994 employment status and depression was moderated by just one variable – change in marital status from 1992 to 1994. However, the group that experienced change from the presence of a spouse in 1992 to the absence of a spouse in 1994 (i.e., respondents who were divorced, widowed, or separated) included just 5.1% of the total sample. Consequently, the cell sizes of those who both lost a spouse and were either adequately employed or underemployed were very small ($n \leq 3$). Because results based on such small cell counts might be unstable, this interaction was not included in Table 7.4. With that caveat, the pattern of this interaction suggests that the beneficial effect on depression of having employment (either adequate employment or inadequate employment) was greater for those who lost a spouse than for others.

DISCUSSION

Conclusions

Summary of Findings. Among those with adequate jobs in 1992, adverse employment change was positively related to 1994 depression after controlling for prior psychological well-being and other potential confounders. In the OLS model, both the unemployed and inadequately employed groups reported significantly more depression than those continuing in adequate employment but were not different from each other. A potential mediator of these effects, loss of spouse between interview years, was significantly associated with increased depression, but its inclusion did not substantially reduce the direct effects of job loss or entering inadequate employment.

Several variables appeared to moderate the effects of adverse employment change. First, being married appeared to buffer the adverse effects of becoming unemployed or inadequately employed, perhaps playing the role of social support during this stressful process. Second, respondent's education appeared to exacerbate the adverse effect of losing a job. Having a job may be more expected, and its loss may be more of a blow to one's self-worth, among those of higher social class, as indexed by education. Finally, among respondents losing jobs, those who were dissatisfied with their jobs in 1992 reported more depression than those who were satisfied. We had expected that losing an unsatisfying job would be less stressful than losing a more satisfying one, as reported elsewhere (Wheaton, 1990). However, the present study's sample is more age-restricted than that of the earlier study, where age played a moderating role in the relationship among job satisfaction, job loss, and outcome. In the present research, those who lost satisfying jobs may have had more optimism about reemployment than those who lost unsatisfactory jobs.

For the group that was underemployed in 1992, any employment in 1994, whether adequate or inadequate, is associated with lower depression in 1994, controlling for 1992 depression. There was no difference in depression between adequate and inadequate employment, relative to unemployment. Prior employment status did not affect this finding. The distress level associated with unemployment in 1994 did not differ between people who had lost inadequate jobs and those without jobs in 1992 or 1993. Moreover, there was no difference in 1994 depression between those who were unemployed and those who were out of the labor force (OLF). This agrees with prior work suggesting that being unemployed and being OLF are functionally equivalent (Goldsmith, Veum, & Darity, 1995). The major difference between being unemployed and being OLF is the degree to which the respondent claims to want work and to have tried to find work. In either case, the respondent is nonworking and missing those latent functions of work that may promote psychological well-being (e.g., sense of time structure).

Prior research found an interaction of favorable employment change with prior dysfunction (specifically, binge drinking), suggesting a restorative effect of improved employment (Dooley & Prause, 1997c). However, the present study found no interaction of employment change with prior depression, implying that all respondents, not just those acutely depressed by inadequate employment, could gain psychological benefit from work.

Symptoms, Caseness, and Selection. In the analysis of dichotomous 1994 depression, adverse employment change was, as in the analysis of continuous symptoms, associated with elevated levels of depression. However, after adjusting for prior depression and other confounding variables, the effect for inadequate employment reached statistical significance, but that for unemployment did not. Why would job loss, the seemingly more serious stressor, fail to produce as strong an effect as that of becoming inadequately employed? One ever-present possibility is that this difference is a statistical fluke that would disappear upon replication. However, a prior study gave results consistent with the finding that the adverse effect of unemployment is clearer in its effect on depressive symptoms than on caseness (Dooley et al., 1994). That study had a superior method for identifying clinical cases of major depression, using the Epidemiologic Catchment

Area data. However, it had an inferior measure of job loss (based on receipt of unemployment compensation) and no way to operationalize inadequate employment.

One plausible explanation for the seemingly differential effect of job loss and inadequate employment involves the role of selection. Among the adequately employed in 1992, those who later lost their jobs had substantially higher levels of depression than did those who became inadequately employed. Both types of adverse employment appeared to increase depressive symptoms, even after adjustment for this selection effect. But in the categorical analysis, it is possible that the selection adjustment was greater (thus suppressing the apparent adverse employment effect more) for those with high levels of depression at time one (and a correspondingly higher likelihood of job loss) than for those with lower levels of depression. In any event, these results do not imply that a high level of depression is more likely in a group of inadequately employed than in a group of unemployed. Rather, it suggests that a high level of depression in the unemployed group is more likely to stem from a mixture of causes, including both selection and social causation.

Intervention and Research Implications

Favorable Employment Change in Context. The findings for the favorable employment change hypothesis showed that later employment status was more important than either prior status or the particular type of change. Of the four 1992 underemployed groups that were employed in 1994, only two enjoyed clearly favorable change – the unemployed to adequately employed and the inadequately employed to adequately employed. One group experienced change of an ambiguous nature – those moving from unemployment to inadequate employment. The research on adverse change described earlier suggests that inadequate employment differs little from unemployment, relative to adequate employment, for those who have been adequately employed. Apparently, for those who have been unemployed, moving into an inadequate job may seem to be a step in the right direction. In contrast to this view, an earlier study found that the transition from unemployment to a dissatisfying job did not produce mental health gains (Wanberg, 1995). One explanation for these different findings is that, unlike the earlier study, the present study measures employment adequacy in terms of objective economic characteristics rather than in terms of subjective self-assessment of job satisfaction. These two aspects of work may contribute differently to a worker's overall sense of well-being.

The fourth of the 1994 employed groups experienced no change at all – those who were inadequately employed in both 1992 and 1994. Nevertheless, this group fared better than another group with no change, those who were unemployed in both years. Why should remaining inadequately employed prove better than remaining unemployed? One explanation is that long-term unemployment may involve more adverse changes. For example, unemployment compensation is time-limited, typically restricted to about six months. Those remaining unemployed may experience the loss of this compensation as a new stressful life event. Those without unemployment insurance may have to dip into their savings in order to make ends meet. This financial drain may also be perceived as a stressful life event, as dreams of a child's education or a comfortable retirement evaporate. In contrast, workers continuing in inadequate employment do not experience these kinds of losses. To the extent that these workers were aware of the high unemployment levels of the early 1990s, they may even have experienced gratitude for avoiding the unemployment that was occurring to others in their communities.

In sum, the effect of inadequate employment on depression may depend on respondents' comparison levels. Falling into inadequate employment from adequate employment is associated with rising depression that is comparable to that associated with falling into unemployment. Thus an economy that substitutes inadequate jobs for adequate ones may well produce mental health effects similar to those generated by an economy that allows jobs to disappear altogether. On the other hand, for individuals who have become unemployed or inadequately employed, any employment, even economically inadequate work, will prove beneficial compared to unemployment. Thus, for an economy climbing out of a recession, the provision of any employment should prove helpful to the overall level of depression.

Clarifying the Causal Relationships. Based on its correlational design, this study cannot demonstrate a causal linkage between employment status change and depression. Even after controlling for spuriousness and checking at least partially for reverse causation, there still remains a reverse causation possibility – that an intervening change in depression, between 1992 and 1994, caused a still later employment change. Because the depression measure reflects symptoms of the past week, this late-developing reverse causation scenario requires some complicated assumptions.

If the depression change occurred after 1992 but months before the job change, it must have then held stable until the week prior to the 1994 interview. Alternatively, if the depression change only appeared shortly before the 1994 interview, then the employment change must also have appeared very late in the two-year period, even nearer the 1994 interview. In order to check this rival explanation, we would need data such as weekly diaries that track change in employment and mood more precisely. However, a few longitudinal studies of the sequential relationship between unemployment and depression onset have also reported that job loss appeared prior to increased depression (Eales, 1988; Montgomery et al., 1999).

Nevertheless, this is an area that warrants further clarification, less to establish whether depression or employment change comes first than to illuminate what is very likely a reciprocal process, in which each influences the other. The present data suggest that social causation and selection are not mutually exclusive processes. What remains to be explored are the mechanisms by which each of these processes operate, both the mediating variables that transmit their influence and the moderating variables that could help us to identify those most vulnerable to their operation.

8

Extending the Employment Continuum
Well-Being in Welfare Transitions

> Nothing is so certain as that the evils of idleness can be shaken off by hard work.
>
> Seneca, *Epistles*, 56: 9

> The most immediate route by which the ex-welfare population can find jobs is by competing with and displacing unqualified workers who are already employed, either by being in some way a more suitable employee or, more likely, by offering to work for less than the incumbent is getting. Unqualified workers are presumably excellent substitutes for one another, so only a very small wage cut would be needed. But pure displacement is just musical chairs: more players and the same number of chairs.
>
> Solow, 1998, pp. 27–28

INTRODUCTION

Welfare in the Employment Continuum

Welfare as Underemployment. Welfare may appear to be outside the domain of work and employment. In the United States, the term "welfare" has come to refer to public funds used to assist parents in the care of their young children. Usually, this has meant cash payments supplemented by other benefits such as food stamps and health coverage. In order to limit such assistance to the legitimately needy, eligibility rules have sometimes specified that the adult recipient (almost always the mother) have no source of income, such as her own job or the job of a working spouse. When such a recipient is neither working nor looking for work, she is officially counted as out of the labor force (OLF).

In practice, however, welfare recipients have significant connections to the labor market. First, income eligibility for welfare sometimes derives from economic events such as job loss, either by the mother or by her spouse. Thus transitions into welfare often correspond to the ebbing of employment opportunities in the surrounding job market. Others have observed that certain OLF categories may be functionally similar to unemployment (Goldsmith et al., 1995). When job opportunities decline, some people may be able to choose the form of their joblessness, electing to take a socially approved OLF status such as full-time student or homemaker, while those with fewer options may be forced to accept the less desirable status of being unemployed or on welfare.

Second, policies aimed at moving people from welfare to work will, if successful, have implications for those already in the labor force. As indicated in one of the quotations that opened this chapter, an influx of job seekers from the welfare rolls might very well increase the incidence of adverse employment changes for those now employed, with the initial impact being felt by the inadequately employed (Solow, 1998).

Third, whether encouraged or forbidden by the prevailing eligibility rules, current welfare recipients frequently engage in paid employment. Welfare stipends often fail to cover all of a family's living expenses, and recipients do what they must to make up the difference. Such jobs typically provide only part-time work at low wages and generally qualify as inadequate employment as defined here. Nevertheless, such jobs may provide enough income to motivate the welfare recipient to run the risk of losing eligibility – that is, to take the chance of being found out and disqualified (Edin & Lein, 1997). Thus, following the paradigm of the preceding chapters, we locate welfare on the employment continuum. Although welfare may not always involve working or seeking work, it resembles an employment status at the boundary between unemployment and inadequate employment and interacts similarly with the prevailing employment climate.

Welfare Transitions as Employment Status Changes. If welfare can be located on the employment continuum, it follows that transitions between welfare and other employment statuses can be analyzed in the same way that other, more frequently studied transitions, such as job loss, are analyzed. Thus, we place this approach to welfare research in the stressful life event tradition, focusing not on the static qualities of welfare recipients (e.g., low socioeconomic status) but rather on the predictors and sequelae of their changing experiences (Stueve et al., 1998).

Organizing employment statuses on an ordered continuum implies that the statuses vary in their desirability, ranging from high-status and high-pay employment to unemployment. Thus transitions involving welfare can represent either favorable or unfavorable life events. In turn, events with different valences could be expected to produce either beneficial or harmful effects on the well-being of the people involved. This chapter explores the relationship of welfare transitions to two indicators of psychosocial functioning – depression and alcohol abuse.

Selection, Social Causation, and the Welfare Reform of 1996

Causal Direction between Welfare and Well-Being. Like the links between underemployment and health discussed in prior chapters, the connection between welfare transitions and psychological changes can be located in the larger context of the social causation–selection debate. Researchers recognized early that poverty is associated with elevated levels of psychiatric disorder (Faris & Dunham, 1939). By extrapolation, we expect behavioral problems to be more prevalent in impoverished welfare recipients than in the general population. And this association could be explained by two different mechanisms that have long competed for primacy (Dohrenwend & Dohrenwend, 1969). In the social causation view, the stress of poverty or other aspects of being on welfare might lead to disorder. In the selection view, preexisting disorder handicaps individuals in their occupational functioning, leading to their descent into poverty and welfare.

In research on poverty and health, efforts to determine the more important mechanism, social causation or selection, have often been hindered by reliance on cross-sectional data. A correlation between being poor and being unhealthy at any point in time not only does not tell us which factor caused the other, it also leaves open to question of whether the association is causal or spurious. Some prior factor, such as parents' education, may account for both the health problems and the poverty of the respondent at a later time. Even if such potential confounding variables can be statistically controlled, cross-sectional research still leaves unclear the causal direction of the remaining association. To overcome this problem, different research approaches have been used.

One cross-sectional method exploits ethnicity data in order to provide differential tests of the competing hypotheses (e.g., Dohrenwend et al., 1992). More often, researchers rely on longitudinal methods to control for prior economic or health status and to assess change over time. Both multigenerational prospective data (e.g., Johnson et al., 1999; Miech et al., 1999; Timms, 1996) and shorter-term panel data have been used to contrast these causal mechanisms (Moos et al., 1998; Weich & Lewis, 1998). Taken as a whole, this literature suggests that both processes occur but that each operates differently depending on the type of disorder. On balance, it appears that selection and social causation work together in a sequential reciprocal process (Timms, 1996). Although this literature on selection versus social causation has illuminated the connection between poverty and health, it includes few studies that specifically address welfare transitions in relation to health.

TANF and the Heightened Interest in Selection. In 1996, the United States modified its welfare system. The Personal Responsibility and Work Opportunity Reconciliation Act changed the name of the welfare program from Aid to Families with Dependent Children (AFDC) to Temporary Assistance to Needy Families (TANF). This new federal law required the states to make major changes in welfare programs, while allowing them flexibility in crafting state-specific rules. The most important change involved time limits on federal support. Unlike AFDC grants, federal funds for TANF assistance have a five-year cumulative lifetime limit regardless of the recipient's employment status and are cut off after two years unless the recipient engages in approved work or training. Any extension of these time limits must be funded from state rather than federal sources.

When welfare recipients faced no time limits under the earlier AFDC rules, the inability to leave welfare because of disabling emotional or substance abuse problems had little administrative consequence. However, the TANF rules have raised concerns about potential behavioral barriers to leaving welfare that might cause recipients to exceed the new time limits. Under TANF, states may exempt, without federal penalty, up to 20% of their TANF caseloads from the time limits. But research has raised fears that the rates of substance abuse or other behavioral disability among the welfare population may exceed this 20% level (Green et al., 2000; Weisner & Schmidt, 1993). As a result, the role of such health factors as alcohol abuse and depression in selecting people into or keeping people on welfare became much more salient after 1996.

In addition to the research on selection into poverty already noted, there have been some studies of selection into underemployment, particularly job loss, as described in Chapter 4. For example, several studies have found selection into unemployment by depression (Hamilton et al., 1993; Hammarström & Janlert, 1997; Mastekaasa, 1996). Because alcohol misuse can harm productivity through absenteeism, job-site accidents, and inefficiency (Gill, 1994), we are not surprised to find that alcohol abuse also predicts adverse employment change (Dooley et al., 1992). Together, such findings provide ample reason to suspect that selection also operates in the welfare domain.

Underemployment Research and the Plausibility of Social Causation. The 1996 reform has stimulated much less attention to the social causation mechanism involved in welfare transitions. Historically, people who go onto welfare have generated more suspicion than sympathy. The political hostility toward welfare may derive in part from the assumption that some recipients prefer welfare to work. In response to this perception, one argument for welfare reform anticipates moral benefits from restoring individuals to economic self-sufficiency – for example, increased self-respect, responsibility, and ambition. Such views would predict no adverse health effects, such as depression and alcohol abuse, from either entering or exiting welfare. Moreover, any potential adverse effects, such as embarrassment at entering welfare, would not be seen as health problems.

Rather, they could be welcomed as health-promoting insofar as they motivated appropriate reactions, such as working harder to avoid or to exit welfare.

By contrast, research from other domains points strongly to social causation effects of stressors that are akin to entering welfare, such as unemployment and impoverishment. For example, studies have linked job loss to both increased alcohol abuse (Dooley et al., 1992) and depression (Dooley et al., 1994). In previous chapters we have provided further evidence consistent with the social causation of adverse changes in self-esteem, alcohol misuse, and depression by various forms of underemployment (Chapters 5, 6, and 7). From a public health perspective that seeks to identify and ameliorate the causes of illness, it is essential to explore potential social causation pathways between welfare transitions and health outcomes.

Prior Research on Health and Welfare. Surprisingly little research has examined the relationship between welfare and health. The 1996 TANF reform did raise interest in health barriers to leaving welfare, but it did little to stimulate concern about selection into welfare by health problems or about the social causation consequences of either entering or exiting welfare. Because research on this relationship has often relied on cross-sectional data, findings of an association can rarely be interpreted in causal terms. Nevertheless, the literature does generally point to a link between being on welfare and an elevated risk of having emotional or substance abuse problems.

Studies of the mental health of welfare recipients have typically focused on depression (Olson & Pavetti, 1996). One selection study found that welfare recipients with elevated depression had lower postwelfare earnings (Neenan & Orthner, 1996). This result parallels a study of a nonwelfare unemployed sample in which higher depression predicted subsequent unsatisfactory rather than satisfactory reemployment (Leana & Feldman, 1995). Social causation theory suggests that welfare entry may resemble job loss in its emotional impact. For example, one study linked welfare entry to loss of self-esteem, perhaps due to the stigma of welfare (Nichols-Casebolt, 1986). It follows that leaving welfare for employment could elevate mood, but this may depend on the quality of the new job. School-leaver research has shown that transitions into the workforce can have either good or bad mental health consequences depending on how satisfactory the new job is (Winefield et al., 1993).

More welfare research has been done on substance abuse than on other mental health variables, but the results have been mixed. For example, one study found that the prevalence of alcohol and illicit drug indicators among persons on public assistance was no different from that among the general population (Grant & Dawson, 1996). However, other studies have found higher rates of alcohol abuse among welfare recipients than among the general population (Olson & Pavetti, 1996). For instance, one large-scale study found that women on AFDC were twice as likely to abuse alcohol or illicit drugs as women not receiving AFDC (National Center on Addiction and Substance Abuse, 1994). This echoed another study that also found the odds of problem drinking in a welfare sample to be double the odds among the general population (Weisner & Schmidt, 1993). A third study of female AFDC recipients estimated the prevalence of alcohol abuse at 11.4%, with another 14.7% possibly alcoholic, both higher than the rates for women in the general population (Sisco & Pearson, 1994). Although these studies tend to find an association between welfare and mental health, they were generally not designed to specify the causal direction of this association.

Framework of Hypotheses: Four Possible Links between Health and Welfare

The foregoing analysis implies that any association between welfare status (being on welfare versus not being on welfare) and risk of mental health problems could result from a variety of causal processes. Of course, no association between mental health status and welfare status may remain after controlling for confounding variables. Consequently, any test of a causal connection must adjust for spuriousness.

One causal process involves selection, and this process could take either of two forms. Starting with a sample of people not on welfare, those with existing symptoms and in employment might have greater difficulty performing their jobs and thus be at higher risk of falling into welfare (as one economic safety net). Alternatively, starting with a sample of people already on welfare, those with more symptoms might have more difficulty in becoming or appearing employable and thus might tend to remain on welfare longer than welfare recipients with fewer mental health problems. Either of these two selection mechanisms could account for a greater prevalence of mental symptoms among those on welfare than among those in the general population.

The other major causal process involves social causation and sees welfare status not as a consequence of preexisting symptoms but rather as a cause of new or increased symptoms. Social causation could also take two forms. Among people not on welfare, and controlling for their prior symptoms, those who experience the transition into welfare may suffer more stressful life changes that in turn lead to elevated symptoms. Alternatively, among those already on welfare, the experience of leaving welfare may produce changes in symptom levels (although the direction of such changes is less clear). One hoped-for outcome of the 1996 reform was that people who had become adapted to and dependent on welfare would enjoy a positive change in their sense of worth, self-control, and optimism as a result of shifting into paid employment. By this reasoning, people exiting

TABLE 8.1. *Four possible causal mechanisms*

	Sample of All Women Not on Welfare at Time One	Sample of All Women on Welfare at Time One
Selection hypothesis	Question 1: Does depression or alcohol abuse at time one predict selection into welfare at time two?	Question 2: Does depression or alcohol abuse at time one predict selection out of welfare at time two?
Social causation hypothesis	Question 3: Controlling for time-one depression or alcohol abuse, does the transition into welfare correlate with time-two depression or alcohol abuse?	Question 4: Controlling for time-one depression or alcohol abuse, does the transition out of welfare correlate with time-two depression or alcohol abuse?

welfare for good jobs could be expected to gain in self-respect, independence, self-discipline, and confidence. On the other hand, people who shift from welfare into insecure, poorly paid, or stressful types of employment might perceive their situation as being no better than before, and possibly even worse. Either way, leaving welfare might produce noticeable changes in emotions or behavior.

In sum, if a nonspurious association exists between welfare status and mental health problems, it might result from any of four possible causal processes. Table 8.1 summarizes these possibilities in the form of questions in the four cells defined by crossing two factors. One dimension consists of the causal mechanism – selection or social causation. The other refers to the nature of the transition – whether into welfare (based on people not initially on welfare) or out of welfare (based on people who are initially on welfare).

METHODS

Samples

The NLSY includes measures of both depression and alcohol abuse for one pair of years: 1992 and 1994 (see Chapter 3 for more details on the NLSY). The data from these years should reflect the experience of respondents with transitions into and out of AFDC during the time period just before the 1996 welfare reform. Although the NLSY did not measure depression in other years, it did include alcohol items in three other pairs of years: 1982/84, 1984/85, and 1988/89. This chapter will focus on depression and alcohol abuse measured in the 1992/94 pair of years, and then briefly summarize the findings for alcohol abuse in these three prior pairs of years as replications of the 1992/94 alcohol findings.

Because very few AFDC recipients were male, either in the NLSY or in the national population, this study considers only female respondents. In 1992, the NLSY had 3,678 women with responses on the depression, alcohol, employment, and welfare items for the years 1992 and 1994. Because of changes to the number of individuals interviewed (part of the supplemental sample was not interviewed after 1990; see Chapter 3 for details) and attrition over the course of the NLSY, sample sizes were even larger (exceeding 4,000) in the years prior to 1992. Of the 3,678 women available for analyses in 1992, 347 received income from AFDC during the month of the 1992 interview and were classified as on welfare. The remaining 3,331 did not receive income from AFDC during the month of the interview and were classified as not on welfare. These two samples are compared in Figures 8.1 through 8.6.

The demographic profiles of the two samples (women on welfare and women not on welfare) differed in many important aspects. More than one-third of the women who were on welfare had not completed high school, versus only 10.2% of the women who were not on welfare. A majority of the welfare sample was African American (54.6%), as compared to about one-fourth of the sample not on welfare. Approximately one-half (47.6%) of the sample on welfare had never married and 40% were divorced, separated, or widowed, versus 21.7% and 17.9%, respectively, of the sample not on welfare. All members of the welfare sample had children in their household; about one-third (31.5%) of the sample not on welfare did not

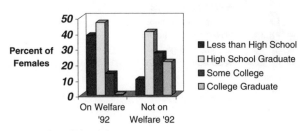

FIGURE 8.1. Education.

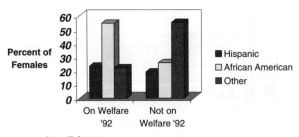

FIGURE 8.2. Ethnicity.

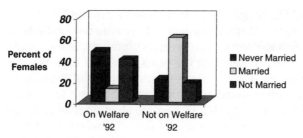

FIGURE 8.3. Marital status.

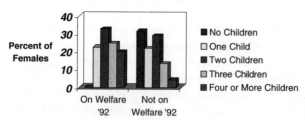

FIGURE 8.4. Number of children in household.

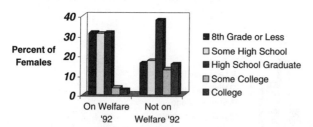

FIGURE 8.5. Parental education.

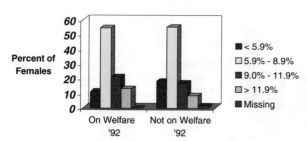

FIGURE 8.6. Unemployment rate.

have children in the household. Twenty percent of the sample on welfare had four or more children in the household, versus only 4.3% of the sample not on welfare. Approximately two-thirds of the welfare sample (62.3%) had a parent (the more highly educated parent) who had not completed high school, versus about one-third of the sample (33.6%) not on welfare. The sample on welfare also lived in areas with less favorable economic conditions, as measured by the unemployment rate, when compared to the sample not on welfare. About one-third of the welfare sample lived in areas with more than 9.0% unemployment, versus about one-fourth of the sample not on welfare.

Variables

Alcohol. An earlier chapter (Chapter 6) provides more details on the nature of the NLSY alcohol measures along with findings for their relationship to adverse employment change in the general sample. The alcohol variable definitions used here differ somewhat from those used earlier, for two reasons. One is that different alcohol items were included on different survey waves. The second is that women generally report less drinking and fewer alcoholic symptoms than males, and the present definitions were tailored to an all-female sample (for more details, see Dooley & Prause, 2002).

The 1992 NLSY did not ask for respondents' symptoms of alcohol abuse, but it did measure the number of drinks per drinking day during the thirty days preceding the interview. This measure was the best available proxy for binge drinking and proved to be more highly correlated with later alcohol abuse symptoms than the only other available measure – number of days in the past month that the respondent reported drinking alcohol. The consumption variable is coded here as follows: 1 = nondrinker over the past thirty days; 2 = two or fewer drinks per drinking day; 3 = three or more drinks per drinking day.

In 1994, respondents who drank gave information on both symptoms over the past year and binge drinking over the past month. The NLSY defined a binge as six or more drinks on a single occasion. The present binge variable is defined as follows: 1 = nondrinker over the past thirty days; 2 = no episode of binge drinking during the past thirty days; 3 = binge drinking on one or more occasions during the past thirty days.

The 1994 NLSY included twenty-five possible symptoms of alcohol abuse that could have been experienced over the past year. Many of these items parallel the DSM-IV diagnostic criteria for alcohol abuse or dependence (American Psychiatric Association, 1994). In order to maximize comparison across years of the NLSY in which different sets of alcohol symptoms were used, we did not use these items to create DSM-IV diagnostic categories. Rather, we used a simple count of the number of reported symptoms to categorize respondents as follows: (1) nondrinker over the past thirty days (not asked about past-year symptoms); (2) current drinker with low (three or fewer) symptoms; (3) current drinker with high (four or more) symptoms. We chose the cut-point of four or more symptoms because that defined approximately the top 10% of the symptom distribution for female respondents in 1994. Perhaps because of the different recall time periods (a month for consumption, a year for symptoms), the 1994 measures of binge drinking and symptoms had only moderate agreement (kappa = .37).

Depression. The previous chapter provides more details on the nature of the Center for Epidemiologic Studies Depression scale (CES-D), along with findings for its relationship to adverse employment change in the general sample. The original twenty-item scale was administered in 1992, and an abbreviated seven-item version was collected in 1994. Although not designed to assign patients to official diagnostic categories, the original CES-D has shown the ability to detect major depressive disorder using the conventional cut-point of 16 or higher (on a scale ranging from 0 to 60). Although the short version has no agreed-upon cut-point for identifying clinical-level depression, it correlates well with the full twenty-item scale.

Employment and Welfare Status. In addition to the various adequate and inadequate types of employment defined in earlier chapters (see especially Chapter 3), the respondents were all evaluated for AFDC status. Women who received AFDC income during the month of the interview were considered to be on welfare. Women without AFDC income during the month of the interview were classified as not on welfare. A woman who was not on welfare in 1992 but on welfare in 1994 was considered to have entered welfare. A woman who was on welfare in 1992 but not in 1994 was considered to have exited welfare. Each respondent was categorized at each of three interviews (1992, 1993, and 1994) into one of the following categories: received AFDC income (whether also employed or not), adequately employed (no AFDC), inadequately employed (involuntary part-time or poverty-wage employment but no AFDC), unemployed (including discouraged workers but no AFDC), or out of the labor force (OLF but no AFDC).

Control Variables. Any variable that might cause both later welfare status and health status might contribute to a spurious association between those variables. For example, low socioeconomic status might increase the respondent's risk both of falling into welfare and of having health problems. For this reason, we controlled for such variables as prior family poverty and respondent's educational level. Moreover, such variables might contribute as moderators in such a way that the causal connection between health and welfare might be stronger for one type of person than for another – for example, married people versus unmarried people. Also, such variables would function as mediators if some of the causal influence between welfare transitions and health changes were transmitted by change in another variable – for example, change in marital status. Thus numerous potential confounding, moderating, and mediating variables were routinely checked in the analyses.

Analyses

Cross-Sectional Analyses. Before exploring possible longitudinal causal linkages between mental health status and welfare transitions, we checked to see whether there were any cross-sectional connections between these variables. Chi-square and single-factor ANOVA methods were used to describe these associations in 1992.

Selection. The longitudinal analyses of the two selection hypotheses used measures of depression and alcohol consumption in 1992 to predict change in employment and welfare status one year later in 1993. Although depression and alcohol abuse measures were available only in certain years (for example, 1992 and 1994), employment status items were asked in every survey wave. Although for symmetry we could have used 1992 depression and alcohol abuse to predict 1994 employment and welfare changes, we judged that the shorter lag would provide a more sensitive test of possible selection effects. By 1994, any adverse selection effects of 1992 depression or alcohol consumption would have had another year in which to be diluted by passing events or canceled by intervening changes in mood or alcohol use.

The 1993 outcome variable in the selection analyses consists of the several different categories of employment or welfare status to which the respondent might move. In this situation, it is appropriate to employ polytomous logistic regression. The effects of each of the predictor variables can then be expressed as odds ratios (OR). For example, the chances of transition from AFDC relative to continuing on AFDC can be estimated in the form of a ratio of the odds for two groups of respondents – for example, the odds for the high-depression respondents divided by the odds for the low-depression respondents.

Social Causation. The analyses of the two social causation hypotheses used 1994 measures of depression or alcohol abuse as the outcomes predicted by the change in welfare status between 1992 and 1994. Although it would have been possible to use employment or welfare status change between 1992 and 1993, this could have obscured the more potent effects of the most recent employment status (i.e., status in 1994).

The 1994 alcohol abuse variables consist of categories, for which it is appropriate to use polytomous logistic regression. Because of the continuous nature of the 1994 depression variable, it is appropriate to use ordinary least squares regression. In both cases, 1992 measures of these variables were statistically controlled in the analyses so as to remove the selection component from the association.

RESULTS

Cross-Sectional Association

The cross-sectional analyses of the 1992 data confirmed earlier reports of an association between welfare status and mental health indicators. Women who were receiving AFDC reported substantially higher levels of depression than women who were employed or out of the labor force. Over two-fifths (43.8%) of women on welfare ($n = 347$) met the conventional CES-D criterion (scores $\geq$ 16) for elevated depression, and this level matched that of women who were unemployed (39.5%, $n = 195$). By comparison, the proportion of women meeting this depression criterion was only 20.3% for those in adequate employment ($n = 2,060$) and 24.6% for those out of the labor force ($n = 639$). Falling between the adequately employed and the unemployed women, 26.3% of the inadequately employed women ($n = 437$) had elevated levels of depression in 1992. This pattern of differential depression across AFDC and employment groups was highly significant ($p < .001$). And the mean level of CES-D in the welfare group ($M = 15.9$, almost at the cut-point for serious depression) suggests a surprisingly high level of distress for many if not most of these women.

The results for alcohol consumption appeared to be more complex. As might be expected, the AFDC and unemployed women reported the highest rates of consuming three or more drinks per drinking day (26.7% and 28.2%, respectively). However, the AFDC and OLF groups reported the highest rates of no drinking during the past thirty days (49.6% and 58.1%, respectively). Although generally more depressed than other women, the AFDC respondents evidenced two opposite tendencies in alcohol consumption – either abstaining completely or high levels of consumption. This bimodal drinking pattern suggests that care must be taken in assessing alcohol misuse in this population. If average drinks per drinking day were used as the indicator, the abstaining and heavy drinkers would tend to cancel out, leaving the false impression that AFDC women showed the same drinking pattern as the general population. Whether such cross-sectional associations reflect causal connections depends on the results of the multivariate, longitudinal analyses to be described in the following sections.

Longitudinal Relationships for Depression and Alcohol Misuse

Selection into Welfare: 1992–93. In 1992, there were 3,331 women in the NLSY sample who were not on welfare, and 46 of these women had entered welfare by 1993. The first selection question is whether elevated levels of depression or alcohol consumption in 1992 predicted transition into welfare a year later. Just as there was a cross-sectional association between welfare status and both depression and alcohol consumption in 1992, so also there were significant bivariate associations for each of these latter two variables in 1992 with 1993 employment status. Ignoring possible confounding for the moment, women who drank three or more drinks per drinking day in 1992 were about twice as likely to be on welfare relative to being adequately employed in 1993 as women who drank only one or two drinks per drinking day (borderline significance, $p < .06$). Women with CESD scores of 16 or more in 1992 were about three times as likely to be on welfare in 1993 as women with lower depression scores ($p < .05$).

But do these associations indicate selection into welfare? No, these apparent links disappear when likely confounding variables are controlled. After adjusting for ethnicity, years of education, and family's prior poverty status, the 1992 alcohol to 1993 welfare association disappeared. After adjusting for ethnicity, marital status, and family poverty status, the 1992 depression to 1993 welfare association also disappeared. That is, these other variables appear to explain the increased risk of entering welfare and, coincidentally, help to cause or are correlated with the alcohol and depression of these women.

Going further, we considered the possibility that alcohol consumption or depression would predict welfare entry in interaction with some other variable, even after controlling for confounding factors. None of the interactions involving 1992 alcohol consumption predicted 1993 welfare entry. However, there was one significant interaction between depression and marital status in 1992. Among women with lower levels of depression, having a spouse present greatly reduced the odds of entering welfare within a year (OR = .19), but for those with higher levels of depression, having a spouse present did not reduce the risk of entering welfare (OR = 1.26).

The absence of selection into welfare by alcohol consumption (either alone or in combination with any other variable) might be attributed to either of two aspects of this test. One is the reliance on a single, potentially unreliable item measuring 1992 consumption, and the other is the use of only a one-year follow-up. To double-check the negative finding for alcohol, we repeated the selection analysis using a different alcohol measure and a longer follow-up period. We had to go back to the 1989 survey to find an extensive set of alcohol abuse symptom items that permitted assigning respondents to DSM-IV-type diagnostic categories of abuse and dependence. We then used these categories to predict not one-year welfare entry, but instead cumulative months of AFDC for the five years from 1989 to 1994. These follow-up analyses were also negative. In a later section, we will check this selection hypothesis again in the alcohol abuse and welfare status analyses for the years 1982/84, 1984/85, and 1988/89.

Selection out of Welfare: 1992–93. In 1992, there were 347 women on welfare, and 48 of them were no longer receiving AFDC payments by the 1993 interview. Using those who remained on welfare as the reference group, the second selection question asks whether 1992 depression or alcohol consumption predicted leaving welfare by 1993. Neither of these predictors alone, nor any interaction between them and other variables, predicted welfare exits. The same difficulty with using the single 1992 alcohol consumption item to predict one-year change that was earlier noted for testing selection into welfare might also account for some of these negative findings. Following the same procedure, we repeated the test using 1989 alcohol symptoms to predict cumulative months on AFDC between 1989 and 1994, starting with women on welfare in 1989. As before, the results remained negative.

Because the starting sample of women on welfare was so small in 1992, the tests of transitions into various employment categories were limited by small respondent counts in the various analytic cells. This problem would be compounded in any attempt to test interactions involving subgroups (e.g., employed or not employed in 1992) of these categories (e.g., becoming employed or not employed by 1993). In such cases, the critical cells sometimes had just two or three respondents, making a sensitive test (high statistical power) impossible and increasing the risk of missing a real selection effect. Nevertheless, we tested whether any variables overcame this sample size limitation and predicted the likelihood of exiting welfare. The only significant predictor of exiting AFDC by 1993 was 1992 employment. Welfare recipients who held jobs in addition to receiving AFDC payments in 1992 were over ten times more likely than those without jobs to leave welfare and be employed in 1993 (relative to continuing on AFDC). Surprisingly, no other factor contributed to this prediction, including the local unemployment rate, age, years of education, history of being on AFDC prior to 1992, and self-esteem.

Social Causation by Entry into Welfare. Of the 3,331 women not on welfare in 1992, 2.6% were receiving AFDC support as of the 1994 interview. The first social causation question asks whether, controlling for prior depression and alcohol misuse, entry into welfare was associated with elevated levels of depression or alcohol abuse. Table 8.2 shows two models for various significant predictors of 1994 depression. Model 1 shows the main

TABLE 8.2. *Social causation by entry into welfare: predictors of 1994 depression* $(n = 3,175)^a$

	Model 1			Model 2		
	b	se(b)	Beta	b	se(b)	Beta
CES-Depression 1992	.19*	.01	.41	.19*	.01	.41
Years of education 1992	−.11*	.03	−.06	−.11*	.03	−.06
Marital status 1992 (1 = spouse present; 0 = no spouse present)	.02	.15	.002	.02	.15	.002
Change in marital status 1992–94 (1 = lost spouse; 0 = no change/gain spouse)	1.66*	.32	.09	1.68*	.32	.09
Ever on AFDC prior to 1992 (1 = yes; 0 = no)	.60*	.19	.05	.60*	.19	.05
Self-esteem 1987	−.09*	.02	−.08	−.09*	.02	−.08
Unemployment rate 1992^b						
Missing	1.56*	.58	.04	1.55*	.58	.04
≥9.0%	−.07	.16	−.01	−.08	.16	−.01
Employment status 1992 (1 = not employed; 0 = employed)	−.32	.19	−.03	−.39	.32	−.04
Employment status 1994^c						
AFDC	1.47*	.44	.06	.34	.61	.01
Unemployment	.93*	.30	.05	.72	.39	.04
Inadequate employment	.21	.22	.02	.32	.25	.03
Out of labor force	.70*	.21	.06	.81	.30	.07
Emp. status 1994 × emp. status 1992						
AFDC × emp. status 1992				2.29*	.89	.06
Unemployment × emp. status 1992				.54	.65	.02
Inadequate emp. × emp. status 1992				−.35	.53	−.02
OLF × emp. status 1992				−.10	.47	−.01
Intercept	6.35	.69		6.38	.69	
R^2_{adj}		.238			.240	
F (df)	77.1(13, 3161), $p < .001$			59.6(17, 3157), $p < .001$		

* $p < .05$.
^{a} Women not receiving AFDC during the month of the 1992 interview.
^{b} Relative to < 9.0%.
^{c} Relative to adequately employed in 1994.
Source: Adapted from Dooley and Prause (2002, Table 4).

effect terms, and Model 2 adds the interactions between 1994 employment status and 1992 employment status ($n = 3{,}175$ with complete data on all variables in these models).

Model 1 shows that transitions into welfare were significantly associated with increased depression in 1994 after controlling for 1992 depression and a host of other predictors, including education, prior experience on AFDC, and self-esteem. The experience of another stressful event – losing a spouse – was also significantly associated with increased depression, and this term might be construed as a mediating variable. That is, falling into welfare might cause marital change or other undesirable life events and thus indirectly influence depression. When losing a spouse is excluded from the analysis, AFDC entry has a somewhat higher regression coefficient (1.73 as opposed to 1.47 as in Model 1). However, even after it is controlled, the effect of AFDC entry remains significant, and its standardized coefficient remains the same (beta = .06, with or without change in marital status). Moreover, the magnitude of this AFDC-entry effect is comparable to that of other known stressors, such as being unemployed (beta = .05) and losing a spouse (beta = .09).

However, the main effects of Model 1 can be interpreted only in the context of the interactions found in Model 2. The impact of entering AFDC in 1994 depends on the individual's employment status in 1992. This significant interaction can be interpreted as follows. For those employed in 1992, there was little difference in depression between women who entered AFDC and those who were adequately employed in 1994. But for those not employed in 1992, entering AFDC was associated with elevated levels of depression compared to being adequately employed in 1994.

The effect of entering welfare was tested on two different 1994 alcohol measures – binge drinking over the past month and alcohol symptoms over the past year, both using 1992 alcohol consumption as a control for prior drinking behavior. Transition into welfare, relative to adequate employment in 1994, appeared to be associated with higher odds of binge drinking in 1994, controlling for 1992 alcohol use (OR = 2.06, $p < .05$). However, adding further controls for such variables as marital status, education, and ethnicity dropped this association below the level of significance. Nor did any interaction with welfare entry predict an increased risk of binge drinking. By contrast, years of education, being married with a spouse present, and higher 1992 depression did predict a higher risk of binge drinking by 1994.

Welfare entry also appeared to be associated with 1994 alcohol abuse symptoms (OR = 2.05, $p < .05$), but this bivariate relationship disappeared with control for 1992 alcohol consumption. The interaction between welfare entry and family poverty status did reach significance after adjustment for all of the control variables. For women living below the federal poverty level in 1992, entering welfare was associated with greatly increased odds of alcohol symptoms in 1994 (OR $=$ 9.23), while for those above the poverty level, welfare entry had little effect on alcohol symptoms (OR $=$ 1.44).

Social Causation by Exit from Welfare. Of the 347 women on welfare in 1992, 72.9% were still on welfare in 1994, and 13.3% were employed (7.5% adequately and 5.8% inadequately), with the remainder either unemployed (5.2%) or out of the labor force (8.6%). The second social causation question asks how leaving welfare compares to remaining on welfare. Exiting welfare by 1994, either for employment or for unemployment, was unrelated to depression in 1994 after controlling for 1992 depression. Nor were there any significant interactions between any employment transition and any of the other control variables.

By contrast, there appeared to be a significant beneficial effect of leaving welfare for employment with respect to symptoms of alcohol abuse. Compared to women remaining on welfare and not looking for work in 1994, women who were employed had decreased odds of having elevated symptoms (four or more symptoms) relative to having few symptoms (three or fewer symptoms; OR $=$ .16, $p <$ .05). Interestingly, their odds of being nondrinkers were also decreased relative to the low-symptom group (OR $=$ .34, $p <$ .05). No other group, including those who left welfare and were without work, showed a significantly increased or decreased risk of having high alcohol symptoms. There were no significant welfare exit effects for 1994 binge drinking after controlling for 1992 alcohol consumption. Nor did any interaction between any of the employment transitions and the other control variables reach significance for either binge drinking or alcohol symptoms.

Alcohol Abuse and Welfare Transitions over Time

Three Replications. The extended nature of the NLSY makes it possible to track welfare transitions over a series of different pairs of years. Unfortunately, the NLSY measured repeatedly only one well-being indicator – alcohol abuse. As described in Chapter 6, in some years the NLSY had no alcohol items, and varying items appeared in the survey in different years. Making allowances for these varying or missing measures, we were able to construct parallel tests of the two selection and two social causation hypotheses for three additional pairs of years.

Besides the already reported findings for 1992/94, these three pairs of years include 1982/84, 1984/85, and 1988/89. For the first year of each pair of years, we identified the women who were either receiving AFDC payments (on welfare) or not receiving AFDC payments (not on welfare). Table 8.3 summarizes the sample sizes for each of these groups for each of the pairs of years for the respondents reporting complete data for the

TABLE 8.3. *Sample sizes for welfare transition and alcohol abuse analyses*

	On AFDC Time One	Off AFDC Time One
1982–84	318 (395)	4,550 (5,491)
1984–85	404 (449)	4,406 (4,915)
1988–89	377 (434)	4,019 (4,392)

Note: Sample sizes prior to excluding cases with missing data are in parentheses.

studied variables (sample sizes without excluding cases with missing data in parentheses).

Interpretive Issues. If additional analyses were to prove similar to the 1992–94 results just reported, they might be interpreted as confirming replications. But a different pattern of findings would raise an interpretive choice. On the one hand, a complete absence of any significant findings might cast doubt on the few significant findings from the 1992–94 analyses, implying Type I error (results appearing statistically significant only because of sampling error).

On the other hand, if a number of statistically significant results appeared for different hypotheses, it might suggest some developmental process. That is, the welfare entry social causation effect observed in 1992–94 might hold only for women in their late twenties or early thirties, and a different selection or social causation mechanism might operate for women in their late teens or early twenties. As seen in Chapter 6, the impact of adverse employment change on alcohol abuse appeared to change over time in the full sample. Such potential developmental changes might also occur for women in relationship to welfare transitions, implying that developmental stage moderates the selection or social causation processes.

Results. The same four hypotheses tested in 1992/94 for binge drinking over the past thirty days and alcohol abuse symptoms reported over the past year were tested in each of the three earlier pairs of years. As before, the hypotheses were first tested adjusting for the primary control variable – either time-one alcohol abuse for the social causation questions, or time-one employment status for the selection hypothesis. Then the analytic models were adjusted for all of the other relevant control variables. Table 8.4 summarizes the results for all four pairs of years.

These analyses provide no support in any of the four test periods for either of the two selection hypotheses, after adjusting for appropriate control variables. By contrast, there were several findings in support of the social causation hypotheses. The most frequently replicated finding was

TABLE 8.4. *Summary of findings for pairs of years with significant main or interaction effects (1982/84, 1984/85, 1988/89, and 1992/94)*

		Women Not on AFDC at Time One	Women on AFDC at Time One
Selection: Time-one alcohol abuse predicts transition to or from AFDC at time two	*Binge* Time-one employment controlled	1988/89	1982/84
	All other controls	None	None
	Symptoms Time-one employment controlled	1988/89	None
	All other controls	None	None
Social Causation: Transition to or from AFDC predicts time-two alcohol abuse	*Binge* Time-one alcohol controlled	1982/84, 1988/89, 1992/94	1982/84, 1988/89
	All other controls	None	1982/84, 1988/89
	Symptoms Time-one alcohol controlled	1982/84	1992/94
	All other controls	1982/84, 1988/89,[a] 1992/94[b]	1992/94

[a] The main effect for transition to AFDC in 1989 was not significantly associated with increased alcohol symptoms in 1989. However, there was a significant interaction between transition to AFDC and time-one (1988) alcohol symptoms, suggesting that among women with no alcohol symptoms in 1988, transition to AFDC (relative to adequate employment) was associated with increased odds of alcohol symptoms in 1989 (OR = 4.3). By contrast, among women with symptoms of alcohol abuse in 1988, transition to AFDC in 1989 was not associated with increased symptoms of alcohol abuse in 1989 (OR = 1.03).

[b] The main effect for transition to AFDC in 1994 was not significantly associated with increased alcohol symptoms in 1994 after controls, but welfare entry did interact with family poverty status in 1992 at a significant level. Among women living below the federal poverty line (corrected for family size), transition to AFDC relative to adequate employment was associated with increased odds of alcohol symptoms (relative to no symptoms) in 1994 (OR = 9.44). By contrast, among women living above the federal poverty line, there was little association between transition to AFDC and alcohol symptoms (OR = 1.44).

Note: In 1992, number of drinks per drinking day was used as a proxy for binge drinking and alcohol symptoms, which were not measured that year.

of an increase in symptoms of alcohol abuse associated with entry into welfare. This appeared in three of the four pairs of years (although only in the form of interactions in two of those years). During the 1988–89 period, welfare entry raised the risk of symptoms primarily for women low on initial symptoms. During the 1992–94 period, welfare entry raised the risk of symptoms primarily for women initially living below the poverty line. There was also some evidence for a social causation effect for welfare exit, especially a reduction in binge drinking during the 1982–84 and 1988–89 periods. The 1992–94 association of a reduction in alcohol symptoms with welfare exit was not found in any of the other periods. One possible reason for this failure to replicate is that, unlike the 1992–94 analyses, the other periods all had stronger time-one measures of symptoms to serve as controls.

DISCUSSION

Findings and Limitations

Summary of Results. These analyses confirm the existence of a nonspurious association between being on welfare and such indicators of distress as depression and alcohol misuse. Four possible causal explanations of this association were examined. Little support emerged for the two selection hypotheses. There was no support for selection out of welfare by either depression or alcohol misuse. Nor did alcohol misuse predict selection into welfare. However, there was one significant interaction between depression and marital status that predicted selection into welfare. The combination of low depression and having a spouse present at time one was associated with a decreased risk of receiving AFDC payments one year later.

By contrast, these analyses provided more support for the social causation hypotheses. Welfare entry was associated with increased depression and, in three of the four test periods, increased alcohol symptoms. Moreover, welfare exit was associated with decreased alcohol symptoms in one test period and decreased binge consumption in two others.

Study Limitations. Although the overall sample was quite large in each of the study periods, relatively few women made welfare transitions during any one- or two-year period. Small cell counts reduce analytic power and may have contributed to the negative findings for the selection hypotheses. On the other hand, with similar small sample sizes, the social causation analyses tended to produce significant results.

A particular limitation for the 1992–94 analyses derives from the narrow age distribution of the NLSY women in those years – predominately in their early thirties. The findings for depression, both positive for social causation and negative for selection, might not generalize to other age groups. However, the collection of alcohol measures in earlier years permitted several replications for younger women, and these tended to agree with the 1992–94 alcohol findings.

As with all of the analyses reported in previous chapters, we must recall that this correlational research design remains vulnerable to the threat of unmeasured confounding variables. Moreover, even if neither depression nor alcohol abuse selects women into or out of welfare, some other unmeasured trait might do so.

Alcohol versus Depression. Although moderately correlated with each other, the present alcohol and depression measures not only reflect different constructs but also behaved differently in the 1992–94 analyses. Prevalence and incidence research suggests that women and men differ in their typical symptomatic responses to stress, with women more likely to become depressed and men more likely to misuse alcohol (Aneshensel, Rutter, & Lachenbruch, 1991). Other research has also reported evidence for social causation of depression in women and of substance abuse in men (Dohrenwend et al., 1992), although other studies have reported different patterns (Johnson et al., 1999; Miech et al., 1999).

Another possible explanation for the difference between depression and alcohol misuse in this study involves the offsetting tendencies in alcohol consumption sometimes observed in reactions to employment stressors. The stress of a welfare transition can be expected to affect depression in just one direction – adversely. But people threatened with the economic challenge of seeking work or living with reduced income may modify their drinking in two offsetting ways – coping adaptively by abstaining altogether, or coping maladaptively by increasing their drinking (Catalano et al., 1993; Lee et al., 1990; Warr, 1987). In the present analyses, high 1992 depression was associated with both elevated heavy drinking and increased abstinence in 1994. This bimodal pattern may be amplified in this sample of mothers by the presence of children. An increase in the number of children between 1992 and 1994 predicted increased abstinence rather than increased binge drinking in 1994. This may reflect a mobilization of adaptive coping by the demands of motherhood.

Policy Implications

Generalizability. The present findings describe the behavior of women in the period before passage of the 1996 welfare reform legislation and, thus, may not generalize to the new situation under the current TANF rules. However, the first occasion on which the TANF time limits began to take effect may likewise fail to generalize to future situations under different economic circumstances. Even before the 1996 reform went into effect, with its rules that could force women off TANF, the welfare rolls were already dropping, apparently in response to the economic expansion that began during the early 1990s. The unemployment rate in the United States fell from 7.5% in 1992 to 6.1% in 1994 over the period of this study, and it continued to fall to 5.4% by 1996 and 4.2% by 1999 (U.S. Department of Labor, 2000). How welfare transitions under the TANF system will affect recipients during the next major economic downturn will not be known until the country experiences high unemployment levels similar to those experienced by the NLSY sample in the early 1990s.

In addition, it must be noted that, compared to the period before 1996, the new federal guidelines permit much greater state-to-state variability in the specification of TANF rules (Gallagher et al., 1998). The question of generalizability will become more complicated in the future, as some states may choose to provide extended support to welfare recipients, using state or local funds, after the federal time limits have run out. The welfare environment in such states may resemble the pre-1996 AFDC situation as much as or more than the welfare environment envisioned under the strict application of TANF time limits. Thus the present findings, using data gathered under the old AFDC rules, may hold lessons for some states under TANF.

At least one early study evaluating the new TANF system has reported results similar to those found in this analysis on the selection question. In a study of California welfare recipients conducted in 1998–99 (initial sample $n = 512$), alcohol abuse and mental health problems were not found to be significant barriers to working (Green et al., 2000). Rather, lack of work skills and child care proved to be the most important barriers to employment. In a follow-up at fifteen months of this same sample ($n = 449$), mental health and alcohol dependence problems were still not found to be significantly related to being on or off welfare (Dasinger et al., 2001).

Targeting Health Problems as a Means or an End. The new TANF rules have increased the concern of the managers of the welfare system for the health and behavioral problems of their clients. Fearing that welfare recipients will fail to find work and leave the rolls because of substance abuse or emotional problems, they are turning more of their attention to the question of selection, and looking especially at barriers to exiting welfare. However, the present study suggests that this concern may be exaggerated for welfare recipients as a whole, however accurate it may be for some individual cases. If these largely negative findings for selection hold up on replication, such behavioral problems as alcohol abuse and depression may be redefined as being outside of the mission of welfare system managers, whose primary responsibility is to move women off the rolls.

However, substance abuse and serious depression, especially among mothers of young children, should not be viewed only as barriers to reaching some other goal such as employment. Even if these signs of dysfunction appear to be unrelated to employability, they should still hold intrinsic interest for another social system, that of public mental health. For the sake of their well-being and that of their children, women experiencing adverse transitions into or out of the welfare system warrant the attention of those charged with monitoring and reducing the incidence of mental disorder in the community. The present findings of social causation effects invite the community mental health system to develop primary and secondary preventive efforts, especially for women entering welfare.

Research Implications

Mediators of the Social Causation Effect. The field of unemployment research has provided theories intended to explain the psychological impact of job loss (e.g., Jahoda, 1982), but the adverse psychological effects of entering welfare have received less attention. Perhaps this derives from a tendency to suspect the motives of those going on welfare ("welfare cheats" who presumably want to take public assistance and avoid work). However, the present finding of an adverse social causation effect invites attention to the mediators linking welfare entry to outcomes such as increased depression.

The apparently simple event of welfare entry may represent a bundle of several different stressful events, any of which might provoke increased symptoms. For example, a woman might qualify for welfare if she lost her job, lost her spouse, or had a new child join her family. We checked the main effects of several such potential mediators and found that only one significantly affected later depression – loss of a spouse. However, even with this variable controlled, welfare entry was still associated with increased depression. One possibility is that these potential mediators amplify each other, so that two or more combine to account for the effect of welfare entry on depression (e.g., a triple interaction among loss of spouse, added child, and loss of job). Unfortunately, our sample's small number of welfare entrants precluded testing such higher-order interactions, leaving this possibility for further study.

Another possible mechanism involves some unmeasured variable that is caused by welfare entry and in turn causes increased depression. Other researchers have noted one such variable – feelings of degradation, shame, and embarrassment brought about by the stigma of accepting welfare (e.g., Nichols-Casebolt, 1986). Future studies could usefully include measures of both the individual's perception of the prevailing social attitudes toward welfare (stigma) and their own emotional reaction (shame or embarrassment) to welfare entry.

Welfare as an Employment Status. As suggested at the beginning of this chapter, people on welfare can be viewed as having connections to the labor force even if they do not meet the official definition of currently working or seeking work. Under the new TANF rules, welfare recipients are being urged to leave the welfare rolls for employment as soon as possible, under the threat of having time-limited financial assistance cut off. These recipients will probably view their chances of leaving welfare as rising or falling with the prevailing economic climate. Whether formally seeking work (officially unemployed) or biding time until their employment prospects improve (discouraged-worker status), these people have as sensitive a link to the economy as any employed worker.

If, as we argue, welfare recipients belong on the employment continuum, they might be located near those who are unemployed or inadequately employed. From the present analyses, it appears that falling into welfare has psychological effects paralleling those of becoming underemployed. In the next major recession, when TANF recipients are forced to seek ever scarcer jobs, it seems likely that they will be competing for the jobs now held by the inadequately employed (Solow, 1998). Future research on employment transitions could usefully monitor those involving movements between welfare and employment of varying adequacy in order to delineate the effects on welfare recipients. Moreover, such research should also consider the influence of welfare exits in dislocating those already in the least adequate jobs.

9

The Next Generation

Underemployment and Birthweight

> A major task for research on the social costs of economic stress is to trace how macrosocial changes affect increasingly smaller social units and ultimately those microsocial phenomena that directly influence children in their families.
>
> Elder & Caspi, 1988, p. 25

INTRODUCTION

Intergenerational Effects

Do parents' adverse employment events affect their children? That parents' financial and psychological well-being might influence their children seems intuitively likely. Parents' loss of income should lower the whole family's standard of living and thereby threaten future opportunities to obtain important goals. Emotional stress on the parents following employment setbacks could infect other family members sensitive to the psychosocial climate of the family. But do such effects, if they exist, reach socially significant levels, and what form do they take? This chapter represents not the end of our exploration of underemployment and well-being but rather the beginning of an extension of this research across generations. We will explore the effect on the birthweight of firstborn children of adverse employment change experienced by women in the year before giving birth.

Evidence for a cross-generational impact of underemployment comes from various sources. Studies going back to the Great Depression have followed the lives of children whose parents coped with massive macroeconomic change (Elder, 1974). More recently, aggregate-level time-series studies have linked unemployment rates with community variations in levels of child abuse (Steinberg et al., 1981) and foster care placement (Catalano et al., in press). However, the literature connecting parents' underemployment with the well-being of their children remains rather sparse. By contrast, an extensive literature on women's employment and their children has focused on the presumed harm of working (e.g., neglectful childcare environments) rather than on the costs of underemployment (Menaghan & Parcel, 1990). This chapter addresses the potential adverse effects for children's well-being of a parent's becoming underemployed.

The NLSY provides an especially good opportunity for exploring this linkage because it has surveyed both the women of the NLSY79 and their children. Using these data, Menaghan and her colleagues have already studied the relationship between certain psychological characteristics of parents' employment and their children's outcomes. For example, she has reported positive relationships between the occupational complexity of the mother's job and the well-being of children three to six years old (Menaghan, 1997). These parental employment effects appeared to operate indirectly through family resources and environmental conditions. Persistent unemployment and starting new jobs of average or low complexity were both associated with declines in the quality of the home environment. Although not based on the employment framework that we have used in this book, such results suggest that adverse employment change (becoming unemployed or inadequately employed) might also affect the children of the NLSY.

Birthweight

Parents' employment might influence children in a variety of ways, on a host of outcomes, and with different delays or lags. We will focus on one potential outcome of adverse employment experience that has received attention in recent years – child's birthweight. Past research has linked pregnancy outcomes to the mother's number of hours worked (Peoples-Sheps et al., 1991), the amount of psychosocial stress on the job (Homer, James, & Siegel, 1990), the intensity of occupational fatigue, and the type of occupation (Spinillo et al., 1996). Most of this research has focused on specific job characteristics, with fewer studies looking at unemployment or underemployment. Some studies have linked income loss with low birthweight (Norbeck & Tilden, 1983; Nuckolls, Cassel, & Kaplan, 1972). Other studies have reported no relationship between unemployment and birthweight, but these were conducted in countries where medical insurance is not dependent on employment (Najman et al., 1989; Stein et al., 1987).

Some studies have found that father's but not mother's unemployment was related to birthweight (Hiroshige, Matsudy, & Kahyo, 1995). Researchers using aggregate research methods have also linked the incidence of low birthweight to community unemployment levels. One study found an association between threatened reduction in the number of state workers and elevated rates of low birthweight (Catalano & Serxner, 1992).

Another study found an association between low-birthweight incidence and male unemployment levels (Johnson, Dack, & Fogarty, 1994). This association between male unemployment and low birthweight has been replicated in aggregate time-series analyses in Scandinavia (Catalano, Hansen, & Hartig, 1999; Catalano & Hartig, 2001).

The mechanism by which unemployment might cause reduced birthweight remains unclear. However, low birthweight is associated with both slow intrauterine growth (Kramer, 1987) and preterm delivery (Crouse & Cassaday, 1994). These variables may in turn be associated with stress (Copper et al., 1996). Stress may raise the risk of preterm delivery by increasing levels of corticosteroids in pregnant women (Lockwood, 1999) or by compromising their immune systems (Arnetz et al., 1987), which, in turn, increases the risk of infections that can affect intrauterine growth or duration of gestation (Goldenberg et al., 1990). Employment stressors also might lead to low birthweight because of maladaptive maternal coping involving risky health behaviors. For example, smoking during pregnancy is known to be associated with low birthweight (Hofvendahl, 1995; Li, Windsor, & Hassan, 1994). Underemployment might also influence a pregnant woman's marital or economic status, resulting in nutritional or other lifestyle changes that could affect birthweight (MacDonald, Peacock, & Anderson, 1992).

Birthweight provides a useful outcome measure for these analyses for several reasons. First, birthweight is linked to a variety of important health and social sequelae. Very-low-birthweight children and their parents experience considerable suffering, and the care needed for such children exacts a high price from the health care system. Birthweight predicts overall health and well-being during the early years of life. For example, extremely-low-birthweight children have a higher incidence of infant mortality (Wise, Wampler, & Barfield, 1995) and exhibit slowed cognitive development (Dammann et al., 1996).

Second, weight at birth provides the first possible measure of child well-being following any employment or other recent life stressors experienced by the mother. Of course, mother's adverse employment experiences may also show up in the child's cognitive functioning, social relationships, or physical health in infancy or childhood. But such distal effects will likely be mediated by a variety of intervening experiences (e.g., family social environment) and moderated by other events in the life of the mother and the child (e.g., subsequent employment change, both desirable and undesirable). Focusing on the more proximal outcome of birthweight should help to reveal the effects of mother's employment change with minimal dilution by other variables.

Finally, the available literature on parental employment and child's birthweight gives good reason to predict a link between these variables. Moreover, the varying research methods employed suggest that the causal linkage, if any, may operate through more than one process. The stress model suggests that personal experience of an adverse life event (e.g., mother's job loss during pregnancy) may produce physiological or behavioral changes that in turn cause low birthweight. On the other hand, some studies find that community-level measures of economic climate are associated over time with aggregate measures of low birthweight (e.g., Catalano & Hartig, 2001). Thus, both personal and community labor force experiences may influence birthweight in ways that our cross-level research methods are well suited to capture.

Hypotheses

In this chapter we will test the hypothesis that mothers who experience adverse employment change in the year leading up to their child's birth will have children with lower birthweights than those who remain adequately employed. Moreover, following the findings from aggregate time-series studies, we test the hypothesis that mothers living in communities with higher unemployment rates will have a higher risk of having firstborn children of low birthweight.

Of course, these potential associations might be influenced by a host of confounding, mediating, and moderating variables in the previous and current life experience of the mothers. As will be detailed in the next section, our analyses will include as many of these potentially influential variables as the NLSY mother-child data set allows.

METHODS

Data

Sample. The relationship between adverse employment change and birthweight was studied using first births to female respondents of the NLSY. Because the respondents were fourteen to twenty-one years old at the onset of the survey in 1979, many of these women were of peak childbearing age during the 1980s. We based our sample on 907 female respondents who gave birth to a first child during this decade (1981 through 1990), who were adequately employed at the pre-pregnancy interview (the interview immediately preceding the pregnancy), and who were reinterviewed sometime during their pregnancies. Of these 907 female respondents, 896 provided usable, complete data on the study variables. We note that these women represent a select group of female respondents to the NLSY, in that all of them were working in adequate jobs prior to their pregnancies. They differed in several ways when compared to other female respondents to the NLSY, as shown in Figures 9.1–9.6. These figures compare the demographic composition of this group of 896 women to that of the remaining

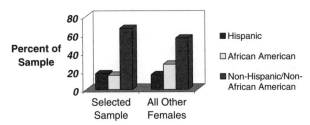

FIGURE 9.1. Ethnicity.

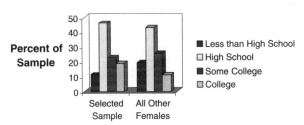

FIGURE 9.2. Education.

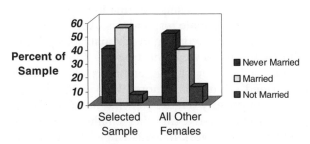

FIGURE 9.3. Marital status.

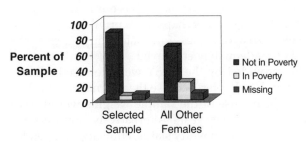

FIGURE 9.4. Family poverty status.

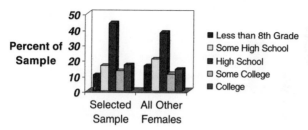

FIGURE 9.5. Parental education.

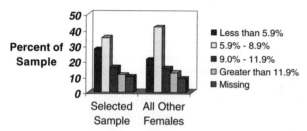

FIGURE 9.6. Unemployment rate.

group of female respondents ($n = 4{,}671$), using information from 1985 to characterize the remaining group of female respondents. Approximately two-thirds of the 896 women who were working in adequate jobs prior to their first pregnancies during the 1980s were non-Hispanic/non–African American, compared to 56.2% of the other females (Figure 9.1). This smaller group was also better educated (Figure 9.2), more likely to be married (Figure 9.3), less likely to live in poverty (Figure 9.4), and had better educated parents (Figure 9.5) when compared to the other female respondents. This group also appeared to live and work in areas where the economic climate was slightly more favorable (see Figure 9.6) when compared to the other female respondents, as evidenced by the larger percentage who lived in areas with unemployment rates of less than 5.9% (27.8% as compared to 21.1% for the other female respondents). Thus our findings apply to this somewhat well-functioning and perhaps more privileged group of women and may not generalize to other, less fortunate groups such as the chronically unemployed or inadequately employed.

The sampling weights provided by the NLSY were not used for any of the analyses presented in this chapter. Because the pregnancies studied here occurred in different years, use of the sample weights would have required combining them across survey years. Alternatively, controls were included in our statistical models for poverty status, ethnicity, and gender (only females were used), which are primary factors used in determining the weights for a given survey year.

Measures. The data used in this chapter come from two different NLSY data sets, the adult files and the child/young adult files. All children born to female members of the original NLSY survey were followed from birth into young adulthood, and these data make up the NLSY child/young adult data files. These files contain a rich collection of data describing the mother's prenatal care, work history, and family structure during the pregnancy, as well as a comprehensive collection of measures characterizing the birth, health, and social and psychological development of the children. During adolescence, additional information was collected describing school activities, peer relationships, work history, and alcohol/drug use.

The outcome variables used in the present analyses came from the child/young adult data files and include infant birthweight in ounces and a dichotomous variable measuring "low birthweight," defined as less than 5.5 pounds at birth (World Health Organization, 1950). Using the birthweight of the child in ounces, it is also possible to define another measure that is often used to identify at-risk infants – "very low birthweight" (e.g., Catalano & Hartig, 2001). Very low birthweight is defined as less than 1,500 grams at birth. Unfortunately, we were unable to use this definition in the present research, because there were only 6 such very-low-birthweight infants in our sample of 896.

The key independent variable was change in the mother's employment status from the pre-pregnancy interview (when all were adequately employed) to the interview during the pregnancy. Of the 896 females who were adequately employed at the pre-pregnancy interview and had usable data on the study variables, 627 (70.1%) remained adequately employed, 39 (4.3%) became unemployed, 75 (8.3%) became inadequately employed (either poverty-wage or involuntary part-time), and 155 (17.3%) were out of the labor force (OLF).

Other variables describing the mother and the pregnancy were also examined. These variables included demographic characteristics such as age, years of education, ethnicity, and marital status; economic characteristics, including family poverty status and the local unemployment rate; and variables describing the pregnancy, such as weight gain, gestational age, and smoking and alcohol intake during pregnancy. Many of these variables were incorporated into our analyses in order to control for potential confounding of the relationship between employment change and birthweight. Others were evaluated for their potential to explain the mechanism by which adverse employment change is associated with lower birthweight. As an example, either mother's weight gain during pregnancy or gestational age might be affected by the stress associated with adverse employment change and, in turn, associated with birthweight. We also evaluated whether changes in poverty status and changes in marital status from the pre-pregnancy interview to the follow-up interview acted as mediators of the relationship between adverse employment change and birthweight. Summary statistics describing these variables appear in Table 9.1.

TABLE 9.1. *Demographic characteristics of respondents with first births in 1980s (n = 896)*

	M	%	SD
Background variables			
Age in years	23.0		3.2
Years of education	13.0		2.1
Ethnicity			
Hispanic		17.3	
African American		15.7	
Non-Hispanic/non–African American		67.0	
Marital Status			
Married		54.7	
Divorced/separated/widowed		6.0	
Never married		39.4	
Geographic/economic variables			
Region			
Northeast		18.7	
North Central		22.9	
South		36.2	
West		21.7	
Unemployment rate			
Missing		9.9	
Less than 6%		27.8	
Greater than or equal to 6%		62.3	
Family poverty status			
Missing		7.2	
Not in poverty		87.3	
In poverty		5.5	
Health/pregnancy variables			
Weight prior to pregnancy (pounds)	131.8		25.3
Weight gain during pregnancy (pounds)	33.8		13.9
Length of gestation (weeks)	38.9		2.1
Sex of child (% male)		52.7	
Smoking during pregnancy			
Did not smoke		75.7	
Smoked		24.3	
Alcohol during pregnancy			
Did not drink		57.7	
Less than once a month		19.8	
Once a month or more		22.7	
Birthweight (ounces)	117.2		18.4
Birthweight below 5.5 pounds		5.7	
Employment status			
Remained adequately employed		70.1	
Change from adequate employment to:			
Unemployment		4.3	
Inadequate employment		8.3	
Out of the labor force		17.3	

Analyses

The key hypothesis predicts that mothers who experience an adverse employment change during pregnancy will have children of lower birthweight than those who remain adequately employed. Single-factor analysis of variance was used to assess the bivariate association between employment change and birthweight in ounces. Odds ratios were used to evaluate the bivariate association between adverse employment change and low birthweight (defined as less than 5.5 pounds).

Ordinary Least Squares. Multivariable models, including both ordinary least squares (OLS) regression and logistic regression, were used to adjust for the effects of potential confounding variables. The relationship between birthweight in ounces and employment change was evaluated using OLS multiple regression. This same procedure was also used to test the significance of the mediating variables and to examine interactions between employment change and the other variables in the model. Testing interactions checks the possibility that the effect of adverse employment change on birthweight differs depending on the values of other variables – for example, the effect of adverse employment change might depend on the mother's education, age, or ethnicity.

Logistic Regression. The relationship between birthweight as measured using a dichotomous variable (<5.5 pounds vs. ≥ 5.5 pounds) and change in employment status was evaluated using a multivariable logistic regression. When the number of events is small relative to the number of predictor variables or when the cell sizes become extremely small, the model can become "over-fit," yielding unrealistically extreme estimates of the logistic regression parameters and standard errors (Bagley, White, & Golomb, 2001; Hosmer & Lemeshow, 2000). To help avoid this problem, the potential confounding variables were individually screened in order to identify those that were significantly related to low birthweight. Only this small subset of variables was used in the multivariable logistic regression model, and interactions were screened on an individual basis using this subset of potential confounding variables.

RESULTS

Bivariate Associations

Table 9.2 describes the bivariate association between employment change and both birthweight in ounces and low birthweight. Mothers who experienced an adverse change in employment, specifically a change from adequate employment to unemployment, had children who weighed

TABLE 9.2. *Birthweight and number of low-birthweight infants among first births to NLSY females during the 1980s, by change in employment status (n = 896)*

	Birthweight[a] (Ounces)		Birthweight less than 5.5 Pounds		
	M	SD	N	%	OR[b]
Remained adequately employed (n = 627)	118.5	18.3	31	4.9	—
Changed from adequate employment to:					
Unemployment (n = 39)	108.4	18.0	6	15.4	3.5*
Inadequate employment (n = 75)	113.8	19.2	8	10.7	2.3*
Out of the labor force (n = 155)	115.1	18.4	6	3.9	.8
TOTAL (n = 896)	117.2	18.4	51	5.7	

* $p < .05$.
[a] Birthweight is significantly different among the employment groups (F(df) = 5.5(3, 892); $p < .005$). Children of women who became unemployed weighed significantly less at birth than children of women who remained adequately employed (Bonferroni corrected level of significance equal to .05). None of the other groups were different from one another.
[b] Odds of a child weighing less than 5.5 pounds at birth for the given employment change relative to remaining adequately employed.

significantly less than those who remained adequately employed (M = 108.4 ounces and M = 118.5 ounces, respectively; $p < .05$). Additionally, women who experienced an adverse employment change were more likely to give birth to low-birthweight infants than those who remained adequately employed. The odds of a low-birthweight infant were 3.5 times greater for women who became unemployed relative to those remaining adequately employed ($p < .05$), and 2.3 times greater for women who became inadequately employed relative to those remaining adequately employed ($p < .05$).

Multivariable Analyses

Ordinary Least Squares. Table 9.3 presents the results of an OLS regression predicting birthweight from the set of potential confounding variables (Model 1), the confounding variables and the employment-change variables (Model 2), and with the mediating variables included (Model 3). These results suggest that age of the mother, living in a community with an elevated unemployment rate (above 6.0%), smoking during pregnancy, and being African American were all significantly negatively associated with birthweight. Male infants tended to weigh more than female infants, and the mother's pre-pregnancy weight and alcohol use during pregnancy were positively associated with birthweight (both $p < .05$). Other background variables were tested and not found to be significant predictors of birthweight. Among these were family poverty status and marital status.

TABLE 9.3. *Ordinary least squares regression: adverse employment change and birthweight (ounces) (n = 896)*

Predictor Variables	Model 1 b	Model 1 Beta	Model 2 b	Model 2 Beta	Model 3 b	Model 3 Beta
Age (years)	−.33	−.06	−.50*	−.09	−.22	−.04
Unemployment rate[a]						
Missing	−3.52	−.06	−3.60	−.06	−2.77	−.05
≥6.0%	−2.79*	−.07	−2.72*	−.07	−2.55*	−.07
Child's sex (1 = male)	3.51**	.10	3.39*	.09	2.89**	.08
African American (1 = yes)	−4.27*	−.09	−4.14*	−.08	−5.05**	−.10
Weight prior to pregnancy (pounds)	.09**	.13	.09**	.12	.08**	.11
Alcohol use during pregnancy[b]						
Less than once a month	3.25*	.07	3.15*	.07	1.99	.04
More than once a month	1.14	.03	.89	.02	1.08	.03
Smoking during pregnancy (1 = yes)	−6.77**	−.16	−6.48**	−.15	−7.37**	−.17
Employment status[c]						
Change to unemployment			−9.41**	−.11	−6.61*	−.07
Change to inadequate employment			−4.76*	−.07	−4.52*	−.07
Change to OLF			−1.72	−.04	−3.09*	−.06
Weight gain during pregnancy (pounds)					.21**	.16
Weeks of gestation					4.53**	.51
Constant	113.94		119.63		−68.28	
F(df)	6.34 (9,886)*		5.90 (12,883)*		37.22 (14,881)*	
R^2_{adj}	.051		.074		.372	

* $p < .05$, ** $p < .005$.
[a] Relative to an unemployment rate of less than 6.0%.
[b] Relative to never used alcohol.
[c] Relative to remaining adequately employed.

Controlling for the variables in Model 1, adverse change in employment was significantly associated with birthweight (see Model 2). Specifically, change from adequate employment to unemployment was associated with a 9.4-ounce decrease in birthweight (b = −9.41, $p < .005$), and change to inadequate employment was associated with a 4.8-ounce decrease in birthweight (b = −4.76, $p < .05$) when compared to those who remained adequately employed. Model 3, which incorporates the mediating variables, shows that after statistically adjusting for weight gain during pregnancy and gestational age, the association between adverse employment change and birthweight remains strong and statistically significant. Change in poverty status and change in marital status did not function as mediators, as they were not statistically significant predictors of birthweight, and they were not included in the final model.

In addition to these main-effects models, all interactions between the employment change variables and both the confounding and mediating variables were tested for significance. Only the interaction between weight gain and change from adequate employment to inadequate employment was statistically significant. Further analyses of this interaction showed that weight gain during pregnancy was positively associated with birthweight in mothers who remained adequately employed, but that there was very little association between weight gain and birthweight in mothers who became inadequately employed.

Logistic Regression. Table 9.4 summarizes the results of a multivariable logistic regression showing the relationship between adverse employment change and low birthweight. There was no significant association between low birthweight and use of alcohol during pregnancy, smoking during pregnancy, pre-pregnancy weight of the mother, age, years of education, family poverty status, change in family poverty status, region of residence, marital status, change in marital status, and the local unemployment rate. However, we caution the reader that because of the relatively small sample of low-birthweight infants ($n = 51$), the statistical power (ability of the test to detect an existing relationship) may be somewhat low. Ethnicity

TABLE 9.4. *Logistic regression: adverse employment change and low birthweight (< 5.5 pounds) (n = 896)*

Predictor Variables	Model 1 Odds Ratio	Model 2 Odds Ratio	Model 3 Odds Ratio	Model 4 Odds Ratio
Ethnicity[a]				
Hispanic	2.02*	1.91	1.80	3.19*
African American	2.05*	2.03+	2.02+	4.81*
Change from adequate employment to:				
Unemployment		3.18*	3.16*	2.03
Inadequate employment		2.26+	2.21+	4.10*
Out of the labor force		.74	.77	1.05
Weight gain (in pounds)			.97*	.97+
Gestational age				.41*
Likelihood ratio $\chi(2)$(df)	5.9(2)+	14.6(5)*	21.2(6)*	172.9(7)*
Hosmer-Lemeshow $\chi(2)$(df)	–	2.8(4)	6.3(8)	6.6(8)
		$p = .60$	$p = .62$	$p = .58$

* $p < .05$, + $p < .06$.
[a] Relative to non-Hispanic/non–African American.

was the only potential confounding variable significantly associated with low birthweight (see Table 9.4, Model 1). Relative to non-Hispanic/non–African Americans, the odds of a low birthweight infant were about twice as high for both Hispanic and African American women (OR = 2.02 and OR = 2.05, respectively).

Adverse employment change relative to remaining adequately employed was associated with low birthweight, after adjusting for ethnicity (see Model 2). The odds of a low-birthweight infant were three times greater for those becoming unemployed (OR = 3.18, $p < .05$), and more than two times greater for those becoming inadequately employed (OR = 2.26, $p < .06$).

Interactions between each of the potential confounding variables and employment change were examined. Only the interaction between ethnicity (specifically, African American ethnicity) and becoming inadequately employed was statistically significant ($p < .05$). Approximately 44% (4/9) of the African American women who became inadequately employed had low-birthweight children, compared to only 6.1% (4/66) of non–African American women who became inadequately employed. This finding is based on such a small sample of inadequately employed African American women that we regard it as tentative and so do not include it in Table 9.4.

We investigated the possibility that either weight gain during pregnancy or gestational age might mediate the relationship between adverse employment change and low birthweight (Models 3 and 4). Although mother's weight gain during pregnancy was negatively associated with the odds of low birthweight, (i.e., each additional pound gained during pregnancy reduced the odds of a low-birthweight child by about 3%; OR = .97), the relationship between adverse employment change and low birthweight is unchanged with the inclusion of weight gain in the model. This suggests that weight gain does not serve as a mediator of the relationship between adverse employment change and low birthweight. (Note the interaction between adverse employment change and mother's weight gain found in the OLS analysis reported earlier.)

Gestational age was also negatively associated with low birthweight (see Model 4). For every additional week of gestation, the odds of a low-birthweight infant fell by about 59% (OR = .41, $p < .05$). Inclusion of gestational age in the model reduced the magnitude of the relationship between low birthweight and unemployment, suggesting that gestational age serves as a mediator of the relationship between this form of adverse employment change and low birthweight. By contrast, the relationship between inadequate employment and low birthweight was strengthened, suggesting that after controlling for ethnicity, weight gain during pregnancy, and gestational age, the odds of low birthweight were about four times greater for women who became inadequately employed (OR = 4.10, $p < .05$).

DISCUSSION

Summary of Findings

Continuous Birthweight Measure. The pattern of findings differed depending on the way in which the birthweight outcome variable was defined and analyzed. The continuous form of this variable allowed analysis by ordinary least squares, which provides good statistical power and, therefore, heightened sensitivity for identifying associations. In this case, personal adverse employment change predicted lower birthweight, with both the unemployment and the inadequate-employment effects reaching significance. Even controlling for these personal employment change variables, living in a high-unemployment-rate community also predicted low birthweight. This latter variable operated as a main effect on all respondents, not as a moderator that increased or decreased the effect for women in just one type of employment status.

These effects also persisted despite controls for a variety of other significant predictors. Some of these variables predicted increased birthweight, including the child's sex (male), the mother's weight prior to pregnancy, the mother's weight gain during pregnancy, and gestational age. Other variables predicted decreased birthweight, including smoking and ethnicity (African American). After all of these controls, underemployment still produced noticeable decreases in birthweight. In the case of unemployment (versus adequate employment), the unadjusted birthweight effect of just over ten ounces fell, with statistical controls, to just under seven ounces (6.61).

Low Birthweight. However, the continuous form of birthweight has an interpretive drawback. A seven- to ten-ounce variation in birthweight, if it occurs in the medium- and high-birthweight range, may not predict developmental problems for the newborn. The highest risk of serious developmental problems is concentrated in the low-birthweight range. Therefore, we tested whether adverse employment change would also affect the risk of low birthweight (i.e., less than 5.5 pounds). The logistic regression analysis confirmed that adverse employment change also predicted greater risk of low birthweight. Moreover, the main-effects analysis showed that both unemployment and inadequate employment were associated with significantly greater risk of low birthweight.

However, this low-birthweight analysis differed in important ways from the OLS analysis. For example, aggregate unemployment rate in the respondents' communities failed to predict low birthweight. Possibly the decrease in power resulting from the shift from OLS to LR modeling accounts for the failure to replicate this cross-level effect. On the other hand, the power explanation does not explain the appearance of a possible new effect involving the interaction between ethnicity (African American) and inadequate employment. Despite its potential policy significance, this interaction effect rests on very small cell counts and so must be replicated before being considered a settled finding.

When gestational age was entered into the mediation model, it appeared to "explain" (i.e., to reduce to nonsignificance) the initial effects of unemployment, but the main effect of inadequate employment survived this control. Apparently, falling into involuntary part-time or poverty-wage work increases the risk of low birthweight by some mechanism other than preterm delivery or decreased maternal weight gain. Research has associated maternal stress with an increase in the incidence of low birthweight (Nathanielsz, 1995) by linking stress to an increase in the production of androgen, which may prematurely activate uterine contractions. Maternal stress has also been associated with increased depression and anxiety, which may lead to increased metabolic expenditure, resulting in lower birthweight (Chomitz, Cheung, & Lieberman, 1995).

In sum, these results offer preliminary support for a cross-generational effect not only of unemployment but also of inadequate employment. Although this finding echoes several similar outcomes in the still-small literature on employment and birthweight, further research is needed to confirm and explain this association. We offer the present analyses as a demonstration of a promising analytic approach that combines unemployment with inadequate employment, individual-level with aggregate-level data, and measures at multiple time points from a long-term longitudinal database. In the next section, we note some of the possible directions for future work on this topic.

Moderators and Mediators

For what kinds of mothers and in which circumstances is adverse employment change more likely to lower a child's birthweight? And by what mechanism or intervening variable does this employment effect proceed?

Possible Interactions. Of the many interactions that we explored in the present analyses, only ethnicity appeared to modify the effect of mother's adverse employment change on low birthweight. Among those who experienced inadequate employment, African Americans (compared to non–African Americans) had a greater risk of low-birthweight babies. However, other variables may also moderate (or exacerbate) such employment effects. For example, research has pointed to the buffering effect on birthweight of such psychosocial assets as social support (Nuckolls et al., 1972).

Among such assets, the mother's spouse's employment status may prove one of the more important factors. Research has demonstrated the potential for a husband's job stressors to harm the psychological well-being of his wife. In one study, undesirable job events experienced by the husband caused as much distress to wives as the women's own personally experienced job stressors (Rook et al., 1991). This effect might operate indirectly via husbands' well-being. Husbands who react to their own employment stress (e.g., job loss) by becoming symptomatic appear to cause increased risk of psychological harm for their wives (Atkinson, Liem, & Liem, 1986; Dew, Bromet, & Schulberg, 1987). If the husband is experiencing both economic stress and emotional symptoms, he may place an even greater burden on his wife for emotional support and caregiving (Kessler & McLeod, 1984).

If the social contagion from spousal employment problems can produce such emotional distress in women generally, it follows that it might amplify women's own employment difficulties, especially during pregnancy. When her personal employment security is threatened, a pregnant woman may rely even more on the financial stability of her husband's job as well as on his emotional support and strength.

Because the NLSY mother-child data do not include detailed measures of the mothers' spouses' employment experiences, their main or interactive effects on birthweight will have to be checked by other studies. However, some of the variables available in the present study may warrant further exploration as possible moderators. Selecting our analytic sample in order to focus on women enjoying adequate employment at time one may have restricted the range of some variables (e.g., education) in ways that attenuated their contribution to our models. Future research should look at chronically underemployed women in order to assess the potential moderating effects of their educational and family status backgrounds as well as the effects of the surrounding economic climate (community unemployment rate). Perhaps favorable employment change helps to lower the risk of low-birthweight babies, just as favorable employment change has been found to be associated with some psychological benefits, as reported in earlier chapters.

Intervening Variables. The present analyses suggest that gestational age mediates at least some of the effect of adverse employment change. Presumably, the stress of adverse employment also affects birthweight by slowing intrauterine growth. However, risky health behaviors, such as smoking and drinking, that might have slowed intrauterine growth did not, when controlled, account for the employment effects. Other factors, such as mother's weight and weight gain, also did not, when controlled, explain the effects of underemployment.

Future research might explore such candidate variables as changes in professional health care, perhaps resulting from loss of or changes in health insurance tied to the mother's employment. Perhaps specific dietary changes related to decreased income or increased demands on the mother's schedule play a mediating role. Our research has shown that adverse employment can reduce self-esteem (Chapter 5) and increase depression (Chapter 7). Such demoralizing effects might reduce the mother's attention to her diet and preventive health care, indirectly affecting the fetus.

Implications and Generalizability

These results tend to confirm some earlier studies linking employment and birthweight. In the context of this book, they add another social cost to be accounted for individuals and populations experiencing adverse employment change. However, important questions remain to be answered. One issue pertains to the external validity or generalizability of these findings. For example, do these results for firstborn children extend to later-born children? Also, do the effects of adverse employment change extend to continued underemployment, or are they limited to the transitional event of falling into underemployment?

These findings invite a program of research designed to follow the long-term sequelae of both low birthweight and employment stress as they operate through other familial factors. Do the effects of maternal underemployment end with the low birthweight observed here, or do they extend through infancy and even into childhood and beyond? What protective factors might be cultivated in order to buffer or prevent such potential long-lasting effects?

The outcome of this study should be regarded as preliminary and interpreted with caution. One possibly erroneous conclusion is that pregnant women should be encouraged to work full-time in the best possible jobs that they can find. The link between child's welfare and mother's employment will probably prove more complex than such simplified interpretations. For example, changes in the U.S. welfare system (see Chapter 8) tend to encourage women to redirect their time away from child care and into careers. Although successful engagement in the world of work may benefit the mother (e.g., less depression, higher self-esteem) and her newborn (higher birthweight), it may not help her older children. For example, three-to six-year-old preschoolers may need a minimum amount of attention and support as they develop their learning readiness.

At a later stage of development, children in grade school are facing an increasingly demanding school system that uses high-stakes tests to prevent social promotion and to control progress toward graduation. If working mothers shift their time and energy away from tutoring their children and monitoring their homework, what will be the consequences for their educational success? We must entertain the possibility that maternal employment has a curvilinear effect on children's well-being. Perhaps it has more favorable effects at some developmental stages and less desirable effects at others. Moreover, the costs and benefits of such employment may vary not only by the child's age and developmental needs but also in interaction with the mother's support system (e.g., spouse's employment status, health insurance, transportation to work, and quality of after-school child care).

10

Conclusions

Jobs are not the issue. Slaves had jobs. The issue is what kind of jobs.
Senator Tom Harkin, quoted by Seligman, 1992, p. 180

PRINCIPAL FINDINGS

Social Causation

Adverse Employment Change. This research has produced the key finding that not only job loss but also other kinds of adverse employment change can carry psychosocial and health costs. Specifically, these studies show that falling into various types of underemployment is associated with a variety of undesirable outcomes. These outcomes include decreased self-esteem (Chapter 5), increased alcohol abuse (Chapter 6), elevated depression (Chapter 7), and lower birthweight (Chapter 9). Both unemployment and such economically inadequate forms of employment as low-wage and involuntary part-time work appear to be linked to each of these outcomes, and these links often have similar magnitudes.

Intermittent Unemployment. Interestingly, intermittent unemployment had opposite associations depending on the outcome. For school-leavers, intermittent unemployment had a negative relationship to self-esteem similar to that of other forms of underemployment. But for alcohol abuse and depression, the intermittently unemployed seemed much more similar to the continuing adequately employed than to any of the other underemployed groups. We can understand this uneven pattern of results by reference to differences in both the outcomes and the employment statuses.

Self-esteem reflects an enduring appraisal based on one's overall record of successes and failures. The school-leaver who falls in the category of intermittent unemployment has a job with adequate wages and hours but, in appraising his or her self-worth, seems to dwell on the recent history of unemployment. By contrast, depression and alcohol abuse symptoms seem to reflect not long-term patterns of success or failure but rather the most recent stressors. Workers who have enjoyed adequate employment, then lost and regained their jobs, appear to connect their current mood and level of alcohol abuse more to their present satisfactory status than to their recent bouts of joblessness.

This finding that depression and alcohol abuse respond more to current than to recent adverse employment experience has some practical implications. One of these is that some but not all forms of inadequate employment can be meaningfully grouped together for research purposes. Our results show that jobs with low pay or low hours seem to produce similar effects across all of the measured outcomes. However, the intermittent unemployment category should not be routinely combined with these other forms of inadequate employment. The other implication is that favorable employment change can have beneficial effects that warrant study in their own right.

Favorable Employment Change. By definition, intermittently unemployed workers have recently been unemployed but have made the positive change of entering jobs with adequate pay and hours. These workers do not appear to be reacting to their prior joblessness or to fears about their future job security. Instead, the depression and alcohol abuse findings show that these recently reemployed workers seem to be functioning as well as workers with no interruption in their adequate employment.

To explore the favorable-employment-change effect, we modified our usual social causation research approach in order to study respondents who were underemployed (unemployed or inadequately employed) at time one. For alcohol abuse, favorable employment change did not reduce symptoms but did reduce binge drinking for those with initially heavy drinking levels. For depression, those who found work (adequate or inadequate) or continued in inadequate jobs were all better off than those who continued to be unemployed. That such favorable or relatively favorable employment experiences might increase the well-being of workers has important implications for interventions, as will be discussed in the next chapter.

Selection

Reciprocal Causation. One of the recurring themes in the literature on underemployment involves the contest between selection and social causation explanations. Cross-sectional studies that find an association between adverse employment states (e.g., being unemployed) and pathology (e.g., depression) now seem fatally flawed by their inability to resolve causal direction. Critics can dismiss such results as resulting from selection and therefore irrelevant to arguments for reducing the social costs of employment stress. In response, scholars concerned primarily with social causation often use longitudinal designs to control for selection, more out of necessity than out of any intrinsic curiosity about possible selection processes.

By contrast, we regard selection as a potentially important mechanism in its own right and view the present longitudinal design as an opportunity to shed light on selection. Because selection may operate in conjunction with social causation in an iterative manner – that is, reciprocal causation – it should interest anyone who is trying to illuminate the relationship between work and well-being. Individuals may well experience adverse employment change because of personal dysfunction (selection), but such adverse employment change may in turn produce a further decrement in functioning (social causation). From this perspective, selection and social causation, far from being mutually exclusive, may take turns to produce a downward spiral in economic and psychological well-being.

Results. Each of the three indicators measured at time one appeared to select individuals into adverse employment statuses by time two (see Chapter 4, Table 4.2, for a summary). High school students with low self-esteem (especially males) had a greater risk of becoming unemployed and of becoming inadequately employed. Workers in their mid-twenties with many alcohol symptoms were more likely to fall into both unemployment and inadequate employment. Adults in their late twenties with high levels of depression had greater chances of losing their jobs but not, interestingly, of becoming inadequately employed. One of our outcome variables had no time one counterpart – birthweight. Thus, the link between the pregnant mother's adverse employment and her baby's birthweight does not lend itself to a selection or reciprocal causation explanation. However, one can speculate that pregnancy complications could contribute both to the adverse employment change of the mother (e.g., the mother is laid off for taking too many sick days) and to the baby's low birthweight.

These selection effects seem to depend not only on the type of predictor but also on other characteristics of the individual, such as race, age, gender, and education. For example, education appeared to buffer the adverse selection effect of binge drinking on later inadequate employment and to buffer the effect of depression on later unemployment. Finally, selection may vary depending on the direction of the employment change. For example, our analyses of welfare transitions found no evidence for selection out of welfare by alcohol abuse or depression but did find evidence for selection into welfare by elevated levels of depression (Chapter 8).

Contextual Variables

The reciprocal relationship between underemployment and mental health takes place in the context of other variables. Some of these variables may operate as confounders, that is, as causes of both employment status and well-being, adding a spurious component to their apparent association. In order to get a clearer picture of the unconfounded part of the causal link, the effects of such variables were removed statistically as a standard part of the analytic process. But contextual variables can also play other important roles in the relationship of interest. When these variables help to determine when or for whom the causal relationship appears, they are called moderators, and they appear in significant interactions with the employment-change variables. When they help to explain the intervening mechanism by which the causal process operates, they are called mediators, and their inclusion in the analytic models tends to reduce the association between employment change and health status outcome. This section will note some of the variables that were found to operate as moderators or mediators in the social causation of dysfunction by adverse employment change.

Moderators

Economic Climate. Individuals deal with their personal employment transitions in the context of the larger economy, typically described by the local unemployment rate. The community's economy functions as an opportunity structure in which workers seek new or improved employment and by which they can gauge their success relative to others in their vicinity. The local unemployment rate might play any of three roles in the process by which underemployment affects mental health. First, as a moderator, the prevailing economic climate might buffer or exacerbate the impact of personal employment change on well-being. Second, the aggregate economy could indirectly affect individual mental health via its influence on the risk of individual employment change. Third, the economic climate might have a direct influence on individuals' well-being, overarching any such indirect effect.

Few data sets permit testing the effect on health status of the interaction between aggregate unemployment and personal employment status. Studies based on a single community cannot support this kind of analysis. In order to provide adequate variability in the aggregate unemployment term, the sample needs to include people from different communities with varying unemployment rates. A few studies have reported a cross-level moderator effect in which the aggregate unemployment rate appears to modify the relationship between personal job loss and symptoms. One such study indicated that unemployment had fewer adverse effects during bad economic times, perhaps because individuals could attribute their employment difficulties to external causes for which they could not be blamed (Cohn, 1978). Another study found the opposite, that unemployment had more adverse effects during bad economic times, particularly for the less well educated, perhaps because prospects for reemployment seemed dimmer (Turner, 1995).

However, other studies have found neither type of moderator effect (e.g., Dooley et al., 1988; Dooley et al., 1994). The present research agrees with these negative findings. Community unemployment rates failed to interact significantly with personal employment change for any of the studied outcome variables. Because prior research on the cross-level moderator hypothesis focused only on unemployment, the present research offers the first test of that interaction for inadequate employment. The results suggest that the social costs of unemployment and inadequate employment do not differ across the range of economic climates experienced by the NLSY respondents.

Does this mean that the unemployment rate of a person's community has no effect on his or her well-being? No, the local economic environment certainly affects the risk of being underemployed and so indirectly influences the social costs of underemployment. As an example, consider the NLSY respondents who had entered the workforce with no college training by 1987 and were studied for the impact of employment status on their self-esteem. Numerous factors contributed to the risk that these individuals would be underemployed rather than adequately employed, including such personal characteristics as gender, marital status, intelligence, high school graduation status, and 1980 self-esteem. But after controlling for these factors, the 1987 unemployment rate in the individuals' communities also significantly influenced their 1987 employment status. For each 1% increase in community unemployment rate, these respondents experienced about a 20% increase in the odds of being unemployed and a 13% increase in the odds of being inadequately employed (Dooley & Prause, 1997a, Table 3).

In addition, there is a third possible link connecting economic climate to individual mental health that involves an overarching direct effect of the economy not mediated by the personal experience of underemployment. Controlling for personal employment status and employment change, individuals may react to the economic situation as they perceive it, perhaps feeling more insecure, pessimistic, and anxious as the economic picture darkens. Testing for such a direct effect requires data for respondents from different communities or industries experiencing a range of economic conditions. This hypothetical direct effect of aggregate unemployment (adjusted for the effects of personal employment status) has failed to appear in some of the few studies that have explored it (e.g., Dooley et al., 1992; Dooley et al., 1994).

On the other hand, a few studies have reported finding this type of relationship (Dooley et al., 1988; Fenwick & Tausig, 1994; Tausig & Fenwick, 1999). Although rare, these positive findings have intuitive appeal. For example, workers currently in economically adequate jobs will probably encounter a host of stressors in a worsening economy. Their opportunities to leave socially irritating work situations and move to more economically or psychologically desirable jobs will decline with rising unemployment rates. Trapped in their jobs, they have little bargaining power to mitigate unpleasant or risky features of their work situations. In the present NLSY analyses, this overarching direct effect appeared for only one of the studied outcomes – birthweight (see the OLS models of Chapter 9). In sum, the direct effect of economic climate may operate on some occasions, for some kinds of outcomes, but it does not have a robust presence across the range of health indicators.

Demographic Differences in Social Causation. Different subgroups of the population might vary in their sensitivity to the stressful effects of underemployment. Our research routinely explored various potential demographic moderators of these effects such as age, gender, and ethnicity.

Age seems a likely moderator of such effects, but by two opposing mechanisms. First, with increasing age, workers are likely to take on increasing economic responsibilities, such as supporting families, mortgages, and children's school tuitions. As a result, older workers, with more to lose, may feel the impact of adverse employment change more acutely than younger workers, who have fewer obligations and social expectations for a stable work role. On the other hand, with increasing age, workers should accumulate more experience in coping with employment setbacks and more assets to help them get through economic hard times. Because the NLSY sample advances in age only from their late teens to their early thirties, this study cannot measure the impact of underemployment in the middle and later years of life.

Another consideration arises from the need to control for prior symptoms in any test of the social causation effect. Typically, such panel studies test short-term change over just one or two years. Consequently, a sample chosen to study the effects of change in any pair of years will have little between-interview variability in age. Thus comparing effects in two more widely separated pairs of survey years offers the best chance to find any age differences in the social causation effect.

Of the various well-being indicators, only alcohol misuse items appeared in more than one pair of survey years. During the 1984–85 period, respondents experiencing job loss or continuing inadequate employment reported increased symptoms, and respondents with prior heavy drinking who became or remained inadequately employed reported more binge consumption. These apparent effects of underemployment seemed to diminish during the 1988–89 period. As discussed earlier (Chapter 6), one plausible explanation for this age-related change involved the respondents' increasing family responsibilities (becoming married with children) along with the stabilizing and supportive elements of those social bonds.

Surprisingly, our data found little evidence of any gender interaction with underemployment. In earlier generations, the cultural norms differentiated work roles by sex, with men expected to be the breadwinners and women to serve as homemakers. For this reason, men might have been expected to feel adverse employment change more acutely than women. However, since World War II, women have entered the labor market in increasing numbers, and the cultural norms now tend to favor gender equity in expectations, if not in reality, about work responsibilities and wages. Gender appeared to moderate the effect of only one type of underemployment on self-esteem (Chapter 5). Among respondents who were intermittently unemployed in 1987, women reported lower self-esteem than men, whereas for the other employment categories, no gender difference emerged after controls for such main effects as 1980 self-esteem. For alcohol abuse and depression, gender did not interact with any of the employment-change variables. Note that the absence of gender interactions does not imply that gender played no role in these latter outcomes. For example, even after controlling for 1992 depression, men reported lower levels of depression than women in 1994. That is, there was a significant main effect of gender on depression but no interaction of gender with employment change.

There was even less evidence for any interaction between underemployment and race or ethnicity. In the case of self-esteem, for example, although there was a significant main effect of race (lower for African Americans than for non–African Americans), there was no interaction of race or ethnicity with employment status. Only for the birthweight outcome did a racial interaction emerge. The elevated risk of low birthweight associated with inadequate employment appeared to be higher for African American mothers (see Chapter 9 for the qualification of this finding by small cell size).

Potential Buffers. Interactions of causal variables with immutable demographic characteristics tell us about the kinds of people who are vulnerable to the impact of stressors such as adverse employment change. Interactions involving more malleable characteristics are often interpreted in terms of buffering. That is, such variables offer the potential to be manipulated in order to reduce or prevent the harmful effects of the stressor. Candidates for such buffer variables include socioeconomic status and human capital, as reflected in the education of the respondent or the respondent's parents. Other potential buffering variables include social support (e.g., as measured by marital status) and employment attitudes such as job satisfaction and psychological commitment to work. Perhaps the most likely candidates for buffering variables consist of prior psychological health as measured by high self-esteem, low depression, and infrequent binge drinking.

Despite numerous tests of possible interactions of these potential buffers and the various employment variables, few reached statistical significance. For example, only one of the several underemployment categories interacted with prior self-esteem in predicting later self-esteem. Among those in the full-year low-income employment category, 1987 self-esteem was lower for those with lower rather than higher 1980 self-esteem, even after adjusting for the main effects of initial self-esteem and other control variables. In the case of alcohol misuse, two employment groups interacted with 1984 heavy drinking – workers who shifted from adequate to inadequate employment and those who continued in inadequate employment. Both groups had higher odds of binge drinking in 1985 if they had been heavy drinkers in 1984. However, prior alcohol abuse symptoms did not interact with underemployment for the prediction of later symptoms. Similarly, the analyses revealed no interaction of prior depression with adverse employment change in predicting subsequent depression.

Various personal, economic, and social assets offer the potential to buffer the stressful effects of adverse employment change. In the case of depression, three such moderators appeared – marital status, education, and job dissatisfaction. Of these, only the first operated in the expected buffering manner. For respondents with a spouse present, the depressive effects of both losing a job and falling into inadequate employment were reduced compared to the depressive effects on other respondents (divorced, separated, widowed, or never married). This finding may reflect the beneficial value of social support in dealing with stressful events.

By contrast, among respondents who lost their jobs, those with more years of education reported more depression than those with less education. Perhaps this anti-buffering or exacerbation effect stems from more educated respondents' having more to lose, both economically and psychologically (e.g., status), in becoming unemployed. Finally, job dissatisfaction also appeared to increase the harmful effect of job loss on depression. Some prior research has suggested that losing a job with more work problems might prove beneficial relative to losing a job with fewer such problems (Wheaton, 1990). However, among NLSY workers who became unemployed, those who were unhappy with their jobs reported more depression than their more satisfied counterparts. We speculate that job losers who had found or created satisfying jobs may have had more optimism about their chances for finding and enjoying a new job and also may have been more creative and energetic agents in finding satisfying activities during their hiatus from employment (Fryer, 1986).

Analyses of alcohol abuse and self-esteem revealed no additional moderators. Some variables that were identified in prior research as moderators of job loss failed to operate as buffers in these analyses. For example, those low on labor force commitment ("would continue to work even if I could live comfortably without working") were expected to experience less distress with unemployment than those high on this variable (Stafford et al., 1980). But a 1979 measure of this characteristic did not interact with unemployment in predicting 1980–87 self-esteem change (Dooley & Prause, 1995).

In sum, a few interactions involving underemployment effects did appear in these analyses, and they invite further exploration as potential moderators. But taken together, these sparse results show little pattern of such interactions across different categories of underemployment and outcomes. Absent more consistent or frequent interaction effects involving the same moderator(s), the present evidence does not add up to clear support for any particular moderating relationship. Put another way, the harmful effects of adverse employment change seem to affect people in general and are not limited to one particular subgroup or another.

Mediators

Explanatory Theories. In contrast to moderator variables that tell us the type of person for whom underemployment threatens the greatest harm, mediators tell us about the mechanism or intervening variable through which the harmful effect operates. In the present analyses, both unemployment and inadequate employment were associated with all of the studied social costs: lowered self-esteem, increased alcohol misuse, increased depression, and decreased birthweight. The similarity in the effects on different outcomes of these two different types of underemployment suggests that a common mechanism might mediate the effects of both.

Various theories suggest different types of potential mechanisms. Perhaps the most intuitive explanation for the mental health effects of underemployment involves the loss of income or the manifest function of paid work (Jahoda, 1982). Workers who lose all of their wages through job loss, or who lose part of their wages through a loss of hours (involuntary part-time work) or a drop in their pay rate (poverty-wage work) will have to reduce their standard of living. Different theorists place varying degrees of emphasis on the importance of income loss in the effect of unemployment on well-being. For example, in his Agency Restriction Theory, Fryer asserts that income loss operates to a great extent by reducing the workers' personal agency or capacity to plan and execute a satisfying lifestyle (Fryer, 1986).

If declining income is the crucial mediator, then those respondents whose family incomes drop below the poverty line should feel income loss most acutely. The variable reflecting this change in family poverty status should significantly predict a mental health outcome such as depression, and its inclusion in the model should reduce the explanatory power of the employment-change variables. However, this expected pattern did not appear in the present analyses. Change in poverty status was unrelated to depression and failed to account for (reduce the magnitude of) the adverse effects of any of the employment-change variables (Dooley et al., 2000).

While acknowledging in her Deprivation Theory that income loss could account for some of the harm associated with unemployment, Jahoda (1982) identified another potential mediator – a set of latent psychosocial functions of employment. These functions include status, time structure, and participation in collective purpose, among others, and their loss through unemployment might provide the mechanism for any negative mental health consequences. Although specified for the case of job loss, such functions might also diminish in the transition from adequate to inadequate employment and could thus help to explain the array of underemployment effects found in this study. By contrast, Fryer has argued that some jobs might not supply Jahoda's latent functions of work at all. Furthermore, he suggests that workers are not dependent on their jobs for these functions but can, with adequate income, generate them on their own. These two perspectives need not be mutually exclusive. Some workers may lose and sorely miss both manifest and latent functions of work in the course of adverse employment change. Unfortunately, the items necessary to measure the loss of Jahoda's latent functions were not asked in the NLSY surveys, and we could not test their role in mediating the effects of underemployment.

Still another possibility is that adverse employment change might trigger other stressful life events, which might account for the observed emotional and behavioral effects of underemployment. For example, employment shocks may provoke changes in marital status, such as divorce and separation, leading in turn to increased depression. When change in marital status was entered into the model for depression, it did explain a significant amount of variability in depression, but it did not reduce (i.e., explain) the adverse effects of underemployment (Dooley et al., 2000).

Other mechanisms for the mental health effects of underemployment have appeared in the literature. One of these involves one's sense of employment security (see, e.g., Catalano et al., 1986). Adverse job changes may breed fear of the future and a loss of optimism and confidence in one's economic prospects. Unfortunately, the measures necessary to check this potential intervening variable were also unavailable for these analyses.

Multiple Mechanisms. Our study failed to identify a common causal mechanism by which different types of underemployment lead to increased depression and other mental and physical health outcomes. Of course, the assumptions that the same mediator transmits the influence of both unemployment and inadequate employment and that any mediator holds constant over time may prove to be false. Workers' personalities, their jobs' characteristics, and the degree of fit between job and worker all vary in ways that may not conform to a single mediation theory.

For example, one person who becomes unemployed may initially experience job loss mainly as the loss of status. By contrast, a worker falling into poverty-wage employment may primarily feel the strain of unpleasant workplace conditions, such as increased demands for production, decreased decision latitude, and lack of respect from coworkers. Over time, both these individuals may come to fear future financial difficulties, such as the inability to make mortgage payments or to cover their children's college tuition. But it may not be until these financial stressors lead to interpersonal strife within the family that serious mental health symptoms begin to appear. The mechanism connecting underemployment and symptoms of mental disorder may well consist not of a single mediating variable but rather of a long chain of intervening links, with each chain unique to the individual–job–outcome combination.

LIMITATIONS

Methods

Measures. Like all research endeavors, these studies had constraints that placed limits on the conclusions that can be drawn. The questions included in the NLSY surveys generally provide reliable and valid measures of their target constructs. For example, measures of the key employment variables parallel the items on official government questionnaires such as the Current Population Survey. The key measures of such outcomes as self-esteem and depression consisted of widely used and respected scales. However, one inevitable measurement limitation was the finite number of questions that could be asked of the NLSY respondents.

As described earlier, various potential mediators of the underemployment–social cost relationship went unmeasured, thus limiting our ability to check rival theories. Some core questions were asked in only one or two of the survey waves, thus preventing study of the stability of some relationships over different years and developmental periods. On the other hand, even if adding such measures would have provided more interpretive richness, their addition seems unlikely to have reversed the major conclusions of this study.

Design. Another concern has to do with the research design. That underemployment is associated with social costs in these data is undeniable. However, our confidence in the interpretation of this association depends on the plausibility of any rival explanations. We have interpreted this association as being due, at least in part, to the causation of the observed social costs by adverse employment change. Unfortunately, this judgment rests on a correlational or passive observational design that has limited internal validity. The nature of these variables precluded the use of more convincing designs, such as randomized experiments. As a result, we can check rival explanations of the observed association, such as reverse causation or confounding, only by statistical control of the pertinent variables collected in the survey. There remains the possibility that some important but unmeasured confounding variable could, if it were included in the analyses and statistically controlled, reduce to insignificance the apparent association of our key variables. Although this threat cannot be ruled out (the impossibility of proving a negative), the numerous variables that were measured and checked in this study make that scenario implausible.

Another design-related problem involves the sequencing of events. Our causal explanation assumes that the adverse employment change from being adequately employed to being underemployed (e.g., between 1992 and 1994) preceded the change in well-being (e.g., moving from lower depression in 1992 to higher depression in 1994). In a true experimental design, the presumed causal event would be administered as a treatment, so as to leave no doubt that it occurred prior to the outcome measure. But the present correlational design leaves open the possibility that the change in depression (or drinking or self-esteem) took place before the employment change.

Taking more frequent measures of employment status and well-being between the annual surveys (e.g., by diary or other retrospective methods) could have provided evidence on the timing of these employment and psychological events. Although the NLSY did not collect such data, other studies have, and their results tend to show the employment event (e.g., job loss) occurring before emotional changes such as increased depression (Eales, 1988; Montogomery et al., 1999). In our analyses, moreover, the birthweight results seem especially resistant to this timing explanation. That is, the adverse employment change experienced by the pregnant mother occurred unambiguously before the birth of the child.

Sample

Generalizability. The sample surveyed in the NLSY provides one of the strengths of this study. Its large size provides statistical power sufficient to detect even small associations. Its sampling design ensures fair representation of all types of young Americans growing to maturity after 1979. But no sample can represent all populations and assure universal external validity. As a sample of residents of the United States during the last decades of the twentieth century, these respondents cannot inform us about their age peers in other countries or in other eras.

But they do reflect the experience of young people living in a large multiethnic and multicultural society passing through a very interesting economic period. They entered a labor market experiencing not only the usual business cycle variation but also more secular shifts. They participated in the ongoing transition from an industrial economy to one based more on service and information technology. They found themselves working less for local and national commercial organizations and increasingly as employees of global enterprises. Whether their experiences illuminate those of future workers depends on the extent to which these economic trends continue in the new century.

Age. One feature of the NLSY data provides both a special advantage and a serious limitation – the age restriction of the sample. That we can follow a panel of respondents from their high school years until well into their thirties provides a great opportunity. These data permit exploration of potentially important developmental changes – especially in early adulthood, when the employment–well-being relationship may be especially critical.

On the other hand, the absence of data on respondents in their middle or later years limits any conclusions that can be drawn. Are young adults more or less sensitive to adverse employment change than people in their forties, fifties, or sixties? How does removal from the workforce by retirement compare with unemployment by plant closing? Perhaps these questions will be answered in future analyses of the NLSY as its sample continues to mature and be reinterviewed.

11

New Directions

> It is quite easy to provide work for everyone, if no one minds how low his pay is. But quite rightly most people do mind a great deal. . . .
>
> A. G. B. Fisher, 1945, p. 28

RESEARCH IMPLICATIONS

Expanding Measures

Including Inadequate Employment. The present findings argue for expanding the usual paradigm of research on unemployment that contrasts people with and without jobs. On several well-being indicators, people who fall from adequate to economically inadequate employment resemble those who become unemployed altogether. This finding implies that researchers can no longer treat all jobs as functionally equivalent. If the changing nature of work brings a rising share of economically inadequate jobs, the health consequences linked to these changes will increasingly demand our attention.

Researchers could, with little extra effort, subdivide employees on the basic economic dimensions of hours and wages. Are employees getting sufficient hours of work, or are they working involuntarily part-time? Are workers receiving hourly wages that, on a full-time basis, provide an adequate standard of living (e.g., relative to the federal poverty guideline or to local cost-of-living measures)? Our research suggests that small-sample studies with too few respondents in either the low-wage or the low-hours subgroup could combine such subgroups into a single group for analytic purposes. This subdivision by hours and wages offers an inexpensive, objective, and theoretically appealing way of categorizing workers for the purposes of social epidemiological research. Of course, numerous other characteristics, besides hours and wages, suggest themselves as potentially useful for the study of employment types and transitions. We will consider a more comprehensive approach in a later section.

In the first instance, new studies need to check these employment categories in replications of the present findings (e.g., Friedland & Price, in press). Numerous job loss studies were required before the general acceptance of unemployment's adverse effects. Similarly, inadequate employment's adverse effects will need more documentation than the present sparse literature provides. Beyond the problem of confirming the health effects of various forms of underemployment, there remains the problem of external validity. The NLSY sample, young Americans in the 1980s and 1990s, limits the conclusions that can be drawn with respect to nationality, era, and respondent age. For wider generalizability, research will have to check these results in older Americans, in representative samples from other countries, and periodically during future phases of the business cycle.

Improving Unemployment Research. This recommendation to divide employment into categories based on economic adequacy may seem irrelevant to scholars whose primary focus remains on unemployment. On the contrary, this new approach may be vital to such researchers, for two reasons. First, the traditional way of estimating the effect of unemployment is to contrast it with employment. But if jobs are being downgraded with respect to hours and wages, the contrast between the average (often inadequately) employed person and the average unemployed person will tend to narrow or even disappear. As Fryer says, "it may only be a matter of time until the deteriorating mean mental health of employed people obliterates this formerly largely reliable difference" (1999, p. 1).

Our findings show that the mean level of functioning of the inadequately employed typically falls between the mean level of functioning of the adequately employed and the unemployed. Combining the inadequately and adequately employed into a single group must necessarily bring the mean of that combined group below the level of the adequately employed and nearer the level of the unemployed. Even when, as in the present NLSY analyses, the samples are so large that either contrast would reach statistical significance, the different effect sizes might still be worth noting. As reported in Chapter 5 on self-esteem, the apparent adverse effect of unemployment was about 18% greater when the unemployed were contrasted with the adequately employed than when they were contrasted with all employed. This method effect (the reduced effect due to comparing the unemployed with all employed rather than with the adequately employed) will no doubt vary over different outcomes and samples. However, in studies with low power it may make the difference between finding and missing a significant effect of unemployment.

There is a second reason why unemployment researchers should pay attention to the adequacy of employment. As noted in the first chapter, there are worrisome indicators that the level of inadequate employment is rising. The social costs of job loss (self-evident to workers and corroborated by social scientists) have helped to sensitize employers and governments to the human and political problems of unemployment. As a result, policies designed to reduce official unemployment rates seem very attractive. Unfortunately, such policies may sometimes operate by buying lower joblessness with higher inadequate employment (e.g., work-sharing schemes that divide full-time jobs into several part-time jobs, or plans that reduce higher-paid middle-management positions in favor of more lower-paid entry-level positions). Such efforts may result in an increase in disguised unemployment even when official unemployment rates seem to remain flat or to decline. In order to monitor such changing forms of unemployment, researchers will need to expand their operational definitions to include various forms of inadequate employment.

Employment Continuum

Rationale. Expanding the range of employment statuses need not stop with the distinction between economically adequate and inadequate jobs as defined in the present research. The time now seems ripe for research on work and health to move toward a new paradigm based on a comprehensive employment continuum. Such a continuum could include subdivisions of employment not only by hours and wages but also by other economic (e.g., pension, health insurance) and psychological (e.g., perceived job security, demand/latitude) factors. This continuum could also include subdivisions of unemployment (e.g., acknowledging welfare recipients and discouraged workers in addition to the officially unemployed).

Why should we complicate the research task by adding further categories to the basic ones studied here? First, there is a long-standing recognition that employment statuses are multifaceted in ways that can affect health. For example, Warr's Vitamin Model (1987) defines nine dimensions on which both employment and unemployment can be assessed, including such concepts as opportunity for control, opportunity for skill use, availability of money, opportunity for interpersonal contact, and value of social position. Warr explicitly recognized the possibility not only of good and bad jobs but also of good and bad unemployment depending on each situation's profile on these dimensions.

Undesirable forms of employment can result not only from their economic inadequacy, as examined here, but also from other economic and psychological characteristics, such as those proposed by Warr. Various studies have documented that these unsatisfactory types of employment can in turn function much like unemployment in relation to health outcomes. Two longitudinal school-leaver studies using different measures of "bad" jobs illustrate such findings. Feather (1990) used longitudinal methods to compare school-leavers who entered good employment versus poor employment as defined in terms of one of Warr's dimensions – opportunity for skill use. On various outcomes, including depression and life satisfaction, respondents in poor employment (low opportunity for skill use) more closely resembled the unemployed than those in good employment. Using another approach, Winefield and his colleagues (1993) divided employed school-leavers into those with high and low job satisfaction. Respondents in "bad" jobs (low satisfaction) resembled the unemployed more than the satisfactorily employed on outcomes such as self-esteem. We considered the possibility that characteristics such as job satisfaction operate as mediators between a job's economic adequacy, as measured in this study, and outcomes such as self-esteem. However, when we controlled for job satisfaction, the association between economic adequacy and self-esteem in school-leavers remained (see Chapter 5). This suggests that different job facets can independently influence well-being and thus warrant recognition in a more comprehensive employment typology.

A second reason for capturing more gradations of employment quality is that it would permit improved study of employment transitions. Without the distinction between economically adequate and inadequate jobs used in this study, the effect of job loss could not be properly estimated. Losing an undesirable job and losing a desirable job represent psychologically different phenomena that can be studied only if the gradations in job adequacy are measured. Extending this logic, it seems plausible that economically adequate jobs could usefully be subdivided into those that are barely adequate (no benefits, poor psychological features) and those that provide long-term security, pension plans, health insurance, high income, status, and so forth. Surely the meaning and impact of job loss would differ between two such "adequate" types of jobs. By a similar logic, differences in unemployment might affect the meaning and effect of job loss – for example, whether the individual has unemployment insurance or not.

Third, a more refined system for categorizing good and bad employment and good and bad unemployment can acknowledge and synthesize the multiple theories and conceptual schemes that exist but that seldom converge in the same study. For example, one theory focuses on the psychological quality of work and identifies "bad" jobs as offering the worker low control or latitude in combination with high work demand (Karasek & Theorell, 1990). Evidence from studies using this approach show that people in bad jobs will be more likely to have health problems. But how does this dimension of work relate to others, such as economic adequacy of employment? And does employment change (e.g., job loss) vary depending on whether one is leaving a "good" or "bad" job, defined in combinations of high and low economic adequacy and high and low psychological desirability?

Finally, a multidimensional approach to categorizing employment will facilitate our search for moderators and mediators of the relationship between employment change and health. The present study, like most research in this field, included a limited number of potential contextual variables, making it impossible to assess the role played by constructs from some other relevant theories (e.g., Warr's "vitamins," Jahoda's latent variables, Karasek and Theorell's work characteristics). Bringing together the key variables from diverse research domains could help us to identify which of them overlap as different facets of the same constructs, which explain adverse employment change effects (mediators), and which identify the conditions or subgroups for which adverse employment change has the greatest impact (moderators).

Approaches. How might we proceed toward a more comprehensive employment-status measurement system? One possible approach would combine any two existing systems by assigning people to mutually exclusive cells of a matrix defined by crossing the categories of one with those of the other. For example, the categories of the Labor Utilization Framework (LUF) could be combined with high versus low levels on a factor such as social status (found among both Warr's "vitamins" and Jahoda's latent variables). In order to add another psychological factor, such as opportunity for socialization or opportunity to use one's skills, this matrix would have to expand by one dimension per added factor. Given that some theories include numerous factors, any attempt to cross all possible categories of even a small subset of theories would produce a conceptually daunting multidimensional matrix. Making this approach dynamic would require still further complication in order to reflect a worker's changing location in such a matrix over different time points. As a practical matter, the application of such an elaborate system to any but the largest samples would necessarily yield cells with too few subjects for analysis.

As a more feasible alternative method for synthesizing different employment categorizing systems, we suggest a simpler initial approach that locates employment statuses on a single dimension rather than in numerous cells of a multidimensional matrix. Using a typology suggested by Warr's terminology, we can imagine an ordered set of mutually exclusive employment situations starting with "good" (or "best") jobs at one end, through "bad" jobs and "good" unemployment in the middle, to "bad" (or "worst") unemployment at the other end. Others have explored such good-versus-bad job typologies that take into account employment characteristics such as nonstandard employment (e.g., on-call, day labor, temporary-help agency) and access to health insurance and pension benefits (Kalleberg et al., 2000).

Starting with an economically defined employment continuum such as the LUF used in this research (see Chapter 3), it is possible to incorporate additional gradations drawn from other conceptual systems. For example, one exploratory approach elaborated the LUF continuum by subdividing the large group of workers who fall into the economically adequate category (Grzywacz & Dooley, 2003). Workers with above-poverty wages were assigned to the "barely adequate" category if their jobs were deficient on additional criteria, both economic (e.g., unstable employment, lacking employer-paid health insurance) and psychological (little decision latitude, unsatisfying coworker relations). Economically adequate jobs that met one type of additional criteria but not the other could be "psychologically good" or "economically good," and jobs that met both types of additional criteria were considered "optimal employment."

In two different large surveys, analyses of this employment status continuum revealed significant associations between less-than-optimal jobs and poorer physical and mental health. Although preliminary, such findings invite further development of such "good-bad" employment status continua. Such simplified categorizing approaches may facilitate research by helping scholars from different domains to combine their focal variables in manageable ways. As will be discussed later, employment typologies with a few mutually exclusive, ordered levels might serve as templates for expanding the current official measures of the labor market (unemployed versus employed) on which we base most of our policy discussions. Finally, such one-dimensional continua can facilitate dynamic employment-change research by capturing the direction and magnitude of shifts up or down the scale.

APPLICATIONS TO POLICY

Interventions

Social Significance. The statistical significance tests reported in previous chapters show that the associations between adverse employment change and the well-being indicators are probably not due to chance (i.e., the result of sampling errors). But relationships, especially ones measured in very large samples such as the NLSY, can reach statistical significance without being socially significant. Do these findings provide any basis for reassessing social policies or clinical practice?

The studied relationships might fail to reach social significance in either of two ways. First, the outcome measures might reflect relatively minor symptoms of distress (e.g., feeling blue) rather than signs of more severe disorder (e.g., major depression). Unlike psychiatric epidemiological surveys, the NLSY generally did not use standard diagnostic instruments designed to identify cases of clinical disorder. However, the questions used to tap symptoms of alcohol abuse and depression did resemble those used for such case-finding surveys. But it is still possible that the observed differences in such symptoms (e.g., the differences between adequately employed and unemployed respondents) fell in the range below the critical levels that reflect serious disorder. As discussed in Chapters 6 and 7, we conducted some analyses based on dichotomous versions of the outcome measures that were designed to reflect high (e.g., the top 10–15%) levels of alcohol abuse and depression. The adverse employment effects persisted even with these quasi-clinical outcomes. Similarly, the harmful effects of adverse employment change on average birthweight (measured in ounces) persisted in dichotomous analysis of more clinically meaningful low birthweight (less than 5.5 pounds; see Chapter 9).

Second, the observed effect sizes may be large enough to reach statistical significance but too small to matter for policy purposes. As reported in the analytic chapters, the pertinent coefficients (even when adjusted for prior symptom measures and other controls) typically reached levels comparable to those of other important explanatory variables.

Moreover, these regression coefficients almost certainly underestimate the total effect of adverse employment change. Members of the underemployed worker's family are likely to feel the effects by social contagion processes. Income loss will lower the standard of living of the whole family. Increases in the worker's alcohol consumption or depressive symptoms may well trigger or exacerbate intrafamily strife. A small literature documents such spillover effects for both children (Steinberg et al., 1981) and spouses (Atkinson et al., 1986; Dew et al., 1987; Rook et al., 1991) of the unemployed. The present study extends the unemployment literature by showing how the stress of a worker's underemployment can also cross generations (the birthweight results of Chapter 9). Thus, the underemployment effects reported here are best viewed as lower-bound estimates of the true total effects. The evidence for such spillover effects invites further work to measure their size and causal mechanisms for both unemployment and inadequate employment and to develop appropriate interventions.

Targeting Interventions. The results of the present study also offer guidance for targeting interventions. The sparse evidence for interactions (moderating variables) implies that adverse employment change is general in its impact, with little variation in the sensitivity of different subgroups. That is, these findings suggest that underemployment causes no more harm when it happens to one type of person (by gender, age, or ethnicity) than when it happens to another.

But the relative absence of interactions does not mean that all groups are equally affected. Different groups experience underemployment at different rates, that is, exposure to this stressor is not evenly distributed throughout the population. Aggregate underemployment levels indirectly influence pathology through the individual worker's personal adverse job experiences. Thus those groups experiencing the highest levels of underemployment will have the greatest exposure to such harmful effects. Underemployment levels vary widely, not only over time and across geographical areas but also by such demographic characteristics as race/ethnicity and age (Chapter 1). Were interventions aimed at those people with the greatest risk of underemployment in the United States, they would certainly focus on young people, especially those from ethnic minorities.

The present study provides other clues for intervention stemming from the findings about the impact of favorable employment change. Conventional wisdom regards reemployment as the best antidote to unemployment. By extrapolation, getting an economically adequate job should provide benefits to those currently in inadequate jobs. This premise, which provides the foundation for many job-training and job-finding interventions, has received surprisingly little scrutiny. For example, does favorable employment change benefit mainly those underemployed individuals who show signs of disorder (i.e., by restoring them to better functioning), or does it assist workers in general, regardless of their level of disorder? Does favorable employment change operate in similar ways and to similar degrees for different types of health outcomes and different kinds of people? Too little is known to answer these questions with confidence.

Our results suggest that there may well be differences in the way favorable employment change contributes to well-being. In the case of alcohol misuse, following the restorative principle, favorable change seemed to reduce the risk of heavy drinking in the short run among those who were heavy drinkers, but not among others. However, similar improvement did not appear in measures of alcohol abuse symptoms. In the case of depression, favorable employment change was associated with a general decrease in depression that was not limited to those who were highly depressed. Such outcome variations invite further study of the mechanisms by which favorable employment change works and of the factors that might amplify or negate its beneficial effects. Although preliminary, the present empirical results, in accord with conventional wisdom, support interventions aimed at moving workers out of underemployment. Comparing such interventions to other strategies, such as those aimed at preventing adverse employment change, requires a more comprehensive picture of the array of possible approaches and their consequences.

Unintended Consequences. This research implies that policy in the employment and health area should no longer focus solely on unemployment but should also treat economically inadequate employment as a comparable risk factor. Seemingly simple, this principle could prove to be very complicated in practice. Some types of unemployment interventions (e.g., training for and placement in good jobs) might easily adapt to the problem of inadequately employed workers. But some approaches to unemployment may have the unintended (or not fully appreciated) consequence of increasing inadequate employment. For example, high unemployment levels frequently elicit calls for work sharing – that is, dividing full-time jobs into enough pieces so that everyone can have a part-time job. Proposals to reduce the statutory work week often draw on this rationale (e.g., the reduction in France in 1998 from thirty-nine to thirty-five hours). If employers continue to pay their workers the same total wages for less work, the employees may well perceive this as a favorable employment change that provides them more leisure at no cost. But if employers reduce wages commensurate with hours, the workers would experience this as involuntary part-time employment, with all of the health consequences documented in these studies.

Any other policy that increases employment by decreasing the economic adequacy of employment risks similar unintended health effects. Another approach to increasing the number of jobs consists of shortening work careers by such tactics as delaying entry into the workforce (e.g., by lengthening mandatory education) and hastening departure from the workforce (e.g., by lowering the retirement age). But for some young people with limited academic interest or ability, an extended stay in school may prove less conducive to psychological maturation than finding an adequate job. Similarly, taking early retirement may prove less desirable and less beneficial to the health of some workers than others. Such career-narrowing policies should be evaluated not just for the number of new jobs created but also for their potential adverse effects.

One way to expand employment is through decreasing wages. In a theoretically frictionless labor market without the rigidities of minimum wages, employers would be able to lower their pay rates to levels at which everyone, even the least productive workers, would be employed. Because the lowest of such free-falling wages would not cover the cost of living, most societies have instituted minimum-wage laws. However, every legislative effort to raise such minimum wages (e.g., to keep pace with inflation) evokes the opposing argument that it will increase unemployment. Thus, efforts to minimize low-wage underemployment can be challenged as threats to full employment. In sum, policies favoring the adequacy of employment will frequently compete with policies trying to reduce unemployment.

Typology of Employment Interventions. A discussion of all of the actual and potential approaches to reducing the social costs of underemployment would far exceed the scope of this chapter. However, it is possible to describe the variety of such interventions, both extant and potential, by noting some of the dimensions along which they can be arrayed. As just described, one relevant dimension involves the degree to which efforts to mitigate one type of underemployment (say, unemployment) produce unintended increases in another type (say, economically inadequate employment). The present study clearly favors those types of policies that can produce reductions in one without creating offsetting increases in the other. Other relevant dimensions on which we might sort employment interventions include the developmental age of the target population (e.g., young school-leavers versus older workers facing retirement) and the efficacy or efficiency of potential interventions (i.e., the probable effectiveness or cost of such programs).

Two other dimensions have proved useful in categorizing interventions for adverse employment change (Dooley & Catalano, 2000). The first consists of the timing of the intervention effort, adapted from Caplan's classic three-tier definition of prevention stages (Caplan, 1964). Caplan's primary prevention category includes interventions taking place before exposure to the risk factor. Secondary prevention takes place after the early appearance of symptoms resulting from such exposure; tertiary prevention consists of rehabilitative efforts to deal with symptoms that have become chronic.

If we consider adverse employment change to be the risk factor, it seems useful to subdivide Caplan's primary prevention into two categories. Proactive primary prevention aims to prevent exposure to the risk factor, whereas reactive primary prevention concedes that the individual may not avoid exposure and instead aims to inoculate the individual against the worst effects of the stressor. This four-level prevention-stage dimension helps us to consider the best timing of efforts to reduce the social costs of employment stress.

The second dimension consists of the level of the intervention, roughly divided between individual or family units at the micro level and larger community or organizational units at the macro level. This dimension helps us to think about the best tactics of intervention – person-by-person clinical or educational efforts versus more group-oriented policies focusing on systems in the aggregate. The matrix defined by crossing these two dimensions provides a conceptual map on which we can locate various types of interventions in this area. Table 11.1 provides a brief summary of this approach, with a few intervention examples for each cell of the matrix (for a more detailed discussion of this approach, see Dooley & Catalano, 2000).

The approaches in each of these cells offer different sets of advantages and disadvantages. For example, macro interventions at the proactive primary prevention stage would, if successful, change the economic environment so as to minimize the number of people experiencing the hazards of adverse employment change. This approach has the advantage of sparing a whole population the distress of adverse employment experiences, but it has the disadvantage of being extremely difficult to achieve in practice. Even if economists could agree on how to arrange the economy so that everyone enjoyed full employment in adequate jobs, there would remain serious political difficulties in executing such policies. Full and adequate

TABLE 11.1. *Intervention typology: examples for economic stress*

Stage	Micro Level (Individual or Family)	Macro Level (Greater than Family)
Preventing adverse employment change	Avoidance: Education and training to prepare workers better for finding and keeping jobs in the changing economy	Environmental: Fiscal and monetary policies to reduce the unemployment rate
Preventing symptoms resulting from adverse employment change	Ecological Coping: Hardiness training; workshops and counseling for the recently unemployed	Ecological Enabling: Early warning of plant closures and layoffs; changing community tolerance of unemployment
Early intervention for symptoms of adverse employment change	Early Detection/Treatment: Crisis intervention for those distressed by recent unemployment	Population Screening/ Education: Advisories to healthcare providers regarding at-risk groups
Managing disease resulting from adverse employment change	Medical Care: Social service assistance to help the disabled find or keep work; clinical treatment for distress due to joblessness	Medical Enabling: Assuring continuing health insurance/care for the unemployed

Source: Dooley and Catalano (2000, Table 2, p. 121).

employment, however attractive it is as a social goal, has remained beyond our reach, with the result that we must consider other options, each with its own mix of pros and cons.

An alternate approach to proactive primary prevention could operate at the micro level by targeting that group at the greatest risk of under-employment – young people leaving school. For example, educational practices at the high school level might be altered to facilitate the transition of young people from school into the workforce. Effective career-centered educational programs tend to be more common outside the United States (e.g., in Germany). However, such programs have appeared in some U.S. schools, along with preliminary evaluations of their effectiveness (Gore et al., in press). America is already struggling to reform its educational system. Whether the present changes will produce better transitions into the labor force for young people remains to be seen. Because such reforms will prove expensive and require long-term commitments by local school districts across the country, they seem likely to encounter both economic and political difficulties.

Similarly, the other potential interventions noted in the cells of Table 11.1 pose their own unique combinations of promised (if not always documented) benefits and probable economic and political challenges. How can we choose from such a widely varying set of potential tools for dealing with the social costs of underemployment? Ideally, each of these options would be thoroughly evaluated to determine the most cost-effective intervention for any given subgroup of the population. Unfortunately, a literature of evaluation studies adequate to provide such comprehensive guidance over the whole range of interventions has yet to emerge (Dooley & Catalano, 2000).

One hindrance to the development of such a systematic set of evaluations is the fact that the necessary research must come from many different disciplines. For example, clinical and community psychologists can evaluate the effectiveness of programs in the micro-level, secondary prevention cell, which involves helping unemployed individuals to manage their distress (e.g., the successful JOBS program – see Vinokur & Schul, 1997). And economists could compare alternative fiscal and monetary policies for reducing unemployment rates for the whole nation. But we have no common metric for comparing the relative advantages of investing in one approach versus another. Each requires a different expertise, and experts in one field (say, behavioral medicine) will rarely have the interdisciplinary knowledge and stature to offer credible guidance to experts from another field working at a different level of analysis with different methods (say, economists). Evaluating and comparing the many alternative approaches to the reduction of underemployment's social costs promises to be a long, complex project.

Measurement as an Intervention

Measuring the Employment Continuum. As a modest first step toward more dialog across the disciplines concerned with underemployment, we offer one practical suggestion. Clinicians, public health professionals, and economists might usefully agree to expand their domain of concern beyond unemployment to include additional categories of inadequate employment. Psychiatrists, psychologists, and social workers concerned with the impacts of job loss could expand their interventions to deal with parallel forms of distress resulting from other forms of underemployment. Social epidemiologists might begin to measure the health costs of different types of adverse employment change in order to insert their findings into the political debate about economic policy. Government and private statisticians who measure the labor force and journalists who report those measures might expand the usual reports of unemployment rates to highlight rates of other forms of underemployment.

The United States has frequently updated its standard labor force measures, both to reflect changing definitions and to improve their accuracy. The present suggestion to expand the categories that are routinely measured and reported thus falls in a long tradition of such adjustments. In the spectrum of possible interventions just noted, this is a rather mild one that should neither require massive new expenditures nor produce any severe side effects. Nonetheless, it holds the promise of stimulating new epidemiological research on the health effects of employment change other than job loss. By raising the public's awareness, such a change could help to promote the invention and evaluation of interventions that treat not just unemployment but also other types of underemployment. In this final section, we will briefly review the historical background and present state of the official U.S. employment measures. After considering some of the arguments against expanding these measures, we will illustrate an alternative approach using data from the NLSY.

The Great Depression made Americans aware of the need to monitor the economic activity of the nation, including employment and unemployment, on a regular basis. In 1937, the Works Projects Administration (WPA) made one of the first attempts to count the number of unemployed persons in the United States (Bregger & Dippo, 1993; also see Jensen & Slack, in press). This effort, called the Enumerative Check Census of Unemployment, consisted of a mail (postcard) survey of the entire nation. Because of the numerous problems associated with accounting for nonresponse and determining who in the household had actually filled out the postcard, a more formal survey, the Monthly Report of Unemployment, was designed in 1940. This survey, which began with approximately 8,000 households, was turned over to the Bureau of the Census in 1942 and has since been renamed the Current Population Survey (CPS). In 1959, the Bureau of Labor Statistics was given the responsibility for creating and publishing monthly employment and unemployment statistics using data from the CPS.

In its present form, the CPS samples approximately 50,000 households and obtains data characterizing the employment status of each member of the household fifteen years of age and older. The survey takes place on a 4-8-4 rotation schedule, where households are interviewed for four months, then exit the survey for eight months, and then reenter the survey for another four months. For a detailed chronology of changes in the survey since its inception and a more thorough discussion of the sampling procedure and design of the CPS, see U.S. Bureau of Labor Statistics (2000b). During the past half-century, the CPS has evolved into the primary data source used to generate the monthly and annual statistics that summarize the labor force activity of the United States.

The Comprehensive Employment and Training Act (CETA) of 1973 first recognized inadequate employment at the federal policy level. The National Commission on Employment and Unemployment Statistics (1978; 1979) was charged with reassessing labor market statistics with regard to how they measure or reflect "labor market hardship" and the "underemployed." This commission recommended the development and publication of indicators of labor market hardship and underemployment.

Even earlier, in 1976, the Bureau of Labor Statistics introduced a range of labor market measures called "alternative unemployment measures," formally referred to as the U1–U7 series (Bregger & Haugen, 1995). These measures, based on different definitions of the labor force and unemployment (the U5 measure was the "official" unemployment rate), were intended to more accurately represent unemployment among certain groups for whom it might have more serious consequences (e.g., full-time workers versus part-time workers) or be underestimated (e.g., among part-time workers). These alternative measures partially addressed employment hardship in that they included measures of involuntary part-time employment (for economic reasons), but they did not include information about income – specifically, about workers making less-than-poverty wages.

When the CPS was redesigned in 1994, the U1–U7 series was revised to include just six measures (U1–U6) and given a new title, "alternative measures of unemployment and other forms of labor resource underutilization." As the title implies, these new measures were intended to reflect various forms of labor underutilization. Beginning in 1994, the U3 measure represented the routinely reported "official" unemployment rate. The redesign of the CPS affected these alternative measures in two important ways (Bowie, Cahoon, & Martin, 1993; Bregger & Dippo, 1993). First, the number of persons classified as employed part-time for economic reasons is now lower than it was before 1994, because respondents are now directly asked about their desire and availability for full-time work, whereas in the past this was inferred from other questions in the survey. Second, the number of persons classified as discouraged was reduced by about one-half because of changes in the definition of discouragement. Beginning in 1994, people classified as discouraged must explicitly want and be available for work and have searched for work during the prior year, even though they are not currently looking for a job because they feel their search would be in vain. The revised measures are described in Table 11.2.

The existence of these various categories shows the feasibility of estimating alternative measures of total underemployment using the present form of the Current Population Survey. We might improve on the routinely reported unemployment rates (U3) in two ways. One would be to encourage the scientific use and journalistic reporting of the measure U-6, which provides the best already-available estimate of the total underemployment rate. This measure includes not only unemployed persons but also the "marginally attached" (including discouraged workers) plus involuntary part-time workers.

The other approach would be to encourage the continued modification of the alternative measures of labor force underutilization. One such adjustment would be to enlarge the number of categories to include one

TABLE 11.2. *Range of alternative measures of unemployment and other forms of labor resource underutilization (1994 annual averages)*

Measure	Percent
U1 Persons unemployed fifteen weeks or longer, as a percentage of the civilian labor force.	2.2
U2 Job losers and persons who completed temporary jobs, as a percentage of the civilian labor force.	2.9
U3 Total unemployed persons, as a percentage of the civilian labor force (the official unemployment rate).	6.1
U4 Total unemployed persons plus discouraged workers, as a percentage of the civilian labor force plus discouraged workers.	6.5
U5 Total unemployed persons, plus discouraged workers, plus all other "marginally attached" workers,[a] as a percentage of the civilian labor force plus all "marginally attached" workers.	7.4
U6 Total unemployed persons, plus all "marginally attached" workers, plus all persons employed part-time for economic reasons, as a percentage of the civilian labor force plus all "marginally attached" workers.	10.9

[a] Marginally attached workers want and are available for a job and have recently searched for work, regardless of their reason for not currently looking. The category includes discouraged workers and those who are not currently looking for work for reasons such as childcare or transportation problems.

Source: Bregger and Haugen (1995, Exhibit 2, p. 23).

of the larger groups of inadequately employed workers that is currently excluded – those in low- or poverty-wage employment. The CPS data could be analyzed in order to identify such workers, as illustrated by the computations reported by Jensen and colleagues (1999; in press) and summarized graphically in Figure 1.1. (p. 13). Such a new category of low-wage employment might then be added to the current U6 to provide a still better estimate of total underemployment.

If estimating and reporting such a total underemployment rate is feasible, why has it not been done? One possibility is that political interests might prefer reporting lower, not higher, rates of unfavorable economic indicators. Certainly high unemployment rates do not help the popularity of incumbents in presidential elections (Monroe, 1984). Some adjustments to the official definitions have tended to lower reported rates. For example, starting in 1983, resident members of the armed forces (military personnel stationed in the U.S.) were added to the workforce, thus decreasing the total unemployment rate by about 0.1% compared to the civilian unemployment rate (Bregger & Haugen, 1995). However, this alternate method was dropped at the end of 1993. Other recent changes have tended to lower the apparent level of underemployment. For example, an older version of total underemployment (called U-7) weighted persons seeking part-time jobs or working part-time for economic reasons by .5, thus reducing their contribution to the estimates. But this downward adjustment was dropped in the new total underemployment measure (called U-6) that came with the 1994 redesign of the CPS (Bregger & Haugen, 1995). On balance, the record does not support the hypothesis that the labor force statistics are tailored to disguise the true level of underemployment in the United States.

Another explanation for the lack of a more comprehensive underemployment measure points to the technical difficulties of estimating some aspects of inadequate employment (Jensen & Slack, in press). For example, workers living in economic hardship are difficult to identify based solely on low wages reported in employment surveys. Hardship stems not only from earned income but also from other nonemployment types of income. Moreover, it depends on the family's total income and the number of family members as well as the cost of living in the local community. The complexity of compiling and synthesizing all of these types of information has discouraged development of a low-wage component for standard labor force reports (Bregger & Haugen, 1995).

Finally, the most likely explanation for the lack of more vigorous reporting of underemployment is the lack of interest. Most consumers of labor force statistics appear to be interested primarily in changes over time in the overall economy – that is, in whether it is expanding or contracting as part of the business cycle. For this purpose, all of the employment indicators (e.g., U1–U7 before 1994) tend to move together. Thus, "there is little 'value added' analytically in tracking the alternative measures over time. While it is true that each indicator provides a different point estimate of 'unemployment,' all seven measures have essentially moved in lockstep across the business cycle" (Bregger & Haugen, 1995, p. 22).

However, even if the present labor force indicators meet most current policy and scholarly needs, they may not satisfy future needs. For example, there are indications that the nature of work is changing (see Chapter 1) in such a way that some forms of underemployment are on the rise. For example, with respect to the range of different labor force indicators, "several of the component series contained in the range have evidenced meaningful long-term trends – such as the upward trend in the incidence of involuntary part-time employment . . ." (Bregger & Haugen, 1995, p. 22). Similar trends may be taking place in other unmeasured components of underemployment such as low-wage jobs, but such long-term shifts will be overlooked if the focus remains narrowly on tracking the traditional business cycle.

Nevertheless, the data necessary to estimate several forms of economically inadequate employment either exist in the official CPS files or can be gathered in smaller social epidemiological surveys. Researchers can generate their own estimates of underemployment from these sources (e.g., Friedland & Price, in press; Jensen & Slack, in press). Perhaps one result of

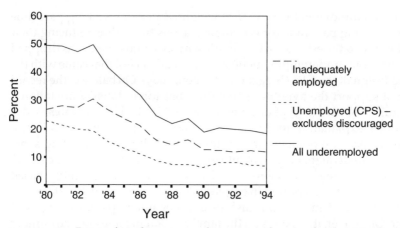

FIGURE 11.1. Rates of inadequate employment and unemployment in the NLSY. *Note:* Inadequately employed includes discouraged, involuntary part-time, and poverty-wage workers.

such scholarship will be to increase the breadth and depth of public and journalistic interest in such measures, which might in turn motivate further development of routinely reported official underemployment statistics.

Illustration from the NLSY. To illustrate how such statistics might add to our understanding of the labor market, we have used data from the NLSY from 1980 to 1994 to estimate two types of rates. One is the unemployment rate as it might be calculated according to the then-prevailing (pre-1994) official definitions. The other is a total underemployment rate that adds discouraged workers, involuntary part-time workers, and low-pay workers as we have defined them in the present study, following the LUF approach. The results appear in Figure 11.1.

Note that these estimates of underemployment do not parallel the official national rates of unemployment as discussed in Chapter 3. Because the NLSY sample is both younger and more heavily weighted toward minorities, the rates in this figure exceed those for the general population. In addition, because the NLSY sample is aging over the period of the survey, the respondents are leaving the high unemployment years of the late teens and early twenties and experiencing ever lower rates of underemployment over time. This age-related trend obscures the ups and downs of the business cycle that would appear in a general population survey such as the CPS. However, these data illustrate the degree to which total underemployment would be increased by adding the categories of discouraged workers and the inadequately employed.

We nominate this approach, not necessarily as the best, but as one reasonable alternative to the present official unemployment rate as a method of describing the U.S. labor force. Our data show that forms of inadequate employment, although not routinely reported, can nevertheless have serious public health consequences. In this changing economy, such forms of inadequate employment may be supplanting traditional unemployment. The existence of such labor force trends and their apparent social costs argue for increased monitoring of such forms of disguised unemployment in order to make them more visible to researchers, policy makers, and the public.

Appendix A

Description of NLSY Sample at Selected Survey Years

TABLE A.1. *Description of NLSY sample at selected survey years*

	1984 (*n* = 12,069)			1989 (*n* = 10,605)			1994 (*n* = 8,889)		
	Mean	%	St. Dev.	Mean	%	St. Dev.	Mean	%	St. Dev.
Demographic characteristics									
Age (years)	22.7		2.3	28.1		2.3	33.2		2.3
Ethnicity									
Hispanic		6.3			6.6			6.6	
African American		13.9			14.2			14.2	
Other		79.8			79.3			79.3	
Gender (% male)		50.9			50.9			50.9	
Education									
Years of education	12.6		2.0	13.1		2.4	13.2		2.4
Enrollment status:									
Not enrolled, less than twelfth grade		14.2			11.9			10.7	
Enrolled in high school		0.5			0.2			0.1	
Enrolled in college		19.0			7.5			4.5	
Not enrolled, high school graduate		66.3			80.3			84.7	
Parental years of education	12.5		3.1	12.5		3.1	12.9		3.1
Armed Forces Qualification Test (AFQT)	48.3		28.8	48.1		28.8	47.6		28.8

(*continued*)

TABLE A.1 (*continued*)

	1984 (n = 12,069)			1989 (n = 10,605)			1994 (n = 8,889)		
	Mean	%	St. Dev.	Mean	%	St. Dev.	Mean	%	St. Dev.
Household characteristics									
Marital status									
Never married		60.9			32.7			21.3	
Married		33.0			54.4			61.6	
Separated		2.5			3.7			4.3	
Divorced		3.6			9.0			12.4	
Widowed		0.1			0.2			0.4	
Number of children in household									
None		73.5			51.5			37.5	
One		15.2			19.6			19.2	
Two		8.7			19.3			27.1	
Three or more		2.6			9.6			16.2	
Family poverty status									
In poverty		13.7			8.9			8.1	
Not in poverty		78.7			73.7			71.4	
Missing		7.6			17.4			20.5	
Family income									
Median	$20,030.00 (n = 9,829)			$30,616.00 (n = 8,757)			$38,000.00 (n = 7,004)		
Environmental factors									
Geographical region									
South		33.7			34.4			35.3	
West		18.2			18.1			18.1	
North Central		27.8			28.1			28.5	
Northeast		20.3			19.5			18.1	
Urban/rural residence									
Urban		71.2			76.7			76.1	
Rural		18.4			20.2			21.7	
Missing		10.5			3.1			2.2	
Unemployment rate									
<3%		0.1			3.1			0.3	
3–5.9%		19.6			65.4			35.2	
6–8.9%		36.3			20.9			45.2	
9–11.9%		15.7			6.9			12.4	
12–14.9%		12.3			0.6			4.0	
15%+		5.4			0.1			0.9	
Missing		10.5			3.1			2.1	

	1984 (n = 12,069)			1989 (n = 10,605)			1994 (n = 8,889)		
	Mean	%	St. Dev.	Mean	%	St. Dev.	Mean	%	St. Dev.
Psychological health									
CES-D (1994)[a]	–			–			3.8		4.1
Self-esteem (1980)[b]	32.4		4.1	32.2		4.1	32.3		4.1
	(n = 11,532)			(n = 10,135)			(n = 8,221)		
Self-esteem (1987)[b]	–			33.7		4.1	33.7		4.1
				(n = 9,971)			(n = 8,298)		
Alcohol									
Frequency of six or more drinks (single occasion, past thirty days)									
Nondrinker past									
thirty days		24.2			33.6			36.6	
Never		32.1			33.5			34.2	
Once		11.5			9.6			9.1	
Two or three times		14.9			11.4			10.1	
Four or five times		7.6			5.6			4.0	
Six or seven times		3.4			2.1			1.8	
Eight or nine times		1.9			1.1			0.8	
Ten or more times		4.4			3.1			3.4	
Number of alcohol symptoms reported during past year[c]									
Nondrinker past									
thirty days		24.2			33.6			36.6	
None		43.3			26.4			29.3	
One		13.3			9.6			8.1	
Two		7.6			6.8			6.4	
Three		4.8			5.9			4.7	
Four		2.6			4.1			4.0	
Five		1.6			3.1			2.5	
Six		1.1			2.4			2.1	
Seven or more		1.4			8.2			6.2	
DSM-IV	–								
Nondrinker past									
thirty days					33.8			42.5	
No alcohol									
dependence/abuse					52.3			45.7	
Alcohol abuse					7.8			6.1	
Alcohol dependent					6.1			5.6	
Family history of alcoholism									
First-degree									
biological only		13.4			14.2			14.2	
Second-degree									
biological only		19.3			20.3			19.9	
First- and second-									
degree biological		10.6			11.2			11.2	

(continued)

TABLE A.1 *(continued)*

	1984 ($n = 12{,}069$)			1989 ($n = 10{,}605$)			1994 ($n = 8{,}889$)		
	Mean	%	St. Dev.	Mean	%	St. Dev.	Mean	%	St. Dev.
Nonbiological relative		2.4			2.6			2.6	
Family history negative		46.0			48.3			46.9	
Missing		8.3			3.5			5.3	
Employment status									
Adequately employed		49.0			67.4			69.1	
Underemployed									
Unemployed		9.2			4.7			4.5	
Discouraged		1.2			0.7			1.0	
Involuntary part-time		3.1			2.0			1.5	
Poverty wages		16.5			9.0			6.7	
Intermittent unemployment		3.7			2.0			2.8	
Out of labor force		17.4			14.1			14.5	

[a] Based on seven items from the original twenty-item CES-D.

[b] Rosenberg Self-esteem Scale, ranging from 1 to 40, with higher values indicating higher levels of self-esteem.

[c] See Appendix B for listing of alcohol symptoms. There were eleven possible symptoms in 1984 and twenty-four symptoms in 1989 and 1994.

Note: Descriptive statistics are weighted using the sample weights provided by the NLSY.

Appendix B

Alcohol Variables by Survey Year: NLSY79

TABLE B.1. *Alcohol variables by survey year: NLSY79*

Item	Survey Years							
	82	83	84	85	88	89	92	94
Quantity/frequency								
Ever had a drink	√	√	√	√	√	√		√
Age when started drinking	√	√						
Age when started drinking at least once a month		√						
Had any alcoholic beverages in last month	√	√	√	√	√	√		√
Frequency of six or more drinks on one occasion in last month	√	√	√	√	√	√		√
Number of days drank in last week	√	√	√	√			√	
Number of bottles/glasses/ drinks of beer/wine/liquor in last week	√	√	√	√				
Number of days drank in last month		√	√	√	√	√		√
Number of days had 1/2/3/4/5/6+ drinks in last month		√	√	√				

(continued)

TABLE B.1 *(continued)*

	Survey Years							
Item	**82**	**83**	**84**	**85**	**88**	**89**	**92**	**94**
Number of days had hangover in last month		√	√	√				
Total number of days had drink in last month		√	√	√				
Frequency of going to bars last month	√	√	√					
Number of drinks per day / number R usually has on days R drinks						√	√	√	√
Abuse dependency symptoms, physiological/ behavioral symptoms								
Felt aggressive/cross while drinking			√	√	√			
Gotten into heated argument			√	√	√			
Gotten into a fight			√	√	√			√
Done things while drinking that caused others to be hurt						√		√
Can't remember activity while drunk			√	√	√			
Tried to cut down or quit but failed			√	√	√			
Afraid might be/become alcoholic			√	√	√			
Spent a lot of time drinking/ getting over drinking						√		√
Sick/vomited after drinking						√		√
Difficult to stop once started						√		√
Sweat/shake after drinking						√		√
Needed drink so badly couldn't think of anything else						√		
Drank more than intended to						√		√
Gotten drunk instead of doing things supposed to						√		

Item	Survey Years							
	82	83	84	85	88	89	92	94
So hung over interfered with things supposed to do						✓		✓
Heard/saw things not there						✓		✓
Difficult to stop until completely intoxicated			✓	✓	✓			
Often take a drink first thing in the morning			✓	✓	✓			
Hands shake in the morning			✓	✓	✓			
Gotten drunk while drinking alone			✓	✓	✓			
Kept drinking after promised self not to			✓	✓	✓			
Had strong desire/urge to drink						✓		
Found same amount of alcohol had less effect						✓		✓
Found you had to drink more than once did to get same effect						✓		
Continued drinking even though caused emotional problems						✓		✓
Lifestyle symptoms (impact on school, work, relationships)								
Drinking ever interfered with schoolwork	✓	✓	✓	✓				
Drinking ever interfered with job	✓	✓	✓	✓				
Kept drinking even though it caused problems with work, home, school								
Stayed away from work because of hangover			✓	✓	✓			✓
Gotten drunk on the job			✓	✓	✓			
Lost/nearly lost job because of drinking			✓	✓	✓			

(continued)

TABLE B.1 *(continued)*

Item	Survey Years							
	82	83	84	85	88	89	92	94
Drinking led to quitting job			√	√	√			√
Drinking hurt chances for promotion			√	√	√			√
Significant other left/threatened to leave						√		√
Arrested/trouble with police after drinking								√
Drink to keep from shaking after drinking/morning after drinking						√		√
Lost ties with/drifted apart from family members						√		√
Gave up/cut down activities/ interests						√		√
Drove a car after drinking too much						√		√
Familial history of alcohol abuse/dependency								
Any relatives been alcoholics/ problem drinkers at any time					√			
Relationship to first/second/ third/fourth/fifth/ sixth alcoholic relative					√			
Number of years lived with first/ second/third/fourth/fifth/ sixth alcoholic relative					√			

Source: Center for Human Resource Research (1997, pp. 66–67).

References

Addams, J. (1910). *Twenty Years at Hull-House*. New York: Macmillan.

Allan, E., & Steffensmeier, D. (1989). Underemployment and property crime: Differential effects of job availability and job quality on juvenile and young adult arrest rates. *American Sociological Review, 54*, 107–123.

American Psychiatric Association. (1994). *Diagnostic and statistical manual of mental disorders*, fourth ed. (DSM-IV). Washington, DC: APA.

Aneshensel, C. S., & Frerichs, R. R. (1982). Stress, support, and depression: A longitudinal causal model. *Journal of Community Psychology, 10*, 363–376.

Aneshensel, C. S., Rutter, C. M., & Lachenbruch, P. A. (1991). Social structure, stress, and mental health: Competing conceptual and analytic models. *American Sociological Review, 56*, 166–178.

Arnetz, B., Wasserman, J., Perini, B., Brenner, S-O., Levi, L., Eneroth, P., Salovaara, H., Hjelm, R., Theorell, T., & Petterson, I. L. (1987). Immune function in unemployed women. *Psychosomatic Medicine, 49*, 3–11.

Atkinson, T., Liem, R., & Liem, J. H. (1986). The social costs of unemployment: Implications for social support. *Journal of Health and Social Behavior, 27*, 317–331.

Babbi, E. (1995). *The practice of social research*, 7th ed. Belmont, CA: Wadsworth.

Bachman, J. G., O'Malley, P. M., & Johnston, J. (1978). *Youth in transition, Vol. VI. Adolescence to adulthood – Change and stability in the lives of young men*. Ann Arbor, MI: Institute for Social Research.

Bagley, S. C., White, H., & Golomb, B. A. (2001). Logistic regression in the medical literature: Standards for use and reporting, with particular attention to one medical domain. *Journal of Clinical Epidemiology, 54*, 979–985.

Baker, P., & Gallant, M. (1984/85). Self-esteem: Measurement strategies and problems. *Humboldt Journal of Social Relations, 12:1*, 36–48.

Baker, R., & Bradburn, N. (1992). CAPI: Impacts on data quality and survey costs. In *Proceedings of the 1991 Public Health Conference on Records and Statistics*. Washington, DC: U.S. National Center for Health Statistics.

Bandura, A. (Ed.). (1995). *Self-efficacy in changing societies*. New York: Cambridge University Press.

Banks, M. H., & Jackson, P. R. (1982). Unemployment and risk of minor psychiatric disorder in young people: Cross-sectional and longitudinal evidence. *Psychological Medicine, 12*, 789–798.

Barron, R., & Kenny, D. (1986). The moderator-mediator variable distinction in social psychological research: Conceptual, strategic, and statistical considerations. *Journal of Personality and Social Psychology, 51*, 1173–1182.

Bartley, M. (1992). *Authorities and partisans: The debate on unemployment and health.* Edinburgh: Edinburgh University Press.

Beck, U. (1992). *Risk society: Towards a new modernity.* (M. Ritter, Trans.). Newbury Park, CA: Sage.

Bernhardt, A., Morris, M., Handcock, M., & Scott, M. (1998). *Inequality and mobility: Trends in wage growth for young adults.* IEEE Working Paper No. 7. Retrieved June 13, 2000, from the world wide web: ⟨http://www.tc.columbia.edu/iee/PAPERS/workpap7.pdf⟩.

Bijleveld, C. C. J., van der Kamp, L., Mooijaart, A., van der Kloot, W., van der Leeden, R., & van der Burg, E. (1998). *Longitudinal data analysis: Designs, models and methods.* Thousand Oaks, CA: Sage.

Billings, A. C., & Moos, R. H. (1982). Stressful life events and symptoms: A longitudinal model. *Health Psychology, 1*, 99–117.

Bocknek, G. (1980). *The young adult: Development after adolescence.* Monterey, CA: Brooks/Cole.

Bolton, W., & Oatley, K. (1987). A longitudinal study of social support and depression in unemployed men. *Psychological Medicine, 17*, 453–460.

Booth, C. (1892). *Life and labour of the people of London, Vol. 1. East, Central and South London.* London: Macmillan.

Borus, M. (1984). A description of employed and unemployed youth. In M. E. Borus (Ed.), *Youth and the labor market* (pp. 13–56). Kalamazoo, MI: W. E. Upjohn Institute for Employment Research.

Bowie, C. E., Cahoon, L. S., & Martin, E. A. (1993). Overhauling the Current Population Survey: Evaluating changes in the estimates. *Monthly Labor Review,* September, 29–33.

Bregger, J. E., & Dippo, C. S. (1993). Overhauling the Current Population Survey: Why is it necessary to change? *Monthly Labor Review,* September, 3–9.

Bregger, J. E., & Haugen, S. E. (1995). BLS introduces new range of alternative unemployment measures. *Monthly Labor Review,* October, 19–26.

Brenner, M. H. (1973). *Mental illness and the economy.* Cambridge, MA: Harvard University Press.

Brenner, M. H. (1975). Trends in alcohol consumption and associated illness: Some effects of economic changes. *American Journal of Public Health, 65*, 1270–1291.

Brenner, M. H. (1976). *Estimating the social costs of economic policy: Implications for mental and physical health, and criminal aggression.* Paper No. 5, Report to the Congressional Research Service of the Library of Congress and Joint Economic Committee of Congress. Washington, DC: U.S. Government Printing Office.

Brenner, M. H. (1979). Mortality and the national economy: A review and the experience of England and Wales, 1936–76. *Lancet, 2*, 568–573.

Brenner, M. H., & Mooney, A. (1983). Unemployment and health in the context of economic change. *Social Science and Medicine, 17*, 1125–1138.

Bridges, W. (1994). *JobShift: How to prosper in a workplace without jobs.* Reading, MA: Addison-Wesley.

Brown, G. W., & Harris, T. (1978). *Social origins of depression: A study of psychiatric disorder in women.* New York: Free Press.

Burkhauser, R. (1986). Disability policy in the United States, Sweden, and the Netherlands. In M. Berkowitz & M. Hill (Eds.), *Disability and the labor market: Economic problems, policies, and programs* (pp. 262–284). Ithaca, NY: ILR Press.

Burkhauser, R. V., Daly, M. C., & Houtenville, A. J. (2000). *How working age people with disabilities fared over the 1990s business cycle.* Paper presented at the NASI Conference on Ensuring Health and Income Security for an Aging Workforce, January 26–27, 2000, Washington, D.C.

Burnett, J. (1994). *Idle hands: The experience of unemployment, 1790–1990.* London: Routledge.

Buss, T. F., & Redburn, F. S. (1983). *Mass unemployment: Plant closings and community health.* Beverly Hills: Sage.

Caetano, R., & Tam, T. W. (1995). Prevalence and correlates of DSM-IV and ICD-10 alcohol dependence: 1990 U.S. National Alcohol Survey. *Alcohol and Alcoholism, 30,* 177–186.

California Work and Health Survey. (1999). *1996 Work and Health Survey.* Retrieved August 17, 1999, from the world wide web: ⟨http://medicine.ucsf.edu/programs/cwhs⟩.

Calkins, C. (1930). *Some folks won't work.* New York: Harcourt Brace.

Caplan, G. (1964). *Principles of preventive psychiatry.* New York: Basic Books.

Caspi, A, Wright, B. R. E., Moffitt, T. E., & Silva, P. A. (1998). Early failure in the labor market: Childhood and adolescent predictors of unemployment in the transition to adulthood. *American Sociological Review, 63,* 424–451.

Catalano, R. (1981). Contending with rival hypotheses in correlation of aggregate time series (CATS): An overview for community psychologists. *American Journal of Community Psychology, 9,* 667–679.

Catalano, R. (1991). The health effects of economic insecurity: An analytic review. *American Journal of Public Health, 81,* 1148–1152.

Catalano, R., & Dooley, D. (1977). Economic predictors of depressed mood and stressful life events in a metropolitan community. *Journal of Health and Social Behavior, 18,* 292–307.

Catalano, R., Dooley, D., & Jackson, R. (1983). Selecting a time-series strategy. *Psychological Bulletin, 94,* 506–523.

Catalano, R., Dooley, D., & Jackson, R. (1985). Economic antecedents of help seeking: Reformulation of time-series tests. *Journal of Health and Social Behavior, 26,* 141–152.

Catalano, R., Dooley, D., Wilson, G., & Hough, R. (1993). Job loss and alcohol abuse: A test using data from the Epidemiologial Catchment Area Project. *Journal of Health and Social Behavior, 34,* 215–225.

Catalano, R., Hansen, H-T., & Hartig, T. (1999). The ecological effect of unemployment on the incidence of very low birthweight in Norway and Sweden. *Journal of Health and Social Behavior, 40,* 422–428.

Catalano, R., & Hartig, T. (2001). Communal bereavement and the incidence of very low birthweight in Sweden. *Journal of Health and Social Behavior, 42,* 333–341.

Catalano, R., & Kennedy, J. (1998). The effect of unemployment on disability caseloads in California. *Journal of Community and Applied Social Psychology, 8,* 137–144.

Catalano, R., Lind, S., Rosenblatt, A., & Novaco, R. (in press). Economic antecedents of foster care. *American Journal of Community Psychology.*

Catalano, R., Rook, K. S., & Dooley, D. (1986). Labor markets and help-seeking: A test of the employment security hypothesis. *Journal of Health and Social Behavior, 27,* 277–287.

Catalano, R., & Serxner, S. (1992). The effect of ambient threats to employment on low birthweight. *Journal of Health and Social Behavior, 33,* 363–377.

Center for Human Resource Research. (1995). *NLS handbook.* Columbus: The Ohio State University.

Center for Human Resource Research. (1999). *NLS: NLSY79 user's guide.* Columbus: The Ohio State University.

Center for Human Resource Research. (2000). *NLS handbook.* Columbus: The Ohio State University.

Chomitz, V. R., Cheung, L. W. Y., & Lieberman, E. (1995). The role of lifestyle in preventing low birth weight. *The Future of Children: Low Birth Weight, 5,* 121–138.

Clogg, C. C. (1979). *Measuring underemployment: Demographic indicators for the U.S.* New York: Academic Press.

Clogg, C. C., & Shihadeh, E. (1994). *Statistical models for ordinal variables.* Newbury Park, CA: Sage.

Clogg, C. C., & Sullivan, T. A. (1983). Labor force composition and underemployment trends, 1969–1980. *Social Indicators Research, 12,* 117–152.

Clogg, C., Sullivan, T., & Mutchler, J. (1986). Measuring underemployment and inequality in the work force. *Social Indicators Research, 18,* 375–393.

Cobb, S., & Kasl, S. V. (1977). *Termination: The consequences of job loss* (Report No. 76-1261). Cincinnati, OH: National Institute for Occupational Safety and Health, Behavioral and Motivational Factors Research.

Cochran, W. (1977). *Sampling techniques.* New York: Wiley.

Cohen, J., & Cohen P. (1983). *Applied multiple regression/correlation analysis for the behavioral sciences,* 2nd ed. Hillsdale, NJ: Erlbaum.

Cohen, L. E., & Felson, M. (1979). On estimating the social costs of national economic policy: A critical examination of the Brenner study. *Social Indicators Research, 6,* 251–259.

Cohn, R. M. (1978). The effect of employment status change on self attitudes. *Social Psychology, 41,* 81–93.

Copper, R., Goldenberg, R., Das, A., Elder, N., Swain, M., Norman, G., Ramsey, R., Cotroneo, P., Collins, B., Johnson, F., Jones, P., & Meier, A. (1996). The preterm prediction study: Maternal stress is associated with spontaneous preterm birth at less than thirty-five weeks' gestation. *American Journal of Obstetrics and Gynecology, 175,* 1286–1292.

Coyne, J. C., & Whiffen, V. E. (1995). Issues in personality as a diathesis for depression: The case of sociotrophy-dependency and autonomy-self-criticism. *Psychological Bulletin, 118,* 358–378.

Craig, T. J., & Van Natta, P. A. (1979). Influence of demographic characteristics on two measures of depressive symptoms. *Archives of General Psychiatry, 36,* 149–154.

Crawford, A., Plant, M. A., Kreitman, N., & Latchman, R. W. (1987). Unemployment and drinking behavior: Some data from a general population survey of alcohol use. *British Journal of Addiction, 82,* 1007–1016.

Crouse, D., & Cassady, G. (1994). The small-for-gestational-age infant. In G. Avery, M. Fletcher, & M. MacDonald (Eds.), *Neonatology: Pathophysiology and management of the newborn,* 4th ed. (pp. 369–387). Philadelphia: Lippincott.

Dammann, O., Walther, H., Aller, B., Schroder, M., Drescher, J., Lutz, D., Veelken, N., & Schulte, F. (1996). Development of a regional cohort of very-low-birthweight children at six years: Cognitive abilities are associated with neurological disability and social background. *Developmental Medicine and Child Neurology, 38,* 97–106.

Dasinger, L. K., Miller, R. E., Norris, J. C., & Speiglman, R. (2001). *Alameda County CalWORKs needs assessment and outcome study: Changes in economic, work, welfare, and barrier status 15 months post-baseline.* Berkeley, CA: Public Health Institute.

Dawes, R. M. (1994). *House of cards: Psychology and psychotherapy built on myth.* New York: Free Press.

Dew, M. A., Bromet, E. J., & Schulberg, H. C. (1987). A comparataive analysis of two community stressors' long-term mental health effects. *American Journal of Community Psychology, 15,* 167–184.

Dew, M. A., Penkower, L., & Bromet, E. J. (1991). Effects of unemployment on mental health in the contemporary family. *Behavior Modification, 15,* 501–544.

Dohrenwend, B. P., & Dohrewnwend, B. S. (1969). *Social status and psychological disorder: A causal inquiry.* New York: Wiley.

Dohrenwend, B. P., Levav, I., Shrout, P. E., Schwartz, S., Naveh, G., Link, B. G., Skodol, A. E., & Stueve, A. (1992). Socioeconomic status and psychiatric disorders: The causation-selection issue. *Science, 255,* 946–952.

Donovan, A., Oddy, M., Pardoe, R., & Ades, A. (1986). Employment status and psychological well-being: A longitudinal study of 16-year-old school-leavers. *Journal of Child Psychology and Psychiatry, 27,* 65–76.

Dooley, D. (2001). *Social research methods,* 4th ed. Upper Saddle River, NJ: Prentice Hall.

Dooley, D. (in press). Unemployment, underemployment, and mental health: Conceptualizing employment status as a continuum. *American Journal of Community Psychology.*

Dooley, D., & Catalano, R. (1980). Economic change as a cause of behavioral disorder. *Psychological Bulletin, 87,* 450–468.

Dooley, D., & Catalano, R. (1984). Why the economy predicts help-seeking: A test of competing explanations. *Journal of Health and Social Behavior, 25,* 160–176.

Dooley, D., & Catalano, R. (2000). Group interventions and the limits of behavioral medicine. *Behavioral Medicine, 26,* 116–128.

Dooley, D., & Catalano, R. (in press). Introduction to special issue on underemployment. *American Journal of Community Psychology.*

Dooley, D., Catalano, R., & Hough, R. (1992). Unemployment and alcohol disorder in 1910 and 1990: Drift versus social causation. *Journal of Occupational and Organizational Psychology, 65,* 277–290.

Dooley, D., Catalano, R., & Rook, K. S. (1988). Personal and aggregate unemployment and psychological symptoms. *Journal of Social Issues, 44,* 107–123.

Dooley, D., Catalano, R., & Wilson, G. (1994). Depression and unemployment: Panel findings from the Epidemiologic Catchment Area Study. *American Journal of Community Psychology, 22*, 745–765.

Dooley, D., Fielding, J., & Levi, L. (1996). Health and unemployment. *Annual Review of Public Health, 17*, 449–465.

Dooley, D., & Prause, J. (1995). Effect of unemployment on school leavers' self-esteem. *Journal of Occupational and Organizational Psychology, 68*, 177–192.

Dooley, D., & Prause, J. (1997a). Effect of students' self-esteem on later employment status: Interactions of self-esteem with gender and race. *Applied Psychology: An International Review, 46*, 175–198.

Dooley, D., & Prause, J. (1997b). School-leavers' self-esteem and unemployment: Turning point or a station on a trajectory? In I. H. Gotlib & B. Wheaton (Eds.), *Trajectories and turning points: Stress and adversity over the life course* (pp. 91–113). New York: Cambridge University Press.

Dooley, D., & Prause, J. (1997c). Effect of favorable employment change on alcohol abuse: One- and five-year follow-ups in the National Longitudinal Survey of Youth. *American Journal of Community Psychology, 25*, 787–807.

Dooley, D., & Prause, J. (1998). Underemployment and alcohol misuse in the National Longitudinal Survey of Youth. *Journal of Studies on Alcohol, 59*, 669–680.

Dooley, D., & Prause, J. (2002). Mental health and welfare transitions: Depression and alcohol abuse in AFDC women. *American Journal of Community Psychology, 30*, 787–813.

Dooley, D., Prause, J., & Ham-Rowbottom, K. A. (2000). Underemployment and depression: Longitudinal relationships. *Journal of Health and Social Behavior, 41*, 421–436.

Dressler, W. W. (1986). Unemployment and symptoms of depression in a southern black community. *Journal of Nervous and Mental Disease, 174*, 639–645.

Druss, B. G., Schlesinger, M., & Allen, H. M., Jr. (2001). Depressive symptoms, satisfaction with health care, and 2-year work outcomes in an employed population. *American Journal of Psychiatry, 158*, 731–734.

Durkheim, E. (1966). *Suicide: A study in sociology.* J. Spaulding & G. Simpson, translators. New York: Free Press. (Originally published in 1897.)

Eales, M. J. (1988). Depression and anxiety in unemployed men. *Psychological Medicine, 18*, 935–945.

Eden, D., & Aviram, A. (1993). Self-efficacy training to speed reemployment: Helping people to help themselves. *Journal of Applied Psychology, 78*, 352–360.

Edin, K., & Lein, L. (1997). *Making ends meet: How single mothers survive welfare and low-wage work.* New York: Russell Sage Foundation.

Eisenberg, P., & Lazarsfeld, P. F. (1938). The psychological effects of unemployment. *Psychological Bulletin, 35*, 358–390.

Elder, G. H., Jr. (1974). *Children of the Great Depression.* Chicago: University of Chicago Press.

Elder, G. H., Jr., & Caspi, A. (1988). Economic stress in lives: Developmental perspectives. *Journal of Social Issues, 44*, 25–45.

Eltis, W. (1996). Unemployment and the economists: A concluding comment. In B. Corry (Ed.), *Unemployment and the economists* (pp. 136–155). Cheltenham, UK: Edward Elgar.

Ensel, W. M., & Lin, N. (1991). The life stress paradigm and psychological distress. *Journal of Health and Social Behavior, 32*, 321–341.

Erikson, E. H. (1959). The problem of ego identity. *Psychological Issues, 1*, 101–164.

Faris, R. E. L., & Dunham, H. W. (1939). *Mental disorders in urban areas*. New York: Hafner.

Feather, N. T. (1990). *The psychological impact of unemployment*. New York: Springer-Verlag.

Feather, N. T. (1997). Economic deprivation and the psychological impact of unemployment. *Australian Psychologist, 32*, 37–45.

Feather, N. T., & O'Brien, G. E. (1986). A longitudinal study of the effects of employment and unemployment on school-leavers. *Journal of Occupational Psychology, 59*, 121–144.

Fenwick, R., & Tausig, M. (1994). The macroeconomic context of job stress. *Journal of Health and Social Behavior, 35*, 266–282.

Firebaugh, G. (1978). A rule for inferring individual-level relationships from aggregate data. *American Sociological Review, 43*, 557–572.

Fisher, A. G. B. (1945). *Economic progress and social security*. London: Macmillan.

Fitzgerald, J., Gottschalk, P., & Moffitt, R. (1998). An analysis of sample attrition in panel data: The Michigan Panel Study of Income Dynamics. *The Journal of Human Resources, 33*, 251–299.

Flett, G. L., Vredenburg, K., & Krames, L. (1997). The continuity of depression in clinical and nonclinical samples. *Psychological Bulletin, 121*, 395–416.

Forrester, V. (1999). *The economic horror*. Malden, MA: Blackwell.

Frank, R. H., & Cook, P. J. (1995). *The winner-take-all society: How more and more Americans compete for ever fewer and bigger prizes, encouraging economic waste, income inequality, and an impoverished cultural life*. New York: Free Press.

Frankel, M., Williams, H., & Spencer, B. (1983). *Technical sampling report: National longitudinal survey of labor force behavior*. Chicago: National Opinion Research Center, University of Chicago.

Frerichs, R. R., Aneshensel, C. S., & Clark, V. A. (1981). Prevalence of depression in Los Angeles County. *American Journal of Epidemiology, 113*, 691–699.

Friedland, D. S., & Price, R. H. (in press). Underemployment: Consequences for the health and well-being of workers. *American Journal of Community Psychology*.

Fryer, D. M. (1986). Employment deprivation and personal agency during unemployment: A critical discussion of Jahoda's explanation of the psychological effects of unemployment. *Social Behaviour, 1*, 3–23.

Fryer, D. M. (1999). Insecurity, the restructuring of unemployment, and mental health. Paper presented at the Social Security and the Restructuring of Unemployment Conference, Graz, Austria, May 27–29. Published in German as Unsicherheit, Strukturwandel der Arbeitslosigkeit und psychische Gesundheit. In H. G. Zilian and J. Flecker (Eds.), *Soziale Sicherheit und Strukturwandel der Arbeitslosigkeit*. Munich and Mering: Reiner Hampp Verlag, 2000.

Fryer, D. M., & Payne, R. L. (1984). Pro-active behaviour in unemployment: Findings and implications. *Leisure Studies, 3*, 273–295.

Gallagher, L. J., Gallagher, M., Perese, K., Schreiber, S., & Watson, K. (1998). *One year after federal welfare reform: A description of state Temporary Assistance for Needy Families (TANF) decisions as of October 1997*. Retrieved March 13, 2000, from the world wide web: ⟨http://newfederalism.urban.org/html/occas6.htm⟩.

Garraty, J. A. (1978). *Unemployment in history: Economic thoughts and public policy.* New York: Harper and Row.

Giesbrecht, N., Markele, G., & MacDonald, S. (1982). The 1978–79 INCO worker's strike in the Sudbury Basin and its impact on alcohol consumption and drinking patterns. *Journal of Public Health Policy, 3,* 22–28.

Gill, J. (1994). Alcohol problems in employment: Epidemiology and responses. *Alcohol and Alcoholism, 29,* 233–248.

Gilroy, C. (1975). Supplemental measures of labor force underutilization. *Monthly Labor Review, 98,* 13–22.

Glyde, G. (1977). Underemployment: Definition and causes. *Journal of Economic Issues, 11,* 245–260.

Goldenberg, R., Iams, J., Mercer, B., Meis, P., Moawad, A., Copper, R., Das, A., Thom, E., Johnson, F., McNellis, D., Miodovnik, M., Van Dorsten, J. P., Caritis, S. N., Thurnau, G. R., & Bottoms, S. F. (1990). The preterm prediction study: The value of new vs. standard risk factors in predicting spontaneous preterm births. *American Journal of Public Health, 88,* 233–238.

Goldsmith, A. H., Veum, J. R., & Darity, W. (1995). Are being unemployed and being out of the labor force distinct states?: A psychological approach. *Journal of Economic Psychology, 126,* 275–295.

Gordon, D. M. (1988). The un-natural rate of unemployment: An econometric critique of the NAIRU hypothesis. *American Economic Review, 78,* 117–123.

Gore, S., Aseltine, R. H., Jr., Colten, M. E., & Lin, B. (1997). Life after high school: Development, stress, and well-being. In I. H. Gotlib & B. Wheaton (Eds.), *Trajectories and turning points: Stress and adversity over the life course* (197–214). New York: Cambridge University Press.

Gore, S., Kadish, S., & Aseltine, R. H., Jr. (in press). Career centered high school education and post–high school adaptation. *American Journal of Community Psychology.*

Grant, B. F., & Dawson, D. A. (1996). Alcohol and drug use, abuse, and dependence among welfare recipients. *American Journal of Public Health, 86,* 1450–1454.

Gravelle, H. S. E., Hutchinson, G., & Stern, J. (1981). Mortality and unemployment: A critique of Brenner's time-series analyses. *Lancet, 2,* 675–679.

Green, R. S., Fujiwara, L., Norris, J., Kappagoda, S., Driscoll, A., & Speiglman, R. (2000). *Alameda County CalWORKs needs assessment: Barriers to working and summaries of baseline status.* Berkeley, CA: Public Health Institute.

Greenberger, E., & Steinberg, L. D. (1986). *When teenagers work: The psychological and social costs of adolescent employment.* New York: Basic Books.

Grzywacz, J. G., & Dooley, D. (2003). The employment continuum and well-being: Replicated evidence from two large cross-sectional surveys. *Social Science and Medicine, 56,* 1749–1760.

Gurney, R. M. (1980a). The effects of unemployment on the psycho-social development of school-leavers. *Journal of Occupational Psychology, 53,* 205–213.

Gurney, R. M. (1980b). Does unemployment affect the self-esteem of school-leavers? *Australian Journal of Psychology, 32,* 175–182.

Hage, J. (1995). Post-indusrial lives: New demands, new prescriptions. In A. Howard (Ed.). *The changing nature of work* (pp. 485–512). San Francisco: Jossey-Bass.

Hall, D. T., & Mirvis, P. H. (1995). Careers as lifelong learning. In A. Howard (Ed.), *The changing nature of work* (pp. 323–361). San Francisco: Jossey-Bass.

Hall, E. M., & Johnson, J. V. (1988). Depression in unemployed Swedish women. *Social Science and Medicine, 27,* 1349–1355.

Ham, J. (1982). Estimation of a labour supply model with censoring due to unemployment and underemployment. *Review of Economic Studies, 89,* 335–354.

Hamilton, V. L., Hoffman, W. S., Broman, C. L., & Rauma, D. (1993). Unemployment, distress, and coping: A panel study of autoworkers. *Journal of Personality and Social Psychology, 65,* 234–247.

Hammarström, A. (1994). Health consequences of youth unemployment: A review from a gender perspective. *Social Science and Medicine, 38,* 699–709.

Hammarström, A., & Janlert, U. (1997). Nervous and depressive symptoms in a longitudinal study of youth unemployment – selection or exposure? *Journal of Adolescence, 20,* 293–305.

Hammer, T. (1992). Unemployment and use of drug and alcohol among young people: A longitudinal study in the general population. *British Journal of Addiction, 87,* 1571–1581.

Handy, C. (1989). *The age of unreason.* Boston: Harvard Business School Press.

Harford, T. C., & Grant, B. F. (1994). Prevalence and population validity of DSM-III-R alcohol abuse and dependence: The 1989 National Longitudinal Survey of Youth. *Journal of Substance Abuse, 6,* 37–44.

Harford, T. C., Hanna, E. Z., & Faden, V. B. (1994). The long- and short-term effects of marriage on drinking. *Journal of Substance Abuse, 6,* 209–217.

Harter, S. (1990). Self and identity development. In S. Feldman & G. R. Elliot (Eds.), *At the threshold: The developing adolescent* (pp. 352–387). Cambridge, MA: Harvard University Press.

Hauser, P. M. (1974). The measurement of labour utilization. *Malayan Economic Review, 19,* 1–17.

Heckhausen, J., & Schulz, R. (1995). A life-span theory of control. *Psychological Review, 102,* 284–304.

Helzer, E., Burnam, A., & McEvoy, L. T. (1991). Alcohol abuse and dependence. In L. N. Robins & D. A. Regier (Eds.), *Psychiatric disorders in America: The Epidemologic Catchment Area Study* (pp. 81–115). New York: Free Press.

Hendry, L. (1987). Young people: From school to unemployment. In S. Fineman (Ed.), *Unemployment: Personal and social consequences* (pp. 195–218). London: Tavistock.

Herzenberg, S. A., Alic, J. A., & Wial, H. (1998). *New rules for a new economy: Employment and opportunity in postindustrial America.* Ithaca, NY: Cornell University Press.

Hill, M. (1992). *The panel study of income dynamics: A user's guide.* Newbury Park, CA: Sage Publications.

Hiroshige, Y., Matsudy, S., & Kahyo, H. (1995). The association between parents' unemployment and birthweight in Japan. *Japanese Journal of Hygiene, 50,* 652–659.

Hofvendahl, E. (1995). Smoking in pregnancy as a risk factor for long-term mortality in the offspring. *Paediatric and Perinatal Epidemiology, 9,* 381–390.

Holmes, T. H., & Rahe, R. E. (1967). The social readjustment scale. *Journal of Psychosomatic Research, 11,* 213–218.

Homer, C., James, S., & Siegel, E. (1990). Work-related psychosocial stress and risk of preterm, low birthweight delivery. *American Journal of Public Health, 80,* 173–177.

Horwitz, A. V. (1984). The economy and social pathology. *Annual Review of Sociology, 10,* 95–119.

Hosmer, D., & Lemeshow, S. (2000). *Applied logistic regression,* 2nd ed. New York: Wiley.

Howard, A. (1995a). Rethinking the psychology of work. In A. Howard (Ed.), *The changing nature of work* (pp. 513–555). San Francisco: Jossey-Bass.

Howard, A. (1995b). Technology and the organization of work. In A. Howard (Ed.), *The changing nature of work* (pp. 89–96). San Francisco: Jossey-Bass.

Hughes, M., & Demo, M. (1989). Self-perceptions of black Americans: Self-esteem and personal efficacy. *American Journal of Sociology, 95,* 132–159.

Isaksson, K. (1989). Unemployment, mental health and the psychological functions of work in male welfare clients in Stockholm. *Scandinavian Journal of Social Medicine, 17,* 165–169.

Iversen, L., & Klausen, H. (1986). Alcohol consumption among laid-off workers before and after closure of a Danish ship-yard: A 2-year follow-up. *Social Science and Medicine, 22,* 107–109.

Jaccard, J., Turrisi, R., & Wan, C. (1990). *Interaction effects in multiple regression* (Sage University Papers series on Quantitative Applications in the Social Sciences, 07-072). Newbury Park, CA: Sage.

Jacobs, D. G., Kopans, B. S., & Reizes, J. M. (1995). Reevaluation of depression: What the general practitioner needs to know. *Mind Body Medicine, 1,* 17–23.

Jahoda, M. (1982). *Employment and unemployment: A social-psychological analysis.* Cambridge: Cambridge University Press.

Jahoda, M., Lazarsfeld, P. F., & Zeisel, H. (1971). *Marienthal: The sociography of an unemployed community.* M. J. Jahoda, P. F. Lazarsfeld, H. Neisel, J. Reginall, & T. Elaesser, translators. Chicago: Aldine. (Original work published in 1933.)

Jang, K. L., Livesley, W. J., & Vernon, P. A. (1995). Alcohol and drug problems: A multivariate behavioural genetic analysis of co-morbidity. *Addiction, 90,* 1213–1221.

Jarvis, E. (1971). *Insanity and idiocy in Massachusetts: Report of the commission on lunacy* (1855). Cambridge, MA: Harvard University Press.

Jensen, L., Findeis, J. L., Hsu, W-L., & Schachter, J. P. (1999). Slipping into and out of underemployment: Another disadvantage for nonmetropolitan workers? *Rural Sociology, 64,* 417–438.

Jensen, L., & Slack, T. (in press). Underemployment in America: Measurement and evidence. *American Journal of Community Psychology.*

Johnson, J. G., Cohen, P., Dohrenwend, B. P., Link, B. G., & Brook, J. S. (1999). A longitudinal investigation of social causation and social selection processes involved in the association between socioeconomic status and psychiatric disorders. *Journal of Abnormal Psychology, 108,* 490–499.

Johnson, R., & Herring, C. (1989). Labor market participation among young adults: An event history analysis. *Youth and Society, 21:1,* 3–31.

Johnson, Z., Dack, P., & Fogarty, J. (1994). Small area analysis of low birth weight. *Irish Medical Journal, 87,* 176–177.

Jones, E. (1971). The elusive concept of underemployment. *The Journal of Human Resources, 6,* 519–524.

Jones, E. G., & Berglas, S. (1978). Control of attributions about the self through self-handicapping strategies: The appeal of alcohol and the role of underachievement. *Personality and Social Psychology Bulletin, 4,* 200–206.

Josephs, R., Markus, H., & Tafarodi, R. (1992). Gender and self-esteem. *Journal of Personality and Social Psychology, 63,* 391–402.

Kalleberg, A. L., Reskin, B. F., & Hudson, K. (2000). Bad jobs in America: Standard and nonstandard employment relations and job quality in the United States. *American Sociological Review, 65,* 256–278.

Karasek, R., Brisson, C., Kawakami, N., Houtman, I., Bongers, P., & Amick, B. (1998). The Job Content Questionnaire (JCQ): An instrument for internationally comparative assessments of psychosocial characteristics. *Journal of Occupational Health Psychology, 3,* 322–355.

Karasek, R. A., & Theorell, T. (1990). *Healthy work: Stress, productivity, and the reconstruction of working life.* New York: Basic Books.

Kasl, S. (1979). Changes in mental health status associated with job loss and retirement. In J. E. Barrett (Ed.), *Stress and mental disorder* (pp. 179–200). New York: Raven Press.

Kasl, S., & Cobb, S. (1982). Variability of stress effects among men experiencing job loss. In L. Goldberger & S. Breznitz (Eds.), *Handbook of stress.* New York: Free Press.

Kasl, S., Rodriguez, E., & Lasch, K. (1998). The impact of unemployment on health and well-being. In B. Dohrenwend (Ed.), *Adversity, stress, and psychopathology* (pp. 111–131). Oxford: Oxford University Press.

Kessler, R. C., & McLeod, J. D. (1984). Sex differences in vulnerability to undesirable life events. *American Sociological Review, 49,* 620–631.

Kessler, R. C., Turner, J. B., & House, J. S. (1988). Effects of unemployment on health in a community survey: Main, modifying, and mediating effects. *Journal of Social Issues, 44:4,* 69–85.

Kessler, R. C., Turner, J. B., & House, J. S. (1989). Unemployment, reemployment, and emotional functioning in a community sample. *American Sociological Review, 54,* 648–657.

Kivimäki, M., Vahtera, J., Elovainio, M., Pentti, J., & Virtanen, M. (in press). Human costs of organizational downsizing: Comparing health trends between leavers and stayers. *American Journal of Community Psychology.*

Kivimäki, M., Vahtera, J., Pentti, J., & Ferrie, J. E. (2000). Factors underlying the effect of organizational downsizing on health of employees: A longitudinal cohort study. *British Medical Journal, 320,* 971–975.

Kivimäki, M., Vahtera, J., Pentti, J., Thomson, L., Griffiths, A., & Cox, T. (2001). Downsizing, changes in work, and self-rated health of employees: A 7-year 3-wave study. *Anxiety, Stress and Coping, 14,* 59–73.

Kleinbaum, D. G., Kupper, L. L., & Morgenstern, H. (1982). *Epidemiologic research.* Belmont, CA: Lifetime Learning Publications.

Kleinbaum, D., Kupper, L., Muller, K., & Nizam, A. (1998). *Applied regression analysis and other multivariable methods,* 3rd ed. Pacific Grove, CA: Duxbury Press.

Koopmans, J. R., & Boomsma, D. I. (1996). Familial resemblances in alcohol use: Genetic or cultural transmission. *Journal of Studies on Alcohol, 57,* 19–28.

Kramer, M. (1987). Intrauterine growth and gestational duration determinants. *Pediatrics, 80,* 502–511.

Lahelma, E., Kangas, R., & Manderbacka, K. (1995). Drinking and unemployment: Contrasting patterns among men and women. *Drug and Alcohol Dependence, 37,* 71–82.

Leana, C. R., & Feldman, D. C. (1995). Finding new jobs after a plant closing: Antecedents and outcomes of the occurrence and quality of reemployment. *Human Relations, 48,* 1381–1401.

Lebergott, S. (1964). *Manpower in economic growth: The American record since 1800.* New York: McGraw-Hill.

Lee, A. J., Crombie, I. K., Smith, W. C. S., & Tunstall-Pedoe, H. (1990). Alcohol consumption and unemployment among men: The Scottish Heart Health Study. *British Journal of Addiction, 85,* 1165–1170.

Lei, H., & Skinner, H. A. (1980). A psychometric study of life events and social readjustment. *Journal of Psychosomatic Research, 24,* 57–65.

Lennon, M. (1999). Work and unemployment as stressors. In A. Horwitz & T. Scheid (Eds.), *A handbook for the study of mental health* (pp. 284–294). Cambridge: Cambridge University Press.

Leppel, K., & Clain, S. (1988). The growth in involuntary part-time employment of men and women. *Applied Economics, 20,* 1155–1166.

Leventman, P. (1981). *Professionals out of work.* New York: Free Press.

Levinson, D. J. (1978). *The seasons of a man's life.* New York: Ballantine.

Levy, P., & Baumgardner, A. (1991). Effects of self-esteem and gender on goal choice. *Journal of Organizational Behavior, 12,* 529–541.

Li, C., Windsor, R., & Hassan, M. (1994). Cost differences between low birthweight attributable to smoking and low birthweight for all causes. *Preventive Medicine, 23,* 28–34.

Lichter, D. (1988). Racial differences in underemployment in American cities. *American Journal of Sociology, 93,* 771–792.

Lichter, D. (1989). Race, employment hardship, and inequality in the American nonmetropolitan south. *American Sociological Review, 54,* 436–446.

Lieberson, S. (1985). *Making it count: The improvement of social research and theory.* Berkeley: University of California Press.

Liem, R., & Rayman, P. (1982). Health and social costs of unemployment: Research and policy consideratons. *American Psychologist, 37,* 1116–1123.

Llangenbucher, J. W., & Chung, T. (1995). Onset and staging of DSM-IV alcohol dependence using mean age and survival-hazard methods. *Journal of Abnormal Psychology, 104,* 346–354.

Lloyd, C. (1980). Life events and depressive disorder reviewed. *Archives of General Psychiatry, 37,* 541–548.

Lockwood, C. (1999). Stress-associated preterm delivery: The role of corticotropin-releasing hormone. *American Journal of Obstetrics and Gynecology, 180,* 264–266.

Long, S. (1997). *Regression models for categorical and limited dependent variables.* Newbury Park, CA: Sage.

MacDonald, L., Peacock, J., & Anderson, H. (1992). Marital status: Association with social and economic circumstances, psychological state and outcomes of pregnancy. *Journal of Public Health Medicine, 14,* 26–34.

MaCurdy, T., Mroz, T., & Gritz, R. (1998). An evaluation of the national longitudinal survey on youth. *The Journal of Human Resources, 33,* 345–436.

Malton, K. (1990). Meaningful involvement in instrumental activity and well-being: Studies of older adolescents and at risk urban teenagers. *American Journal of Community Psychology, 18*, 297–320.

Manello, T. A., & Seaman, F. J. (1979). *Prevalence, costs, and handling of drinking problems on seven railroads.* Washington, DC: University Research Corporation.

Markush, R., & Favero, R. (1974). Epidemiological assessment of stressful life events, depressed mood and physiological symptoms – A preliminary report. In B. S. Dohrenwend & B. P. Dohrenwend (Eds.), *Stressful life events* (pp. 171–190). New York: Wiley.

Marshall, J. R., & Hodge, R. W. (1981). Durkheim and Pierce on suicide and economic change. *Social Science Research, 10*, 101–114.

Martinez, R., & Dukes, R. (1991). Ethnic and gender differences in self-esteem. *Youth and Society, 22*, 318–338.

Mastekaasa, A. (1996). Unemployment and health: Selection effects. *Journal of Community and Applied Social Psychology, 6*, 189–205.

McCord, W., McCord, J., & Gudeman, J. (1960). *Origins of alcoholism.* Stanford, CA: Stanford University Press.

Melville, D. I., Hope, D., Bennison, D., & Barraclough, B. (1985). Depression among men made involuntarily redundant. *Psychological Medicine, 15*, 789–793.

Menaghan, E. G. (1997). Intergenerational consequences of social stressors: Effects of occupational and family conditions on young mothers and their children. In I. H. Gotlib & B. Wheaton (Eds.), *Stress and adversity over the life course: Trajectories and turning points* (pp. 114–132). New York: Cambridge University Press.

Menaghan, E. G., & Parcel, T. L. (1990). Parental employment and family life: Research in the 1980s. *Journal of Marriage and the Family, 52*, 1079–1098.

Menard, S. (1991). *Longitudinal research.* (Sage University Papers series on Quantitative Applications in the Social Sciences, no. 07-076). Newbury Park, CA: Sage.

Miech, R. A., Caspi, A., Moffitt, T. E., Wright, B. R. E., & Silva, P. A. (1999). Low socioeconomic status and mental disorders: A longitudinal study of selection and causation during young adulthood. *American Journal of Sociology, 104*, 1096–1131.

Miller, R. (1988). *The end of unemployment.* Hartfield, UK: Atlas Economic Research Foundation.

Mirowsky, J., & Ross, C. E. (1992). Age and depression. *Journal of Health and Social Behavior, 33*, 187–205.

Mirowsky, J., & Ross, C. E. (1995). Sex differences in distress: Real or artifact? *American Sociological Review, 60*, 449–468.

Mishel, L., Bernstein, J., & Schmitt, J. (1999). *The state of working America 1998–1999.* Ithaca, NY: Cornell University Press.

Mittag, W., & Schwarzer, R. (1993). Interaction of employment status and self-efficacy on alcohol consumption: A two-wave study on stressful life transitions. *Psychology and Health, 8*, 77–87.

Monroe, K. R. (1984). *Presidential popularity and the economy.* New York: Praeger.

Monroe, S. M., & Simons, A. D. (1991). Diathesis-stress theories in the context of life stress research: Implications for the depressive disorders. *Psychological Bulletin, 110*, 406–425.

Montgomery, S. M., Cook, D. G., Bartley, M. J., & Wadsworth, M. E. J. (1999). Unemployment pre-dates symptoms of depression and anxiety resulting in medical consultation in young men. *International Journal of Epidemiology, 28*, 95–100.

Moos, R. H., Cronkite, R. C., & Moos, B. S. (1998). The long-term interplay between family and extrafamily resources and depression. *Journal of Family Psychology, 12,* 326–343.

Mortimer, J. T., & Borman, K. M. (Eds.). (1988). *Work experience and psychological development through the life span.* Boulder, CO: Westview.

Murphy, G. C., & Athanasou, J. A. (1999). The effect of unemployment on mental health. *Journal of Occupational and Organizational Psychology, 72,* 83–99.

Myers, J. K., & Weissman, M. M. (1980). Use of a self-report symptom scale to detect depression in a community sample. *American Journal of Psychiatry, 137,* 1081–1084.

Najman, J., Morrison, J., Williams, G., Keeping, G., & Andersen, M. (1989). Unemployment and reproductive outcome: An Australian study. *British Journal of Obstetrics and Gynaecology, 96,* 308–313.

Nathanielsz, P. W. (1995). The role of basic science in preventing low birth weight. *The Future of Children: Low Birth Weight, 5,* 57–70.

National Center on Addiction and Substance Abuse. (1994). *Substance abuse and women on welfare.* Retrieved February 15, 2000, from the world wide web: ⟨http://www.casacolumbia.org/publications1456/publications_show. htm?doc_id=5940⟩.

National Commission on Employment and Unemployment Statistics. (1978). *Concepts and data needs.* Washington, DC: U.S. Government Printing Office.

National Commission on Employment and Unemployment Statistics. (1979). *Counting the labor force.* Washington, DC: U.S. Government Printing Office.

Neenan, P. A., & Orthner, D. K. (1996). Predictors of employment and earnings among JOBS participants. *Social Work Research, 20,* 228–237.

Neter, J., Wasserman, W., & Kutner, M. (1990). *Applied linear statistical models,* 3rd ed. Homewood, IL: Irwin.

Nichols-Casebolt, A. (1986). The psychological effects of income testing income-support benefits. *Social Service Review, 60,* 287–302.

Norbeck, J., & Tilden, V. (1983). Life stress, social support, and emotional disequilibrium in complications of pregnancy: A prospective, multivariate study. *Journal of Health and Social Behavior, 24,* 30–46.

Norstrom, T. (1987). The impact of per capita consumption on Swedish cirrhosis mortality. *British Journal of Addiction, 82,* 67–75.

Northwest Policy Center and Northwest Federation of Community Organizations (1999). *Northwest Job Gap Study: Searching for Work that Pays.* Retrieved March 25, 2000, from the world wide web: ⟨http://depts.washington.edu/npcbox/publications.html⟩.

Nuckolls, K., Cassel, J., & Kaplan, B. (1972). Psychological assets, life crisis, and the prognosis of pregnancy. *American Journal of Epidemiology, 95,* 431–441.

O'Brien, E. (1985). Global self-esteem scales: Unidimensional or multidimensional? *Psychological Reports, 57,* 383–389.

Olson, K., & Pavetti, L. (1996). *Personal and family challenges to the successful transition from welfare to work: How prevalent are these potential barriers to employment?* Washington, DC: Urban Institute.

Patton, W., & Noller, P. (1984). Unemployment and youth: A longitudinal study. *Australian Journal of Psychology, 36,* 399–413.

Patton, W., & Noller, P. (1990). Adolescent self-concept: Effects of being employed, unemployed or returning to school. *Australian Journal of Psychology, 42*, 247–259.

Pentz, M. A., Dwyer, J. H., MacKinnon, D. P., Flay, B. R., Hansen, W. B., Wang, E. Y. I., & Johnson, C. A. (1989). A multicommunity trial for primary prevention of adolescent drug abuse: Effects on drug use prevalence. *Journal of the American Medical Association, 261*, 3259–3266.

Peoples-Sheps, M., Siegel, E., Suchindran, C., Origasa, H., Ware, A., & Barakat, A. (1991). Characteristics of maternal employment during pregnancy: Effects on low birthweight. *American Journal of Public Health, 81*, 1007–1012.

Phillips, A. W. (1958). The relation between unemployment and the rate of money wage rates in the United Kingdom, 1861–1957. *Economica, 25*, 283–299.

Pierce, A. (1967). The economic cycle and the social suicide rate. *American Sociological Review, 32*, 457–462.

Plant, M. A. (1979). *Drinking careers: Occupations, drinking habits, and drinking problems*. London: Tavistock.

Platt, S. (1984). Unemployment and suicidal behavior: A review of the literature. *Social Science and Medicine, 19*, 93–115.

Pollard, T. (1984). Changes over the 1970's in the employment patterns of black and white young men. In M. E. Borus (Ed.), *Youth and the labor market* (pp. 57–80). Kalamazoo, MI: W. E. Upjohn Institute for Employment Research.

Potthoff, R., Woodbury, M., & Mantou, K. (1992). "Equivalent sample size" and "equivalent degrees of freedom": Refinements for inference using survey weights under superpopulation models. *Journal of the American Statistical Association, 87*, 383–396.

Prause, J., & Dooley, D. (1997). Effect of underemployment on school-leavers' self-esteem. *Journal of Adolescence, 20*, 243–260.

Prause, J., & Dooley, D. (2001). Favorable employment change and psychological depression: A two year follow-up analysis of the National Longitudinal Survey of Youth. *Applied Psychology: An International Review, 50*, 282–304.

Project MATCH Research Group. (1997). Matching alcoholism treatments to client heterogeneity: Project MATCH posttreatment drinking outcomes. *Journal of Studies on Alcohol, 58*, 7–29.

Radloff, L. S. (1977). The CES-D scale: A self report depression scale for research in the general population. *Applied Psychological Measurement, 1*, 385–401.

Reed, D. (1999). *California's rising income inequality: Causes and concerns*. San Francisco: Public Policy Institute of California.

Reynolds, J. R. (1997). The effects of industrial employment conditions on job-related distress. *Journal of Health and Social Behavior, 38*, 105–116.

Rice, D. P. (1993). The economic cost of alcohol abuse and alcohol dependence: 1990. *Alcohol Health and Research World, 17*, 10–11.

Richards, J. M., Jr. (1990). Units of analysis and the individual differences fallacy in environmental assessment. *Environment and Behavior, 22*, 307–319.

Rifkin, J. (1995). *The end of work: The decline of the global labor force and the dawn of the post-market era*. New York: Putnam.

Roberts, R. E., & Vernon, S.W. (1983). The Center for Epidemiologic Studies Depression Scale: Its use in a community sample. *American Journal of Psychiatry, 140*, 41–46.

Robinson, J. (1936). Disguised unemployment. *The Economic Journal: The Quarterly Journal of the Royal Economic Society, 46*, 225–237.

Robinson, W. S. (1950). Ecological correlations and the behavior of individuals. *American Sociological Review, 15*, 352–357.

Rook, K., Dooley, D., & Catalano, R. (1991). Stress transmission: The effects of husbands' job stressors on the emotional health of their wives. *Journal of Marriage and the Family, 53*, 165–177.

Rosenberg, M. (1965). *Society and the adolescent self-image*. Princeton, NJ: Princeton University Press.

Ross, C. E., & Mirowsky, J. (1979). A comparison of life-event weighting schemes: Changes, undesirability, and effect-proportional indices. *Journal of Health and Social Behavior, 20*, 166–177.

Rothbaum, F., Weisz, J. R., & Snyder, S. S. (1982). Changing the world and changing the self: A two-process model of perceived control. *Journal of Personality and Social Psychology, 42*, 5–37.

Rowntree, B. S., & Lasker, B. (1911). *Unemployment: A social study*. London: Macmillan.

Schaufeli, W. B. (1997). Youth unemployment and mental health: Some Dutch findings. *Journal of Adolescence, 20*, 281–292.

Schor, J. (1991). *The overworked American: The unexpected decline of leisure*. New York: Basic Books.

Schuckit, M. A. (1987). Biological vulnerability to alcoholism. *Journal of Consulting and Clinical Psychology, 55*, 301–309.

Schwalbe, M., & Staples, C. (1991). Gender differences in sources of self-esteem. *Social Psychology Quarterly, 54*, 158–168.

Seligman, D. (1992). Keeping up: Two dumb laws: A no-progress report. *Fortune*, December 14, 179–180.

Selye, H. (1956). *The stress of life*. New York: McGraw-Hill.

Shamir, B. (1986). Self-esteem and the psychological impact of unemployment. *Social Psychology Quarterly, 49*, 61–72.

Sisco, C. B., & Pearson, C. L. (1994). Prevalence of alcoholism and drug abuse among female AFDC recipients. *Health and Social Work, 19*, 75–77.

Solomon, S. D., Smith, E. M., Robins, L. N., & Fischbach, R. L. (1987). Social involvement as a mediator of disaster-induced stress. *Journal of Applied Social Psychology, 17*, 1092–1112.

Solow, R. M. (1998). *Work and welfare*. Princeton, NJ: Princeton University Press.

Spenner, K. I., & Otto, L. B. (1985). Work and self-concept: Selection and socialization in the early career. *Research in Sociology of Education and Socialization, 5*, 197–235.

Spinillo, A., Capuzzo, E., Baltaro, R., Piazza, G., Nicola, S., & Iasci, A. (1996). The effect of work activity in pregnancy on the risk of fetal growth retardation. *Acta Obstetricia et Gynecologica Scandinavica, 75*, 531–536.

Stafford, E. M., Jackson, P. R., & Banks, M. H. (1980). Employment, work involvement and mental health in less qualified young people. *Journal of Occupational Psychology, 53*, 291–304.

Steele, C. M., & Josephs, R. A. (1988). Drinking your troubles away II: An attention-allocation model of alcohol's effects on psychological stress. *Journal of Abnormal Psychology, 97*, 196–205.

Stein, A., Campbell, E., Day, A., McPherson, K., & Cooper, P. (1987). Social adversity, low birth weight, and preterm delivery. *British Medical Journal of Clinical Research, 295*, 291–293.

Steinberg, L., Catalano, R., & Dooley, D. (1981). Economic antecedents of child abuse and neglect. *Child Development, 52*, 260–267.

Stueve, A., Dohrenwend, B. P., & Skodol, A. E. (1998). Relationships between stressful life events and episodes of major depression and nonaffective psychotic disorders: Selected results from a New York risk factor study. In B. P. Dohrenwend (Ed.), *Adversity, stress, and psychopathology* (pp. 341–357). New York: Oxford University Press.

Sullivan, T. (1978). *Marginal workers, marginal jobs.* Austin: University of Texas Press.

Tausig, M., & Fenwick, R. (1999). Recession and well-being. *Journal of Health and Social Behavior, 40*, 1–16.

Temple, M., Fillmore, K., Hartka, E., Johnstone, B., Leino, M., & Motoyoshi, K. (1991). A meta-analysis of change in marital and employment status as predictors of alcohol consumption on a typical occasion. *British Journal of Addiction, 86*, 1269–1281.

Tiggemann, M., & Winefield, A. H. (1984). The effects of unemployment on the mood, self-esteem, locus of control, and depressive affect of school-leavers. *Journal of Occupational Psychology, 57*, 33–42.

Tiggemann, M., & Winefield, A. H. (1989). Predictors of employment, unemployment and further study among school-leavers. *Journal of Occupational Psychology, 62*, 213–221.

Timms, D. W. G. (1996). Social mobility and mental health in a Swedish cohort. *Social Psychiatry and Psychiatric Epidemiology, 31*, 38–48.

Tipps, H., & Gordon, H. (1985). Inequality at work: Race, sex, and underemployment. *Social Indicators Research, 16*, 35–49.

Turner, J. B. (1995). Economic context and the health effects of unemployment. *Journal of Health and Social Behavior, 36*, 213–229.

Turner, R. J., & Noh, S. (1988). Physical disability and depression: A longitudinal analysis. *Journal of Health and Social Behavior, 29*, 23–37.

Umberson, D., Wortman, C. B., & Kessler, R. C. (1992). Widowhood and depression: Explaining long-term gender differences in vulnerability. *Journal of Health and Social Behavior, 33*, 10–24.

U.S. Bureau of the Census. (1987). *Poverty in the United States 1987.* (Current Population Reports, Consumer Income Series P-60, No. 163). Washington, DC: U.S. Government Printing Office.

U.S. Bureau of Labor Statistics. (1994). *How the government measures unemployment.* Retrieved September 10, 1999, from the world wide web: ⟨http://stats.bls.gov/cps_htgm.htm⟩.

U.S. Bureau of Labor Statistics. (1996). *Revised data from February 1994 Displaced Worker Survey.* Retrieved April 4, 2000, from the world wide web: ⟨http://www.bls.census.gov/cps/pub/disp_0294.htm⟩.

U.S. Bureau of Labor Statistics. (2000a). *Household data annual averages.* Retrieved May 2, 2000, from the world wide web: ⟨http://stats.bls.gov/pdf/cpsaatab.htm⟩.

U.S. Bureau of Labor Statistics. (2000b). *Current Population Survey: Design and methodology.* (Technical Paper 63). Retrieved March 29, 2002, from the world wide web: ⟨http://www.census.gov/prod/2000pubs/tp63.pdf⟩.

U.S. Civil Rights Commission. (1982). *Unemployment and underemployment among blacks, Hispanics, and women.* Washington, DC: U.S. Government Printing Office.

U.S. Department of Labor. (1990). *Employment and Earnings, 37:1,* 160.

U.S. Department of Labor (1998). *Displaced worker summary: Worker displacement, 1995–1997.* Retrieved March 23, 2000, from the world wide web: ⟨http://stats.bls.gov/news.release/disp.nws.htm⟩.

U.S. Department of Labor (1999a). *A profile of the working poor, 1997* (Report No. 936). Retrieved March 23, 2000, from the world wide web: ⟨http://stats.bls.gov/cpswp97.htm⟩.

U.S. Department of Labor. (1999b). *Employment status of the civilian noninstitutional population, 1935 to date.* Retrieved November 17, 1999, from the world wide web: ⟨ftp://ftp.bls.gov/pub/special.requests/lf/aat1.txt⟩.

U.S. Department of Labor. (2000). *Employment status of the civilian noninstitutional population, 1936 to date.* Retrieved March 23, 2000, from the world wide web: ⟨ftp://ftp.bls.gov/pub/special.requests/lf/aat1.txt⟩.

U.S. Department of Labor, Employment, and Training Administration. (1977). *Dictionary of occupational titles,* 4th ed. Washington, DC: U.S. Government Printing Office.

Vernon, S. W., & Roberts, R. E. (1981). Measuring nonspecific psychological distress and other dimensions of psychopathology: Further observations on the problem. *Archives of General Psychiatry, 38,* 1239–1247.

Vietorisz, T., Mier, R., & Givlin, J. (1975). Subemployment: Exclusion and inadequacy indexes. *Monthly Labor Review, 98,* 3–12.

Vinokur, A. D., Price, R. H., & Caplan, R. D. (1991). From field experiments to program implementation: Assessing the potential outcomes of an experimental intervention program for unemployed persons. *American Journal of Community Psychology, 19,* 543–562.

Vinokur, A. D., & Schul, Y. (1997). Mastery and inoculation against setbacks as active ingredients in the JOBS intervention for the unemployed. *Journal of Consulting and Clinical Psychology, 65,* 867–877.

Wade, T., Thompson, V., Tashakkori, A., & Valente, E. (1989). A longitudinal analysis of sex by race differences in predictors of adolescent self-esteem. *Personality and Individual Differences, 10,* 717–729.

Wagstaff, A. (1985). Time series analysis of the relationship between unemployment and mortality: A survey of econometric critiques and replications of Brenner's studies. *Social Science and Medicine, 21,* 985–996.

Wall, T. D., & Jackson, P. R. (1995). New manufacturing initiatives and shopfloor job design. In A. Howard (Ed.), *The changing nature of work* (pp. 139–174). San Francisco: Jossey-Bass.

Wallulis, J. (1998). *The new insecurity: The end of the standard job and family.* Albany: State University of New York Press.

Wanberg, C. R. (1995). A longitudinal study of the effects of unemployment and quality of reemployment. *Journal of Vocational Behavior, 46,* 40–54.

Warr, P. B. (1987). *Work, unemployment, and mental health.* Oxford: Clarendon Press.

Wechsler, H., Moeykens, B., Davenport, A., Castillo, S., & Hansen, J. (1995). The adverse impact of heavy episodic drinkers on other college students. *Journal of Studies on Alcohol, 56*, 628–634.

Weeks, E. C., & Drengacz, S. (1982). The non-economic impact of community economic shock. *Journal of the Health and Human Resources Administration, 4*, 303–318.

Weich, S., & Lewis, G. (1998). Poverty, unemployment, and common mental disorders: Population based cohort study. *British Medical Journal, 317*, 115–119.

Weisner, C., & Schmidt, L. (1993). Alcohol and drug problems among diverse health and social service populations. *American Journal of Public Health, 83*, 824–829.

Weissman, M. M., Sholomskas, D., Pottenger, M., Prusoff, B. A., & Locke, B. Z. (1977). Assessing depressive symptoms in five psychiatric populations: A validation study. *American Journal of Epidemiology, 106*, 203–214.

Wheaton, B. (1990). Life transitions, role histories, and mental health. *American Sociological Review, 55*, 209–223.

William T. Grant Foundation Commission on Work, Family, and Citizenship. (1988). *The forgotten half: Pathways to success for Americas youth and young families.* Washington, DC: Youth and Americas Future.

Wilson, S. H., & Walker, G. M. (1993). Unemployment and health: A review. *Public Health, 107*, 153–162.

Winefield, A. H. (1995). Unemployment: Its psychological costs. *International Review of Industrial and Organizational Psychology, 10*, 169–212.

Winefield, A. H. (1997). Editorial: Introduction to the psychological effects of youth unemployment: International perspectives. *Journal of Adolescence, 20*, 237–241.

Winefield, A. H., & Fryer, D. (1996). Some emerging threats to the validity of research on unemployment and mental health. *Australian Journal of Social Research, 2*, 115–128.

Winefield, A. H., & Tiggemann, M. (1985). Psychological correlates of employment and unemployment: Effects, predisposing factors, and sex differences. *Journal of Occupational Psychology, 58*, 229–242.

Winefield, A. H., Tiggemann, M., Winefield, H. R., & Goldney, R. D. (1993). *Growing up with unemployment: A longitudinal study of its psychological impact.* London: Routledge.

Winton, M., Heather, N., & Robertson, I. (1986). Effects of unemployment on drinking behavior: A review of the relevant evidence. *International Journal of Addictions, 21*, 1261–1283.

Wise, P., Wampler, N., & Barfield, W. (1995). The importance of extreme prematurity and low birthweight to United States neonatal care and women's health. *Journal of the American Medical Women's Association, 50*, 152–155.

Wittenberg, R. (1968). *Postadolescence.* New York: Grune and Stratton.

Wolman, W., & Colamosca, A. (1997). *The Judas economy: The triumph of capital and the betrayal of work.* Reading, MA: Addison-Wesley.

Woodward, C. A., Shannon, H. S., Cunningham, C., McIntosh, J., Lendrum, B., Rosenbloom, D., & Brown, J. (1999). The impact of re-engineering and other cost reduction strategies on the staff of a large teaching hospital: A longitudinal study. *Medical Care, 37*, 556–569.

World Health Organization, Expert Committee on Maternal and Child Health. (1950). *Public health aspect of low birthweight.* (WHO Technical Report Series, No. 27). Geneva, Switzerland: WHO.

Name Index

Subject Index

abstinence, 116–117, 127, 131, 170, 175, 179
adequate employment, 4, 9–10, 13, 33–34,
    48, 54, 60, 62–63, 70, 72, 77, 81–83, 95,
    99–100, 102–104, 106, 109–110, 118–119,
    123–128, 138–143, 145–155, 168,
    170–171, 174–175, 186, 188–196, 198,
    201–202, 205–206, 208, 210, 214–217,
    219–223
adverse employment change (see also
    inadequate employment;
    unemployment), 13, 15–16, 26–27,
    30–31, 35, 39, 57, 65–66, 68–71, 79,
    81, 85–87, 116–118, 121, 123–127,
    129–130, 132, 135, 138–139, 145–146,
    149, 151, 153–155, 159, 161, 167–168,
    183–186, 189, 191–193, 195–199,
    201–204, 206–210, 212–213, 219–220,
    223, 225
age, 3, 58, 75–76, 206, 213, 215, 220,
    223
    alcohol misuse and, 79, 81, 112, 114,
        117–118, 120–121, 124–125, 127–128,
        130, 132–133, 206–207
    birthweight and, 186, 189–194, 200
    depression and, 134, 141, 149, 154,
        217
    employment status and, 12–14, 20, 50–51,
        91–92, 97, 221, 230
    measurement of, 44
    self-esteem and, 90, 96–97, 100–101
    welfare and, 172, 176, 178
age trap, 90
agency restriction theory, 33, 208–209
aggregate-level analysis, 17, 26–30, 57, 69,
    107, 114, 130, 143, 183–186, 197,
    204–206, 220
Aid to Families with Dependent Children
    (AFDC) (see also welfare), 6, 15, 161,
    163–165, 168, 170, 172–177, 180

alcohol misuse, 15, 32, 57, 111–112, 212, 219,
    220
    age and, 79, 81, 112, 114, 117–118, 120–121,
        124–125, 127–128, 130, 132–133, 206–
        207
    aptitude and, 120, 125–126
    birthweight and, 189, 190, 192–194, 198
    children and, 118, 120–121, 130, 207
    drug use and, 67, 125–126, 128, 162–163,
        180
    economic climate and, 121–122, 130, 132
    education and, 79, 81, 120, 128, 130, 203
    ethnicity and, 81, 120, 124, 132
    favorable employment change and, 82,
        84, 106, 116, 118–124, 127–133, 202, 221
    gender and, 58, 79, 81–82, 111, 114–116,
        120, 124–126, 128, 132, 207
    inadequate employment and, 69, 79,
        81–83, 109, 113, 116–120, 123–133, 137,
        201, 203, 206, 208
    marital status and, 81, 118, 120–121,
        127–128, 130, 207
    measurement of, 37, 53, 55–56, 117, 119,
        122–123, 126, 132, 167–168, 237–240
    mediators, 129, 131
    moderators, 79, 81–82, 118, 130, 132, 203,
        208
    out of the labor force (OLF) status and,
        123, 125, 129
    selection effect of, 65–67, 69, 72–79, 81–87,
        113–114, 116, 161, 203
    unemployment and, 25, 31, 74, 79, 81–83,
        113–116, 118–120, 123–125, 127–130,
        133, 162, 201, 203, 206, 209
    welfare and, 159, 161–165, 167–172,
        174–180, 203
American Psychiatric Association, 133,
    134
anxiety, 6, 67, 74, 137, 197, 205

267